THE WRECKING CREW

*The Inside Story of Rock and
Roll's Best-Kept Secret*

*

Kent Hartman

THOMAS DUNNE BOOKS
St. Martin's Griffin
New York

THOMAS DUNNE BOOKS.
An imprint of St. Martin's Press.

www.thomasdunnebooks.com

www.stmartins.com

Design by Kathryn Parise

THE LIBRARY OF CONGRESS HAS CATALOGED THE HARDCOVER
EDITION AS FOLLOWS:

Hartman, Kent.
    The Wrecking Crew : the inside story of rock and roll's best-
kept secret / Kent Hartman.—1st ed.
        p. cm.
    Includes bibliographical references and index.
    ISBN 978-0-312-61974-9 (hardcover)
    ISBN 978-1-4299-4137-2 (e-book)
    1. Wrecking Crew (Musical group)   2. Rock musicians—
California—Biography.   I. Title.
    ML421.W74H37 2012
    781.66092'2—dc23
    [B]

                                        2011033233

        ISBN 978-1-250-03046-7 (trade paperback)

20   19   18   17   16   15   14   13   12   11

For my late mother, Dorothy Hartman,
who taught me the joy of the written word,
one Beatrix Potter book at a time

Contents

If music be the food of love, play on.

—William Shakespeare, *Twelfth Night*

THE WRECKING CREW

* * * * * * * * *

Prologue

Yesterday Once More

It all began during an automobile trip.

Back in the summer of 1997, after a very quiet, almost-twenty-year hiatus, the hit-making Seventies soft rock group Bread surprised many by deciding to reunite for a grand finale world tour. With the quartet scheduled to play dozens of shows in the United States, Australia, New Zealand, South Africa, the UK, and other countries, their return caused quite a buzz. And by virtue of the company I owned at the time, where I frequently worked with well-known musicians of a certain vintage, I had been asked to design and manufacture all of Bread's concert-merchandising products.

One day mid-tour, while driving a rental car from the Sacramento airport to a beautiful little hideaway resort about two hours to the northwest on Clear Lake, I had along as my co-pilot the band's bass player and keyboardist, Larry Knechtel. I had decided at the last minute to come out on the road for a short stretch to check on things, and Larry, in turn, had asked if he could catch a ride with me to that night's gig.

As we drove in the 100-plus-degree heat along the winding two-lane blacktop road through parched, pine tree–dotted hills, the quiet, self-effacing Knechtel—with some prompting on my part—slowly began to peel back the layers of his long and varied career. I knew that he had done some studio work for other recording artists in his earlier days. And I was well aware of his tenure with Bread, where he had played on David Gates–penned smashes like "Baby I'm-a Want You," "Guitar Man," and "Lost Without Your Love." Those were a part of my youth; I started buying 45s and albums in earnest at the age of ten in the summer of 1970, right around the time of Bread's first hit ("Make It with You").

But what I had no idea about was the sheer magnitude of all the non-Bread work the fifty-seven-year-old Knechtel had done. Like playing the Hammond organ on "Good Vibrations." And the Fender bass on "Light My Fire." Not to mention the killer barrelhouse piano on "Rockin' Pneumonia and the Boogie Woogie Flu." Three classics on which he had played three different instruments. Who *was* this guy, anyway? Well, it didn't take too much more conversation to realize that, in music biz parlance, the mild-mannered gray-haired fellow sitting on my right was a total monster.

Yet there was more. *Much* more. As we drove farther, Knechtel filled me in on the fascinating fact that he wasn't the only one who had done this extraordinary kind of work. He told me that during the Sixties and early Seventies he had teamed with a small number of similarly talented musicians (known today as the Wrecking Crew) who had secretly played the instruments on most of the records of any consequence that came out of Los Angeles. From Phil Spector to the Beach Boys, from the Mamas & the Papas to the Byrds, some combination of these players was responsible for the instrumentation on literally thousands of songs by hundreds of artists.

To say that I was stunned would have been an understatement. Here I was, a guy actually working in the industry, someone who prided himself on knowing a fair amount about who played what on which songs, and I clearly didn't know the tenth of it.

It got me to thinking. If I was so woefully unaware of this stealth-like group of crackerjack players who routinely took the place of the real band members on one chart-topping song after another, then maybe others out there were equally in the dark.

But, with life being life, my discovery somehow managed to fade into the fusty recesses of my mind for almost another ten years. Teaching marketing at a couple of universities, producing a daily syndicated radio feature about classic comedians, and working with various musicians and record labels all seemed to take precedence. Finally, though, I decided that the tale of these great musicians had to be told.

Having started doing some freelance writing for a couple of local newspapers, I thought that the story might make an interesting magazine article. So I e-mailed a pitch letter to Richard Snow, the then-editor-in-chief of *American Heritage* magazine. Remarkably, within hours I had my reply: he had always wondered about this very subject and would be delighted to offer me a contract to write a feature piece about these mysterious sidemen.

After the article came out to a positive reception in 2007, including a mention in *The New York Times*, it became clear to me that the uniqueness of the Wrecking Crew's story—especially regarding what *really* happened behind those closed studio doors—would make an even better book. There was just so much more to tell.

One fantastic literary agent, editor, and publisher later, that book now exists. And there are a few important points to make regarding the contents.

First, about the name. The Wrecking Crew's moniker is undeniably the creation of the drummer Hal Blaine, who, by virtually unanimous agreement, sat front and center as the unofficial dean of the whole bunch. His skills, charisma, and sense of humor were mentioned to me time and again by almost everyone I interviewed—from producers to stars to fellow players—as being the cornerstone of much of what went on during the countless number of recording dates. If you didn't have Hal, you wanted to get Hal.

In the early Sixties, as Blaine and the other young T-shirt and blue jean–clad session musicians began their ascent in the business, some of the older, more established, coat-and-tie-wearing musicians became resentful. They felt that this new breed of rock and roll–playing studio hand was going to somehow wreck the business. It was hard to tell which they hated more: the lack of a dress code or the burgeoning style of music. Maybe it was just a matter of professional jealousy over getting aced out by their more youthful, hipper counterparts. Or, more likely, some combination thereof. In any event, the old guard was headed the way of the Victrola, and they knew it. The Wrecking Crew had become the coveted new set of hired guns in town.

Now, as to exactly *when* people started becoming aware of the Wrecking Crew's name, it is hard to say. Some of the studio musicians I interviewed swear they heard it applied to themselves as early as 1963; others say it was later. One says it was never used at all.

Nevertheless, over the decades the Wrecking Crew's name has become culturally ingrained. So much so that it is now universally used to refer to these great players. Not one person I interviewed ever wondered whom I was talking about. Like "Woodstock" and "Watergate," the term is now a permanent part of our historical lexicon. As proof, no less an institution than the Rock and Roll Hall of Fame made a point of using the Wrecking Crew name when inducting Hal Blaine, Steve Douglas, and Earl Palmer into their ranks (under the sidemen category) a number of years ago. That's plenty good enough for me.

Speaking of the Rock and Roll Hall of Fame, we've all gotten used to seeing the phrase as "rock 'n' roll" and "rock & roll" (among other variations) over the years. Everyone has their favorite way of seeing it and writing it. I've elected to go with "rock and roll" as the standardized terminology throughout this book. Again, I defer to the good folks at the RRHOF, who are the generally accepted standard-bearers of all things that, well, rock and roll.

In doing research for this book (and for the article before it), I conducted several hundred hours of taped interviews over a multi-year period with virtually anybody I could find who had been in the Wrecking Crew or had been associated with them. The vast majority of the anecdotes within these pages came to me firsthand or were told to me by someone who knew the players. Dialogue was taken directly from the tapes. It is of the utmost importance to me to be true to the joyous and sometimes tragic journeys of these marvelous musicians.

I'm often asked about how many people were actually in the Wrecking Crew. Was it fifteen? Twenty? More? The best answer to that question is yes; there was no exact number. But there did exist a small, tight-knit core group of about a couple of dozen who played on a hugely disproportionate share of the hits. The lives and careers of those individuals are the primary focus of this book, with a special spotlight being placed on Glen Campbell (the eventual solo superstar), Carol Kaye (the lone female), and Hal Blaine (the drummer-in-chief, whose name Bruce Springsteen has been known to shout out in joy during concerts when E Street Band drummer Max Weinberg plays a particularly Blaine-like lick). Campbell, Kaye, and Blaine's indelible, interwoven set of experiences provides the backbone of the narrative.

As for why the various members of the Wrecking Crew became the favored choices among so many producers and arrangers, there existed a variety of reasons, almost always relating in some way to the intersection of time and money. And sometimes, understandably, the real band members didn't cotton to being replaced on their own material. But how the individual instrumental parts work *together* is what making a record—a good record, anyway—is all about. That is perhaps the biggest reason why the Wrecking Crew had such an incredible run. They were able to create the appropriate hit-making blend of sounds better and faster than anyone.

Motown had its Funk Brothers. Nashville had the A-Team. New York and Memphis also had their own top-of-the-line sidemen. Every genre and locale had (and has) its own cast of supporting players. But if a rock-and-roll song came out of an LA recording studio from between about 1962 and 1972, the odds are good that some combination of the Wrecking Crew played the instruments. No single group of musicians has ever played on more hits in support of more stars than this superbly talented—yet virtually anonymous—group of men (and one woman). Now it's their turn to step forward and assume center stage.

And, by the way, the next time you listen to some of your favorite groups from the Sixties, please don't be upset. I never knew it was really the Wrecking Crew, either.

1

California Dreamin'

I'd be willing to give you some free lessons.
—Horace Hatchett

Large chicken snakes and twelve-year-old boys are never a good mix. But then, neither are a father's fury and a well-worn leather strap. Unfortunately, these two unpleasant circumstances found themselves on a collision course one very hot Arkansas summer afternoon in 1949.

While desperately trying to avoid yet another stultifying day of picking cotton boles for his father—when he had instead been promised that he could go to a movie—young Glen Campbell hatched a plan to hide under the front porch of his family's dilapidated Arkansas country shack.

"Glen Travis Campbell, where *are* you?" he heard his father bellow.

Filled with thoughts about the terrible beating he would receive if caught, Glen stayed as quiet as a mouse after he deftly slid through broken latticework on the side of the porch. As he silently lay on his belly watching his father's scuffed boots come within inches of his face, he wriggled even farther into the dank, welcoming darkness, ending up in a corner area littered with old cans, empty bottles, and at least one discarded shoe. Thinking that he'd finally made it to a safe haven where no one could find him, he let out a small sigh of relief.

Soon, however, Glen sensed that maybe he wasn't quite so alone after all. As he turned to his left, the faint shafts of sunlight filtering through the porch's warped wooden floorboards caught the image of what he thought at first to be a coil of rope, until the coil suddenly moved. Staring him in the face was a chicken snake, its tongue flicking in and out. The same kind of snake he'd seen devour dozens of rats, mice, and other barnyard critters over the years. Maybe the kind of snake that eats little boys, too, he thought. Trying to scramble as fast as he could to the outside world, Glen raised his head again and again, each time smashing it into the floorboards above. The sounds cracked out into the hot summer air.

Hearing all the racket and fearing that a wild animal was under the porch, his mother came running out the front door. His sisters screamed in hysteria. Glen's father squinted underneath the house, wondering what was going on.

As Campbell fought the fight of his life to extricate himself from the imaginary clutches of a startled snake that was, in all likelihood, heading in the opposite direction just as quickly, his head appeared turtle-like from underneath the porch. While his eyes slowly adjusted to the bright sunlight, he noticed that his father curiously appeared to be standing on only one foot. Even in all the chaos, Glen wondered why that would be. The answer came quickly, as his father's other boot-encased foot came down firmly on Glen's neck, pinning him in place.

"Boy, what were you doing under the house?"

Deciding that his punishment would be less severe if he told the truth, Glen managed to sputter, through tears and a mouthful of dirt, "I was hiding from doing my chores."

With that, his enraged father yanked Glen out of the dirt, bent him over, and pulled out a length of leather used to attach horses to a wagon. He then proceeded to administer a vicious whipping that seemed to go on forever. Even Glen's mother and sisters had to turn away.

At that moment, with each snap of the strap, Glen Campbell became more determined to break away someday, to become his own man. There had to be a better life than being whipped like a mad animal. There just had to be.

✳

As five-year-old Carol Smith sat alone in her father's vintage Ford Model A sedan outside the Elks Club in Everett, Washington, she suddenly felt the hair on her tiny arms stand straight up.

Through the open windows of the aging, long-out-of-production car, Smith could clearly hear the sounds of her father's Dixieland band playing inside the large building. Even for a child quite accustomed to listening to plenty of music around the house—courtesy of two professional musician parents—this particular instance somehow rose to another level. This time it *moved* her. Just listen to that music, she thought, the sheer power of it all. The experience proved to be a defining moment, creating a feeling deep within the little girl that she would never forget.

At its peak, the Benevolent and Protective Order of Elks in Everett boasted more than five thousand card-carrying members, a full one-sixth of the approximately thirty thousand people then living in this mid-sized mill town just north of Seattle. And for the better part of the twentieth century, the Spanish mission–style club located at 2731 Rucker Avenue in the downtown area was *the* place to be. There, at the indisputable hub of civic life, members experienced a sense of belonging, fellowship, and, especially, entertainment.

Big-name stars of the day like Sammy Davis Jr., Sophie Tucker, and George Gobel routinely played shows at the lodge. Local dances, too, were very popular, sometimes stretching into the early-morning hours. And virtually any area musical ensemble worth watching graced the Elks Club's stage at one time or another, including the group Carol Smith's dad played in.

Clyde Smith never did make a lot of money. He had spent the better part of his professional career playing trombone in a World War I military band, various Dixieland bands, and assorted theater orchestras. His wife, Dot, a ragtime and classical pianist, had worked during the Twenties providing piano accompaniment in silent movie houses. Even with two incomes, however, money had always been tight. Betting your livelihood on the instability of being a live musician often meant going without; that was the unfortunate part of the bargain. Decent-paying gigs could be few and far between. Squeaking by became a way of life. And then, during the heart of the Great Depression, along came their only child, Carol, in 1935.

As 1941 drew to a close, Clyde and Dot finally decided they had endured enough of the seemingly endless overcast skies and low pay of the Puget Sound region. At over forty years of age, Clyde Smith was too old to fight, but there had to be some good jobs in the Southern California shipyards with the nation at war, now that Pearl Harbor had been attacked.

They pointed their car due south with their six-year-old daughter and what few possessions they had and headed down U.S. Highway 99 for sunny climes and hoped-for opportunities. Maybe Los Angeles could even use another good musician or two. Any way they looked at it, a little change would be good for the Smith family.

But for Carol Smith, a shy little girl with a pronounced stutter and a blossoming love for all things music, the twelve-hundred-mile trip would prove to be the move of a lifetime.

✳

At first, no one smelled the smoke.

It was a typically hot and sticky July afternoon in Hartford, Connecticut, the kind of oppressively muggy weather some of the locals liked to call the devil's dew. Barely a month before, Allied forces had finally landed on the beaches of Normandy, giving rise to hope that World War II might actually end one day soon.

A seemingly endless stream of happy, sweltering townspeople excitedly walked along leafy Kensington Street toward the northern edge of the city, many with great anticipation clearly evident on their faces. For the circus— yes, the circus!—had just come to town and the first performance of the seventy-third annual Ringling Bros. and Barnum & Bailey spectacular was about to begin at precisely 3:00 P.M. With wartime rationing still in full effect and live entertainment options in short supply, the yearly visit by "The Greatest Show on Earth" was simply not to be missed.

Close to eight thousand circus goers, including a large number of children on summer vacation, descended upon the bustling bluff-top lot, passing by assorted animal cages, portable dressing rooms, and rail cars as they made their way toward the ticket booth and, most important, the fabled big top beyond. Stilt walkers, lion tamers, and bearded ladies, too, meandered about the grass-covered Barbour Street grounds, patiently waiting for their time in the spotlight.

Entering the arena one by one, the lengthy line of buzzing patrons slowly climbed up row after steep row of temporary wooden bleachers in order to find their seats, all strategically arrayed around the interior perimeter of the massive oval portable tent.

From every walk of life they came, sitting elbow-to-elbow, filling the arena to beyond fire code capacity. A little dark-haired Italian girl of about ten sat in the front row, methodically licking her ice-cream cone. An elderly gent in red suspenders and a black bowler hat, rhythmically tamping the tobacco in his meerschaum pipe, said to no one in particular, "I hear this is their best show yet."

Some had great views; others sat in the so-called peanut gallery near the top. But no one cared—it was the circus and that was all that mattered.

While the twenty-man Ringling Bros. band launched into its first notes of fanfare, a procession of colorfully attired clowns, packed improbably into miniature cars, began to slowly wend its way inside the cavernous canvas-covered structure, closely followed by a variety of elephants, giraffes, acrobats, and, of course, the ringmaster himself. An army of snack vendors, too, in red-and-white-striped jackets, began to fan out, offering peanuts, popcorn, and cotton candy to anyone within earshot. The big show had begun.

Unfortunately, as transfixed as they were by the sights and sounds of the world's biggest three-ring circus—particularly by the Flying Wallendas, who were in mid-act on the high wire—only a scattered few in the rapt audience initially noticed a small flicker of flames and puff of smoke beginning to rise from an area over by the back service-entry flap.

Bandleader Merle Evans, always keenly observant, was among the first who did notice. Raising his baton, he instinctively instructed his musicians to quickly switch into playing "The Stars and Stripes Forever," the traditional song to alert circus personnel to possible danger. Hearing the cue, the acts suddenly stopped performing and swiftly leaped into action, some rushing to throw water at the small fire, others trying to calm a growing number of concerned and bewildered audience members.

A fifteen-year-old boy named Harold Belsky noticed the flames, too. He had arrived just in time for the start of the show and had positioned himself, as always, immediately adjacent to the bandstand in order to closely watch every movement the drummer made. As a fledgling percussionist, Hal (as his family called him) hoped to learn as much as possible from every musical act that passed through town, the circus included.

With Belsky coming from a poor background in the Hartford ghetto, watching the pros play in person—major Big Band stick men like Gene Krupa, Dave Tough, and Buddy Rich—had become one of the only affordable methods of instruction he could manage. Even more than that, they were his heroes, the coolest of the cool, the original hepcats. Hal loved to dream of taking their places onstage, sitting behind a big, gleaming kit with his name stenciled on the front, driving the band with every hit of his snare and every thump of his bass drum. And he sure wasn't going anywhere on this day because of a little bit of smoke. Forget that. The circus had good musicians and he wanted to see them. This was his education. Besides, from where he sat, the fire looked relatively minor anyway. Like many others, he assumed it would be extinguished within a matter of minutes, and he paid it little further heed. Hal Belsky, the young drummer-to-be, put his feet up, settled back, and patiently waited for the show to resume.

✳

Growing up poor during the late Forties in tiny Billstown, Arkansas, presented far more challenges, of course, for a youngster like Glen Campbell than just the occasional run-in with a wayward snake. Food was scarce and money even scarcer. Large families of twelve like the Campbells were the norm—free labor to help cultivate what few crops they had. For the children, eking out a meager life on a dirt farm meant a whole lot of family chores and very little emphasis on schooling. Most folks in Pike County were lucky to have had an eighth-grade education. Fewer still graduated from high school. When it came down to eating versus reading, the stomach usually had the stronger vote.

As for when he did get to school, Glen showed little natural interest in sitting behind a wooden desk. Always energetic and outgoing, he much preferred to spend his nonworking time, when he had any, roughhousing with friends, sneaking into the Saturday afternoon picture show, and playing music. Especially playing music.

From the time almost anyone could remember, Glen showed a preternatural aptitude for anything to do with a musical instrument. By the age of ten he'd ably learned to pluck notes and strum chords—all by ear, no less—on a cheap five-dollar acoustic guitar that his father had purchased for him from the Sears & Roebuck catalog. Hum a song for him once and he'd likely play it right back to you, often with an improvised flourish of his own tacked on for good measure. He also had a lovely tenor voice with perfect pitch and he delighted in singing gospel hymns at church every Sunday. Playing and singing came easily to him and he particularly enjoyed the attention it could bring.

By the age of thirteen, with Glen struggling mightily to keep from failing the seventh grade, an answer to his prayers appeared. His uncle Eugene "Boo" Campbell, an accomplished, if somewhat itinerant, professional guitar player, came to ask the family a question: could Glen go on the road with him, make a little money to send home, and have an adventure?

"I've got some club dates lined up between here and Wyoming and I need a second guitar player. The boy would make a good one."

Glen was ecstatic. Compared to the life he'd experienced to that point, the prospect of becoming a real live guitarist alongside his beloved uncle Boo was nothing short of manna from heaven. Thank you, Jesus! No more beatings. No more endless chores. No more senseless schoolwork. And, especially, no more long nights spent lying on his stomach while pressing his fist into his gut, trying to quell the gnawing pangs of hunger.

And so, with hugs all around and a wave to his family, Glen Campbell hit the road to begin the journey of a lifetime. It would be a long journey, longer than most people think, but a little bit of luck and a whole lot of hard work would serve to take him further than even he could ever imagine possible.

✳

Unfortunately for Carol Smith and her parents, things did not work out exactly as planned after the big move to Southern California. With shipyard work proving to be sporadic at best, a lack of money remained a major issue around the house, causing continued hardship, frustration, and arguments. Within a few years, her parents could simply take no more. They decided to divorce, leaving Carol alone with her mother and without any income. For a period of time, Clyde Smith contributed some cash here and there, but the once-and-again trombonist gradually drifted out of their lives. He finally skipped the state altogether just after the end of the war, leaving Carol and her mother to fend for themselves. With nowhere else to turn, the two ended up living in a housing project near the waterfront in a town called Wilmington, by the Port of Los Angeles, accepting welfare in order to survive.

Among those who grow up in extremely limited circumstances, the shame of being poor often sends them in one of two directions. Some give in to the depression and pain, losing their will and their way. With others, the early struggle and stigma help fuel a burning desire to rise above the poverty, to achieve something in life. Carol Smith, from a young age, fell squarely into the latter category.

Knowing that her mother needed all the money she could get, the now-thirteen-year-old Carol wanted to contribute in any way possible. She loved her mother and knew what a burden it was for her to simply put enough food on the table each day. But Carol never complained, even when she had but one pair of shoes to her name. Not even when she had to start working after school at the age of nine to help make ends meet. Her resiliency and inner resolve helped carry her through, giving evidence of a level of maturity far beyond her years. All she really needed was a good break to come her way.

One day, when a door-to-door steel guitar salesman came knocking, Carol's mother decided on the spur of the moment that it was time to finally indulge her daughter, whether they could afford it or not. The little blond-haired girl with the blue eyes and the inquisitive mind had gone without long enough. Her mom pulled out an old piggy bank in which she had painstakingly been saving coins for more years than she could remember and handed the man the required ten dollars. In return, Carol received her very own guitar and a few accompanying lessons.

Thrilled with the gift, even if it was a rather cheaply built instrument, Carol threw herself into practicing with her characteristic industriousness. And she became pretty good.

Shortly after the momentous occasion with the man at the front door, good fortune smiled upon Carol once again. Her girlfriend Jean Blue asked Carol to tag along with her one afternoon to a regular guitar lesson that had been scheduled with a teacher in nearby Long Beach.

"Come on, Carol. It'll be fun."

Seeing no reason not to go, Carol grabbed her little steel guitar and set out with her friend. Maybe it *would* be fun.

After appropriate introductions, the guitar teacher—an esteemed instructor and graduate of the Eastman School of Music named Horace Hatchett—simply could not take his eyes off of Carol's steel guitar. He seemed equal parts appalled and intrigued. After all, it wasn't every day that a thirteen-year-old girl showed up toting *that* kind of instrument. Steel guitars are inherently difficult to play, requiring the precise use of a small glass or metal tube placed on one of the fretting fingers, which then slides up and down the strings. Hardly the best choice for someone just starting out. But there was Carol, ever the trouper, innocently trying to master a musical contraption meant for far more experienced players.

After Jean's lesson, as the two girls prepared to leave Hatchett's small nondescript home on Corona Avenue, something made the longtime teacher stop and take a long look at Carol. Perhaps he recognized a bit of himself somewhere within her youthful earnestness. Or maybe it was her unusual level of talent and desire, which had become evident after he had asked her to play a little bit for him. Whatever the reason, the kid had promise; that much was clear. And Hatch (as his friends called him) had been around long enough to know.

He decided to make her an offer.

"Carol, you're a good player. I'd be willing to give you some free lessons if you'll help me with my teaching."

It was all Carol Smith needed to hear. Suddenly the overwhelming feeling of being poor, of being different, seemed to melt away. A real guitar teacher was offering to become her mentor. Maybe this would lead to being a professional musician, like her parents, and perhaps even making some money to help her mom out with the household expenses.

Carol accepted on the spot. Only later did she learn that Horace Hatchett had played with Jimmy Dorsey, Red Nichols, and Nat King Cole. Someone was smiling down on Carol Smith.

*

Unfortunately for Hal Belsky—and for everyone else in attendance—the show did not resume that day at the circus.

Despite the best efforts of dozens of Ringling Bros. performers and roustabouts, no amount of water seemed to quell the rapidly moving flames as they charged up the side of the big top. As the fire reached the ceiling inside, the giant structure suddenly began to rumble and shudder, acting as a colossal chimney, sucking fresh oxygen in through the side entrances and blowing superheated air out the top. And with the tragic mixture of gasoline and paraffin that had been used as a waterproofing agent, the tent's canvas proved to be the perfect fuel source to ignite a world-class conflagration.

Within moments, the entire roof of the arena exploded into a raging inferno. The big top immediately erupted in chaos, as melting wax rained down like napalm, scorching everything and everyone it touched. Thick white smoke billowed everywhere and the overpowering stench of sulfur hung heavily in the air. Ringmaster Fred Bradna pleaded with the audience not to panic and to leave in an orderly fashion, but the power had failed and his voice could no longer be heard over the loudspeakers.

People began running wildly for their lives in every direction, some with their hair and clothes on fire. Many were trampled; others ended up in giant piles near the exits, with those unfortunate enough to be on the bottom protected from the flames but slowly and cruelly suffocating to death.

Hal Belsky dove under the bottom of the tent's apron and rolled to safety in the grass on the outside, as did the bandleader and his musicians.

"You okay?" one of them asked breathlessly. Hal just nodded, too stunned to speak.

Others were not so lucky. Those who didn't immediately perish inside from the smoke, flames, and violent stampedes were found stumbling and crawling outside around the grounds with broken bones, incinerated lungs, and charred flesh hanging from their bodies.

After making sure their comrades were all accounted for, most of the band members scattered, trying to help the stricken. Fellow circus performers began setting up makeshift triage areas, laying bodies out in rows. They did what they could.

As several ambulances mercifully began to arrive, one of the drivers leaped out and shouted, "Hey, kid, give me a hand here!" Hal didn't have to be asked twice. He immediately grabbed the end of a gurney and helped place a horribly burned older woman into the back of a waiting vehicle. He spent the rest of that day and night riding with the critically injured as they were ferried to local hospitals, making one return trip after another, trying his best to comfort the stricken.

Witnessing all the horrible pain and suffering that day made an indelible mark on Hal Belsky's young mind. Life was precious and for the living. He would redouble his resolve to forge a career as a professional musician, no matter what it might take, no matter where it might take him.

✳

One came from the South, one from the West, and one from the Northeast. They shared little in common other than an innate drive, a work ethic shaped by grinding poverty, and, for now, untapped musical talent. Yet somehow, Glen Campbell, Carol Smith, and Hal Belsky—a country boy, a girl from the projects, and a street-smart city kid—all found it within themselves to relentlessly hold on to their dreams as they went out into the world.

It would be these very qualities that would one day catapult this unlikely trio, along with a couple dozen other equally single-minded freelance musicians, into revolutionizing the music of an era—rock-and-roll music. They would become part of an aggregation known as the Wrecking Crew.

2

Limbo Rock

Man, I can write a song better than that in five minutes.
—BILLY STRANGE

By the end of the Fifties, money had found the music business. Or rather, the substantial amount of cash to be made from selling popular music had suddenly caught the attention of some very shrewd businessmen.

Building on what had begun a few years earlier with the appearances of Elvis, Chuck Berry, and Little Richard on the national scene, the operators of several small, independent LA-based record labels started to sense that perhaps rock and roll, to paraphrase the 1958 hit song by Danny & the Juniors, really *was* here to stay. And their gambles on a handful of new acts paid almost immediate dividends.

Ricky Nelson, with his sultry style and teen-idol good looks—not to mention the pedigree of being Ozzie and Harriet's second son—became a breakout star in the late Fifties for cigar-chomping, streetwise Lew Chudd at tiny Imperial Records on Sunset Boulevard. Bobby Vee, with bouncy songs such as "Rubber Ball" and "Devil or Angel," came along just in time to save Si Waronker's Liberty Records from the ignominy of mostly being known as the home of Alvin and the Chipmunks. And at fledgling Dore Records

over on Vine Street in Hollywood, Jan and Dean made the Top 10 just before the dawn of the new decade with "Baby Talk."

Indie labels all, these record companies were among the first in Los
Angeles to welcome up-and-coming rock and rollers with open arms. No jazz
snobbery here. To a man, the owners implicitly understood the fundamental
tenet that this was always the music *business*. The goal was to give the public
what they wanted, no matter how pedestrian, no questions asked.

Unlike their smaller counterparts, however, some of the major record
labels—corporate behemoths like Columbia, Mercury, and others—were
slow to recognize the revenue potential that this new "kids" music had to offer. Generally looking down their noses at what they assumed to be a passing
fad, the big-label men often opted to stick with more traditional pop offer-
ings by the likes of the New Christy Minstrels, Johnny Mathis, and Tennessee Ernie Ford. Those you *knew* would sell. They had cachet, a legacy.

It wouldn't be until years later, for example, that Columbia Records finally, grudgingly, signed their first bona fide rock-and-roll act (Paul Revere &
the Raiders). Even then, the label showed remarkable hesitancy regarding the
band and, for that matter, the style of music itself: the first Raiders LP
didn't hit stores until a full year *after* the Beatles had already conquered
American record charts during the initial wave of the British Invasion. But,
the Columbia producer Mitch Miller (host of television's terminally bland
Sing Along with Mitch) was also the head of Artists and Repertoire—the department that picks new releases—and he simply *hated* rock and roll.

"It's not music," Miller scornfully proclaimed. "It's a disease."

In the meantime, the ever-observant indie label owners knew exactly
what *they* were going to do. With a variety of factors all simultaneously con-
spiring to create a seemingly insatiable desire among (mostly) teenagers for
an ever-greater supply of new music, it was time to start turning out some
new singles. Fast.

Transistor radios were getting cheaper all the time and practically every
kid had one. In addition, Top 40 AM radio stations were springing up everywhere, catering to the growing throngs of youthful listeners by playing all
the latest tunes. In particular, big-market broadcasters such as KFWB in

Los Angeles, WLS in Chicago, and WMCA in New York became instant success stories, setting the tone for the rest of the country. And the kids just loved the often up-tempo, vaguely suggestive thrill and danger that rock and roll provided. Straightlaced heartthrob crooners of the day like Johnnie Ray, Eddie Fisher, and Pat Boone never knew what hit them.

It was the simplest of business equations, really, one that benefited everyone involved: playing rock-and-roll records on the radio equaled higher ratings, higher ratings equaled more and better-paying advertisers, and more and better-paying advertisers equaled increased revenue for station owners. The owners, in turn, were only too happy to perpetuate the cycle, in the process creating an endless stream of free marketing (via airplay) for the record labels.

From an economic perspective, unprecedented national prosperity also enabled individual households to enjoy larger levels of discretionary income, providing much of the wherewithal for kids to run down to the local record shop and buy those 45s they kept hearing on the radio. And in terms of sheer volume, the post-war baby boom created the largest number of junior high and high school students—and bumper crop of new music consumers—the country had ever witnessed. TV sets, too, were finally in most homes, regularly playing teen-themed music programs like *American Bandstand* to riveted adolescent viewers.

By 1959, new indie label releases recorded in Los Angeles like "Donna" by Ritchie Valens, "Teen Beat" by Sandy Nelson, and "It Was I" by Skip & Flip were routinely selling over a million copies each. Record companies, hungry to cash in on the phenomenon, clamored for ever more product, cutting songs in the studios sometimes twenty-four hours a day. Songwriters, producers, arrangers, engineers, singers, and musicians were booked solid. The musical floodgates were open.

Word soon spread among young, aspiring guitar players, drummers, pianists, bassists, horn players, and anyone else who could strum, bang, pluck, or blow: get to LA as fast as possible. Producers were pumping out new records literally by the stack and there were jobs to be had. Good jobs. Particularly so since a lot of the older, established musicians in town—the blue-blazer-and-necktie, by-the-book, time-clock-punching men who had cut their teeth during the Thirties and Forties playing on movie soundtracks, Big Band records, and early TV shows—simply loathed everything about rock and roll. To them this new music was appallingly primitive, an effrontery on every level. Most refused to play it. In their minds, their careers had been built on decorum and sophistication, not on wearing T-shirts and blue jeans to work while bashing out simplistic three-chord rhythm patterns over and over. That kind of thing was surely going to wreck the business. Because of this, skilled new session aces were increasingly needed to take their places, especially those who could lay down some seriously inspired grooves.

Like the clarion call of a medieval trumpet, the money to be made in the record business at the dawn of the Sixties in Los Angeles would prove to be an irresistible draw to every kind of hopeful. Essentially music's version of the California Gold Rush, the varied and rapidly growing number of opportunities to make some cash and a name in rock and roll began to attract talent, ambition, greed, and egotism, all in seemingly equal measure. And from this diverse migratory mix—aside from the scores of singers, songwriters, and others who made the journey—there evolved a core clique of instrument-playing sidemen who gradually began to stand out from the rest. These particular musicians not only had the willingness and ability to play rock and roll (two qualities that set them uniquely apart from other session musicians in town, both old and new); they also instinctively knew *how* to improvise in just the right doses to make a given recording better. To make it a hit. Which naturally put their services in the highest of demand: producers wanted hits. It also, over time, provided them with a nickname that mirrored their emergence as the new, dominant group of determined young session players who were taking over the growing rock-and-roll side of things: the Wrecking Crew.

Membership in the Wrecking Crew required no club dues. It required no ID card. There were no chapter meetings or other formalities, either. In fact, it couldn't have been more informal. Boiled to its essence, it came down to the simple exercise of show up, play instrument, collect check. But at the same time, it was so much more—an exclusive collaboration created strictly by private invitation. Exemplary skills and some well-placed word of mouth around town might get you a look, a foot in the door. Getting along well with others and, especially, learning how to help turn a song into a million-seller would keep you coming back.

Just like in any industry, those in charge—in this case the producers and arrangers—all liked to hire their favorites time after time. No need to reinvent the wheel on every song. It might be only three pieces, perhaps just guitar, bass, and drums. Or it might be three or four of every conceivable instrument. But they all pulled from the same finite pool of talent, where a hard-won sterling reputation came to mean everything in terms of consistent employment. Though the total number of musicians in the Wrecking Crew fluctuated, a small number of mainstays always seemed to play in some combination on all the most prominent rock-and-roll recordings. People like Glen Campbell, Carol Smith, and Hal Belsky, along with a couple dozen other similarly gifted and ambitious freelancers. And each of them, to be sure, had their own undeniably unique experiences in finally making it to the "show"—*and* in staying there.

✳

A couple of months after Glen Campbell and his uncle Boo made their exhilarating getaway in search of musical fame and fortune across the far reaches of the Continental Divide, the realities of life on the road all came crashing down. Hard.

Finding themselves stranded with little money and no prospects—after a short, dispiriting attempt at performing on a "pass the hat" basis in a string of smoky bars and honky-tonks across Wyoming—the weary duo were forced to weigh their limited options. Uncle Boo had quite clearly miscalculated their potential for earning a livable wage on the road.

Despite the shame of failure, they decided the best move would be to return to Arkansas as soon as possible. Family, friends, and a warm bed surely waited for them there, not to mention a hot meal. Wyoming was rugged, desolate, and bitterly cold, not the kind of place for a pair of gentle-natured, corn-fed country boys.

But in order to cobble together even the small amount of money needed for a couple of bus tickets back home, the two traveling troubadours ended up doing the unthinkable: they pawned their guitars, the indispensable tools of their trade. According to Uncle Boo, it was the only way.

"We'll buy 'em back soon enough; you'll see," he said, trying to reassure his skeptical nephew.

One of the benefits of a large extended family is that there often exists a network of people willing to help a relative in crisis. And this would hold true in Glen's largely rural American branch of Clan Campbell, whose proudly held roots dated back over seven hundred years to County Argyll in the Scottish Highlands. Though his uncle Boo hadn't remotely provided the path to success that Campbell had expected, another uncle—a fellow named Dick Bills—stepped forward with an offer of his own. He invited Glen to come live with his wife and him in Albuquerque, where Bills was an established bandleader and radio personality. Word had gotten to him through the Campbell family grapevine that Glen was a virtual prodigy on guitar and that, more than just taking in a nephew, Bills would be gaining an important addition to his band.

If the Uncle Boo excursion proved to be a fiasco, the Uncle Dick experience proved to be everything Campbell could have hoped for. From the minute he arrived in New Mexico, young Glen found himself strumming his now-out-of-hock guitar for his uncle virtually every day of the week: during the noon radio show, during the nightly dances, and even on Bills's Saturday morning children's show on local television. And for a now-sixteen-year-old young man who would never darken the door of a schoolhouse again, the on-the-job training was just what he needed. For in Glen Campbell's mind, nothing—*nothing*—was going to stop him from his dream of becoming the world's best guitar player.

*

Sitting in a small booth inside a bustling twenty-four-hour diner on the Sunset Strip late one summer night, Billy Strange knew it was time to think about getting sober.

With a thirty-minute drive back to his home in the Northridge section of the San Fernando Valley staring him in the face, Strange had stopped in with a pal to gulp down as much black coffee as they could reasonably hold before attempting the journey. Having a few drinks and a little fun after a full day of recording sessions had become a tradition of sorts for the lanky guitar player, but one that also routinely required gaining intimate knowledge as to whether Maxwell House, per their latest ad campaign, really *was* good to the last drop.

Born in 1930 in Long Beach, California, Billy Strange grew up in a different world from most of his friends. His parents carved out a living as a minor-league, cowboy-style singing duo on local radio and by performing concerts whenever and wherever they could. With little money to provide extravagances for their only son, they passed along the one thing they did have in abundance: a passion for music.

By the age of five, little Billy evidenced enough natural talent to sing along with his mom and dad on the radio and to win a nearby yodeling contest. Music quickly became all he thought about. By the time a family friend gave Strange a beautiful Gibson L-7 archtop acoustic guitar when he turned fourteen, there could be no turning back. He had the chops. He had the drive. He would become a musician, just like his folks.

After dropping out of high school at sixteen to travel the Southwest with a bunch of hell-raising musicians several years his senior (he drove a beat-up converted school bus often hundreds of miles between shows while they slept off their daily hangovers in the back), Strange finally ended up in Los Angeles, working his guitar magic—both acoustic and electric—on a variety of live country music TV shows for stars like the Sons of the Pioneers, Roy Rogers, Cliffie Stone, and others. Sometimes Strange even sang with them, too, being the proud owner of a particularly resonant baritone voice.

During this time, the savvy Strange also made the most of his growing list of local studio connections, which paid off handsomely as rock and roll became a boom industry by the late Fifties. He was a known entity to important LA-based producers and arrangers alike, his estimable skills easily transferable and in high demand from the start.

So perhaps Strange could be excused if upon occasion he imbibed a little more than he should after an especially long day. That's why they made coffee anyhow.

Stubbing out the latest in a chain of unfiltered cigarette butts into a tabletop ashtray, Billy casually exhaled a final lungful of smoke high in the air and then dropped a couple of crumpled dollar bills next to his cup. Time to hit the road.

As the two friends climbed into the car and began heading east toward Cahuenga Boulevard in order to take the Hollywood Freeway over the hill, Strange flipped around on the radio dial, trying to find something, anything, that would help keep him awake. Landing on one of the local country stations, Strange could not seem to get over a record they were playing called "We Need a Whole Lot More of Jesus (and a Lot Less Rock and Roll)."

"Man, I can write a song better than that in five minutes," he said, sounding at least halfway serious.

Before Strange could give the subject any further comment, however, his traveling companion suddenly whipped out his wallet and slapped a hundred-dollar bill on the front seat between them.

"Okay, Billy, you're on!"

Never one to back away from a challenge, particularly when it related to music or money, Strange immediately reached into the backseat and grabbed one of his blank score pads, the kind he used in the studio to sketch out arrangements. A hundred dollars was a whole lot of cash in 1961; it took almost six hours of studio time at union scale for a guy like Strange to earn that much.

Humming to himself while jotting down a series of musical notes as he drove, Strange quickly came up with a basic song he decided to call "Monotonous Melody." As he sang it back to his friend well within the allotted five minutes, they both burst out in laughter. Monotonous or not, Billy's little ditty really *was* better than that crap they had just heard on the radio.

Tossing the pad over his shoulder, a vindicated Strange slid the cash into his pocket and promptly forgot about the whole thing. Just another night on the town in Hollywood for a hardworking, hard-drinking, Stetson-wearing guitar slinger.

*

Several weeks after coming up with his spur-of-the-moment "five-minute tune," Billy Strange found himself hired to play guitar one afternoon on a

TV soundtrack session over at United's Studio B in Hollywood for *The Adventures of Ozzie and Harriet*. The show's music composer and arranger, Basil "Buzz" Adlam, had just created a new music-publishing company on the side and wanted to put out the word that day among the gathered musicians that he was looking to stock it with some fresh songs.

"Anybody have any good material they want me to hear?"

Strange immediately flashed on the forgotten little composition he had so blithely thrown into his backseat.

"Buzz, you know, I might have one," he said. "How about if you give me an hour with the guys so that I can cut you a demo?"

Agreeing to the proposition, the British-born Adlam made himself scarce with his customary cup of tea while Strange and the other players set about laying down the instrumental tracks. Messing around with various tempos and styles, they decided on a basic rhythm section of guitar, bass, and drums employing a calypso feel as the song's foundation. Then, for lack of any real lyrics, they all began singing the words "what a monotonous melody" over and over in unison, eventually sending themselves into a fit of hysterics.

"That's just about the dumbest thing I've ever heard," Strange said, guffawing along with the rest.

When Adlam returned, Billy Strange dutifully handed him the master tape of the recording. Adlam gave it a quick listen, politely said, "Thank you," and left Strange feeling certain that nothing more would come of it. Oh well, he thought, at least we all got a good laugh out of it. Once again, Strange put the song right out of his mind.

But "Monotonous Melody" proved to be anything but.

About a month later, Strange received a phone call at home from Dave Burgess, a guitarist and producer who was the leader of a band called the Champs. It seems that Burgess had not only heard Strange's demo through Buzz Adlam's new publishing company but, in fact, had *already* recorded it with his guys. Thinking that it might have the makings of a decent hit for the Champs—who had been on a dry streak for several years since their breakout chart-topping smash, "Tequila," in 1958—Burgess got right to the point.

"Billy, I want to put out 'Monotonous Melody' as our next single. I think it's got a real shot. But I want to change the title. Would you mind?"

"Mind? I don't give a damn *what* you call it," the ever-blunt Strange replied with a chuckle. "It never had a real name anyway."

Strange well knew from his time spent in the music business that no matter the eventual title of the record, if it actually sold a few copies he would stand to make a little bread out of the deal as the song's writer. No use quibbling over a silly name. Not where money was concerned.

*

After eight years of working in and around Albuquerque, Glen Campbell had pretty much wrung all he could out of the experience. Though grateful for the opportunity provided to him by his uncle Dick, Campbell knew he desperately needed to expand his horizons. Playing in rough-and-tumble cowboy bars like the Chesterfield Club, the Hitching Post, and the Ace of Clubs had proven to be an excellent musical education—the first three hundred times. After that, the fights, the smoke-filled rooms, and the flying beer bottles became a daily, visceral reminder of where he was—and where he was not. Playing the same songs over and over with the same musicians was no way to build a career. If Campbell *really* wanted to make it to the top as a guitarist—to stay true to his dream—he knew he was going to have to somehow get to Los Angeles, the center of music on the West Coast.

Now married to his second wife, with a toddler from wife number one also to support (Glen had been a very busy boy in Albuquerque), the twenty-four-year-old had not been able to save much money. And he had exactly zero connections. The kind of people he knew around town could never help him get anywhere. They were mostly a bunch of small-time catgut scrapers and other musical wannabes who seemed quite content with the notion of spending the rest of their lives right where they were. Of course, slide a pack of Camel straights and a couple of shots of Old Grand-Dad in front of them and they would be happy to oblige you for hours with tales about all the worlds they planned to conquer. How the big time, *this time*, really was just around the corner.

But Campbell knew better, and deep inside so did they. Either way, being around the overpowering aura of so many unrealized dreams was sucking the life out of him. And Campbell wanted no part of that. He just wanted out. Eight years spent in the bush leagues can start to feel like eighty when it represents a full one-third of your life.

And then, one evening, the answer to Campbell's hoped-for exodus unexpectedly materialized. It came in the unlikely form of a little-known Texas-born singer and songwriter with great ambition and charisma by the name of Jerry Fuller.

✳

In 1960, the music business, particularly in Los Angeles, operated much like the American Old West. Back in the nineteenth century, a skilled blacksmith, hide tanner, or cobbler, for example, could usually find plenty of work. As the nation's cattle industry expanded, a variety of supporting occupations like these became vitally important spokes in the wheel of success. Blacksmiths were needed to shoe the horses. Hide tanners were needed to make saddles and durable coats. And cobblers were needed to repair a hardworking cowboy's boot heels.

A hundred years later, the recording industry rewarded the same kind of entrepreneurial spirit. If you could capably write a catchy rock-and-roll melody or convincingly warble a set of lyrics into a microphone, you just might find yourself some work. And if you were skilled at both—as was Jerry Fuller—then the need for your services became virtually assured.

Leaving the Lone Star State at the age of twenty-one with one thing on his mind, the singer/songwriter Jerry Fuller made straight for the glittering lights and musical promise of Los Angeles. Brimming with confidence, the determined young musician made the usual rounds of publishing houses and almost immediately landed a number of jobs singing song demos at ten dollars a pop. Soon, with a winning mixture of drive and obvious talent, Fuller landed his own recording contract with Challenge Records, founded by cowboy singing star Gene Autry. "Betty My Angel," a Top Ten hit on the West Coast, followed, as did several more regional successes. Later in 1960, Fuller's rockabilly-flavored version of "The Tennessee Waltz" squeaked into the national Hot 100 at number sixty-three, earning him an invitation to appear on *American Bandstand*.

Hooking on as the opening act for his Challenge Records label mates the Champs, Fuller found himself playing one night in Albuquerque. After the show, a nervous Glen Campbell—who liked to catch any national act he could that might be passing through town—timidly approached Fuller backstage for an autograph. Despite all his local success, Campbell, almost childlike in his naïveté, still looked up to those with record deals, especially the artists who had actually made the charts. Striking up a conversation, the pair immediately hit it off, realizing a shared musical and cultural kinship when they saw one. Two family-oriented boys from the Mid-South just trying to make it in the biz.

Campbell invited his newfound friend to come watch his show later that night at a local bar. Fuller, accepting the offer, immediately took notice of Campbell's superb, wide-ranging skills.

"You're a *player*, man," Fuller enthused after the gig. "You really ought to get to LA."

"I'd love to, Jerry, but I don't have any connections. I wouldn't even know where to start."

"Let me see what I can do for you."

True to his word, Jerry Fuller did do something for Glen Campbell. A very big something. Jerry got him a job with the touring version of the Champs. Knowing that Dave Burgess wanted to leave the road for good in order to focus on producing more hits for the group in the studio, Fuller suggested Campbell's services as an able replacement on lead guitar. After an impromptu rehearsal, Burgess couldn't help but agree with Fuller's assessment. The kid was *good*. Burgess hired Campbell on the spot for one hundred dollars a week and handed him a bright red suit to wear onstage.

After a stunned and grateful Campbell got in his old car and drove away, he carefully waited a few blocks and then let out a huge scream of joy. From a false start with one uncle to a seemingly dead end with another, how his luck had changed. He was now in a "name" band that had actually charted a number-one nationwide hit.

"We've made it, Billie," he yelled, excitedly turning toward his wife. "We've finally made the big time."

✳

After Billy Strange gave the go-ahead to Dave Burgess and the Champs to retitle "Monotonous Melody," he figured that would finally be the end of it. Maybe some royalties would trickle in, maybe not. He had no idea what they planned to call it and cared even less. In truth, he was just too busy playing studio dates to pay much attention to anything.

But the song he had composed on a bet and on the fly simply refused to go quietly. Burgess did indeed come up with a new name, dubbing the tune "Limbo Rock." And his ad hoc studio lineup of the Champs, featuring, among others, Wrecking Crew players-to-be Earl Palmer (drums), Tommy Tedesco (guitar), and Plas Johnson (sax), took it to number forty on the Hot 100, giving the Champs their strongest showing in over two years.

Though "Limbo Rock" was not nearly as big as "Tequila" had been, the success of the tune did at least temporarily breathe new life into the road version of the Champs. Stellar musicians all, this touring outfit—quite distinct from those who played under the Champs' name in the studio—featured more than just the guitar-playing skills of Glen Campbell. Also on board were a pair of Texans named Jim Seals (sax) and Dash Crofts (drums), who would go on to form the Seventies hit-making duo Seals & Crofts. And on the other guitar was a small, feisty character named Jerry Cole, who would himself become a Wrecking Crew regular in the not-too-distant future.

Perhaps more important, without anyone in the music industry or among the general public paying any real attention, a precedent was also quietly being set. These two versions of the Champs—road and studio—became one of the earliest examples within LA's fledgling rock-and-roll scene of using separate studio players from those who were listed on the record jackets (and elsewhere) as officially being members of the band. It also further helped to cement the art of record making as truly a producer's medium, where those who actually played on any given recording were quite often anonymous and interchangeable at the whim of those behind the glass.

As the Champs's producer *and* owner of its name, Burgess, to his credit, had devised the perfect economic formula: keep one set of guys permanently on the road grinding it out every night—with the band's name plastered front and center on marquees across the country—while hiring a separate group of no-name, on-call players to cut the records back home. It saved a fortune on having to bring the road group home all the time and it kept a steady flow of revenue from ticket sales coming in the door. A major win-win for a producer with a keen eye for the bottom line. Who would know the difference, anyway? And as Burgess discovered, much to his delight, no one ever did.

In the meantime, the newly christened "Limbo Rock" would still have one last, unexpected shimmy to make.

✳

Dancing has always been of central importance in the music industry. It is an age-old axiom that where there is dancing there will be record sales. And virtually nothing can sell a record faster than a red-hot bona fide dance craze, especially one created specifically for that purpose. Cuban bandleader Xavier Cugat, sensing a heightened interest in all things Latin, helped to popularize conga line dancing in the United States with his 1940 hit, "Perfidia." By the mid-Fifties, ex–Glenn Miller Band trumpeter Ray Anthony did Cugat one better by releasing a pair of million-selling singles called "The Bunny Hop" and "The Hokey Pokey." For brief periods after they separately hit the charts, the two novelty songs had Americans everywhere either jumping around on one foot or shaking various body parts "all about."

By the beginning of the 1960s, the tried-and-true formula of capitalizing on a new dance in order to sell more records had evolved into a virtual cottage industry. Rock and roll had become a phenomenon, and now any permutation or subgenre that might also sell a few records was fair game. Accordingly, label executives and producers practically stumbled over themselves in an effort to find songwriters who could come up with some kind of gimmicky new dance tune—anything that might capture the interest of record buyers. The crazier the name, the better, too. "The Stroll," "The Madison," and "The Mashed Potato" were but three examples among the many quickly recorded songs designed to create (and cash in on) the dance du jour.

With dancing being nothing if not visual, the move by ABC in 1957 to begin nationally televising the Philadelphia-based *American Bandstand* show every weekday afternoon also played a crucial role in promoting dance-based records. Dick Clark, the program's handsome, winning host, possessed an almost uncannily shrewd eye for what might excite America's teens next. And *Bandstand* was *the* music and dance showcase of its time. Live artists lip-synched their latest hit records in front of the cameras while dozens of attractive (and handpicked) young men and women cavorted about. So powerful was its appeal that many an adolescent could be found racing home after school just to see which hot new vinyl platter Dick might be spinning next or which new dance steps regulars like Ed and Bunny might be employing.

When the flip side of a Hank Ballard and the Midnighters single called "The Twist" ignited a regional dance fad of the same name, Clark encouraged local label Cameo-Parkway Records—with whom he had a relationship through *Bandstand*—to cut a new version of the song, which he could then spotlight across the country via his show. With an unknown South Philly singer called Chubby Checker (a Fats Domino knockoff in both style and name) tapped to do the honors, "The Twist" rapidly became a national smash, corkscrewing its way to the top of the Hot 100 not once but *twice* in just over a year's time. The corresponding dance's simplicity, which almost anyone could do, also easily made it the most popular of the era. From school kids to college students to jet-setters in trendy Manhattan clubs like the Peppermint Lounge, seemingly *everyone* was doing the twist.

But every dance sensation has its day, and by the summer of 1962 twist mania had finally swiveled itself to a halt. Naturally interested in keeping his now-famous singing client on the charts, Jon Sheldon, Checker's manager, thought he knew of a song that had a chance to become the next big dance floor craze: "Limbo Rock." He had heard the Champs' peppy instrumental version on the radio and liked both the melody and the name. It just needed some happy, danceable, rhyming words, he reasoned.

Sheldon gave Billy Strange a quick call in California and asked his permission to add some lyrics to the composition ("Certainly," Strange had replied), whereupon both men then went back to their respective careers. Billy had heard of Chubby Checker, of course, and was happy that the Philadelphia-based singer wanted to record his little tune. But Strange was a realist, too. He knew that everybody *thinks* they are about to cut the next great hit.

Several months after the now-long-forgotten call from Chubby Checker's manager, Billy Strange sat at his kitchen table one day, going through his mail. As he tore open one of the envelopes sitting before him, he pulled out what looked to be a check of some kind from BMI, one of the two big competing companies that collected airplay royalties on behalf of songwriters and publishers (ASCAP being the other). Strange had become used to seeing the occasional tiny check trickle in from BMI for some minor thing he had written along the way.

As he looked more closely, however, Strange suddenly noticed that this was no tiny check. It was in the staggering amount of sixty-three thousand dollars—more money than he had ever seen in one place, might ever see.

Billy Strange sat back in his chair, stupefied.

Figuring there obviously had been some kind of accounting mistake or mailing error, Strange allowed himself the luxury of enjoying the check for a few minutes, dreaming of what all it could buy. Then, with reality setting in, he decided he had better put in a call to BMI. No use keeping what isn't yours.

"Hey there, this is Billy Strange. I'm a songwriter registered with your company and I've got a check here from you guys for sixty-three thousand dollars that I'm sure isn't really mine. Can you look into it for me?"

After Strange held the line for a couple of minutes, the BMI rep came back with just one question.

"Are you the same Billy Strange that wrote a song called 'Monotonous Melody'?"

"That would be me."

"Well, your song was recorded under the name 'Limbo Rock' by the Champs, and then again by Chubby Checker. Both versions were hits, especially the one by Checker. The money is all yours."

Billy Strange simply could not believe his sheer dumb luck. Here he was gratefully playing his guitar for practically anyone who would pay, and suddenly a huge sum of money appears from nowhere—all because of some silly-assed throwaway song he wrote one night when he was drunk.

But the success of "Limbo Rock," as big as it was, would soon pale in comparison to another piece of good fortune that was about to befall him. For Strange, along with Glen Campbell, Carol Smith, Hal Belsky—now going by the professional name of Hal Blaine—and several other top session players, were all unwittingly just one pint-sized, oddly talented, egomaniacal Svengali away from a coalescence that would put them in position as *the* must-hire musicians in rock and roll.

3

He's a Rebel

Do you think I have a future as a jazz guitarist?
—Phil Spector

As thirty-seven-year-old professional studio guitarist Bill Pitman peered warily through the venetian blinds on his small San Fernando Valley home's living room window, he noticed a short, slightly built, dark-haired high school boy slowly making his way up the front walk.

In one hand the kid carried a large black guitar case almost as big as he was. In the other hand he held an expensive-looking leather attaché case. Dressed to the nines, the teenager had on a sport coat, a necktie, and neatly pressed slacks, topped off by a pair of wraparound sunglasses. Looking like some kind of unusually tiny junior executive on the make who had probably read Sloan Wilson's novel *The Man in the Gray Flannel Suit* one too many times, the strange and incongruent sight gave Pitman pause. What in the world had he gotten himself into?

Several days earlier, Pitman's wife, Mildred, had received a phone call out of the blue from some woman by the name of Bertha, practically begging for her son to be allowed to take jazz guitar lessons from "the great Bill Pitman." All of which sounded quite flattering and reasonable on its face, except for one thing: Bill Pitman didn't give guitar lessons. To anyone.

After spending the better part of two decades honing his talents in more touring Big Bands and combos than he could count, Pitman had finally become, by the mid-Fifties, a first-call guitarist in Los Angeles. In a profession where strong skills and showing up on time were paramount, producers and arrangers loved Pitman's exceptional versatility and rock-solid dependability. He played on radio and TV shows (*The Rusty Draper Show, I Love Lucy*). He played major jazz dates (Tony Bennett, Mel Tormé). And Pitman became, for over three years, the singer Peggy Lee's principal road and studio guitarist, a plum gig with a world-class artist. Sometimes he even sat in on bass or banjo during recording dates, whatever those in charge needed him to do. Pitman wore many hats in the music business and wore them all well. But teaching was decidedly not one of them.

Despite some gentle hinting from Pitman's wife, however, the determined woman with the Bronx accent on the other end of the telephone line had simply refused to take no for an answer.

"Please, just a few lessons, then?"

Whether out of pity or perhaps out of just plain exhaustion, Mildred Pitman—herself a mother of three—felt her resolve begin to crumble. When a child is in need, the shared bond between two mothers can quickly become a force majeure. The next thing she knew she heard herself agreeing to the request, as did her incredulous husband, sitting nearby.

"Mim, you know I don't want to teach," he said as she hung up the phone. "I work all week long in the studios. On weekends, I just want to cool it."

"But she seemed so desperate, Bill."

Pitman thought for a moment. If he had learned anything as a married man it was when to pick his battles. And this was definitely not one of those times. The look on his wife's face said as much. That was a domestic lesson *he* had learned.

"Okay, I'll do it," Pitman replied, sighing. "What's this kid's name anyway?"

"His mother said it was Phillip something." She paused. "Phillip Spector, I think."

✳

By the time the early Fifties rolled around, Carol Smith knew exactly what she wanted to do with her life. She wanted to keep playing guitar.

Her mentor and teacher, Horace Hatchett, had helped her pick up some local work around the Long Beach area, and she had flourished. His connections made the difference in getting her in with a number of local musicians who needed a solid guitarist to play in all sorts of configurations, from trios to combos to Big Bands. Though her knees were shaking during her first gig (as part of a small jazz outfit at a private party), she fortunately knew most of the tunes of the day—standards like "Honeysuckle Rose," "Flying Home," and "Tea for Two"—and managed to play just fine.

Starting with an average of about one booking a week at the almost unprecedented age of only fourteen, Smith rapidly gained acceptance during her high school years among the area's veteran players. She soon found herself in regular demand for live work at a variety of dances, parties, and nightclubs in the South Bay region. Still lacking proper equipment, Carol also had to routinely borrow one of Hatchett's guitars for two full years in order to save enough money to buy her own, top-of-the-line Gibson Super 400. Always versatile, she even found work as a part-time teacher at places like Morey's Music Store in nearby Lakewood.

As the money started to come in, Smith also began to feel a sense of empowerment. She found the ability to finally buy a few things for herself, help her mother with the bills, and enjoy her work, all at the same time. A heady trifecta for the ambitious teenager. And in doing so, she sat side by side on any given night of the week with a bunch of grown men in an era when women in the American workplace commonly limited their employment pursuits to nonthreatening "female" jobs such as nursing, teaching, and secretarial services.

Never satisfied with the status quo, the independent Smith took additional steps on her own to further her musical education by frequently taking the short train ride up to Los Angeles to see acts like Duke Ellington, Ella Fitzgerald, and many of the popular Big Bands of the era. It was in watching these kinds of top-flight pros that Smith began to imagine herself being a part of their world. The sort of world where only the best of the best were able to dwell. Where jazz wasn't just a style of music but a supremely expressive and nuanced art form all its own. A virtual way of life among its most dedicated practitioners. And she felt particularly drawn to the faster tempo of bebop, where improvisational chops mattered and the ability to really *swing it* mattered even more.

Just after high school, Carol caught on for a couple of years with the popular Henry Busse Orchestra, with whom she traveled the country playing dances and other events. She also ended up marrying Al Kaye, the band's string bass player, permanently taking his last name. Soon thereafter came a son and a daughter.

However, by 1957, with the Big Band gig having come to a close sometime earlier (Busse had fallen over dead from a massive heart attack during, of all things, an undertakers' convention), Carol Kaye found herself at a crossroads. Despite her best efforts, her short marriage had not worked out, due in large part to a considerable age difference and her husband's penchant for drinking a little too much wine. Kaye was also no longer on the road making regular money, either. And she now had two kids *and* a mother to support, all on a single income.

Deciding she needed to be practical, Kaye found a day job as a high-speed technical typist within the avionics division of the giant Bendix Corporation. Though the pay was good, she simultaneously moonlighted on guitar sometimes five or six nights a week in the local jazz clubs around Los Angeles. An exhausting schedule for anyone, let alone a working mother of two. But laying down some bebop fed Carol Kaye's musical soul; there was no way to shake that. And the more she played, the more her reputation grew within the higher echelons of the West Coast jazz world.

Unfortunately for Kaye, however, with rock and roll's popularity on the rise in the late Fifties, the number of Southern California clubs catering solely to jazz patrons began to dwindle in direct proportion. It made it almost impossible for an up-and-comer like Kaye to earn a living playing full-time, which had always been her dream. But she persevered, creating the music she loved by night, hoping for the best by day.

One evening, while Kaye took a short break from laying down her inventive lead guitar fills (now on an Epiphone Emperor) as part of the saxophonist Teddy Edwards's combo at the Beverly Caverns nightclub, a man she had never seen before approached her with a very unexpected question.

"Carol, my name is Bumps Blackwell," he said, extending his hand. "I'm a producer here in LA. I've been watching you play tonight and I like your style. I could use you on some record dates. Interested?"

A more-than-surprised Kaye looked at Blackwell and then at her bandmates, not sure what to think, say, or do. She had certainly heard all the rumors that taking on nonjazz recording studio work would be the kiss of death for someone trying to make a career out of playing live bebop. Once someone left, they tended to never come back. And true jazzers tended to look down on those who played what they sometimes referred to as "people's music." It took time to build a name in the clubs, too. But Kaye also knew she needed to get away from her job at Bendix as soon as possible. She had grown to dislike it. Maybe going into studio work would be a chance to finally establish a solid, well-paying career playing music full-time.

With a deep breath, a hesitant Kaye agreed to take the plunge.

"He's a new singer out of Mississippi that I just started producing," Blackwell continued, delighted that she was interested in coming aboard.

"His name is Sam Cooke."

✳

After her serendipitous encounter with the ambitious Bumps Blackwell, Carol Kaye did indeed start working studio dates for his protégé Sam Cooke. And the mental transition on her part in moving from dedicated jazzer to rock-and-roll guitarist proved to be smoother than she expected. Though Kaye had at first never heard of Cooke (few had at the time), she found herself enthused by the caliber of musicians hired to play alongside her. As she gracefully slid into her new role, her particular specialty became adding tasteful and appropriate guitar fills at important points during the songs.

To Kaye's surprise, playing on Cooke's hits at the turn of the decade like "Summertime (Part 2)" and "Wonderful World" didn't seem all that different from playing live in the clubs, either. A quality song was a quality song.

And her work began to lead directly to additional offers from other well-known producers and arrangers, including Bob Keane ("La Bamba" by Ritchie Valens), H. B. Barnum ("Pink Shoelaces" by Dodie Stevens), and Jim Lee ("Let's Dance" by Chris Montez). Word habitually traveled quickly between recording studios whenever a hot new player arrived on the scene. The comparatively lucrative studio pay also proved to be a godsend for Kaye. She soon found herself earning a steady enough income at union scale to finally quit her suffocating day job for good.

As for Glen Campbell, his touring work with the Champs began to wind its way down after a year or so, putting him in a precarious financial position. Without any further hits on the radio, the band had seen its live following diminish accordingly. But that was okay with Campbell. He was tired of the road anyway and wanted to quit. Though he needed the money, he desperately missed his wife and child back home, especially on the nights when he had to sleep five guys to a room in some fleabag motel halfway across the country. At least this time around, though, he was living in Los Angeles, where music jobs seemed more plentiful. And he still had his ace in the hole, Jerry Fuller.

With an unshakeable belief in his own songwriting abilities, Fuller was ever a man on the move. One day in early 1961, on a hunch, he decided to take his latest tune over to a new publishing company on Hollywood Boulevard he had heard about. It's the door you didn't knock on that might have been the one to hire you, he always figured.

Dropping off a demo of his song at SAR, Inc.—owned by none other than the now seemingly ubiquitous Sam Cooke, along with his business partner J. W. Alexander—Fuller hoped to entice the star into recording it. Fuller felt it was the perfect vehicle for Cooke's sublimely smooth singing style.

But when Alexander later played the demo in his small office on the phonograph kept handy for just such purposes, he didn't hear a hit. In fact, he didn't hear anything he liked about the song at all. It was just some tune about a bunch of far-off places like China, Berlin, and Waikiki. Something called "Travelin' Man." Cooke's fans wanted heartfelt love songs they could identify with, not a world atlas.

"This is pure trash," Alexander said to his secretary, flinging the disc into a garbage can next to his desk. "I'm not even going to bother Sam with it."

But at that same moment, directly next door, in another office, a second set of ears had come to a very different conclusion. Joe Osborn, a bass player out of Louisiana currently playing in Ricky Nelson's band, had heard the song, too. And he liked it.

Having stopped by that day to conduct some business at Imperial Records, Ricky's label, Osborn could hear the record being played through the Warner Building's notoriously thin walls. He immediately thought the song might be just right for Nelson. It had a great hook and an easy, carefree feel, something the teen idol's fans had come to expect from his music.

Osborn walked next door and inquired about the song's name and writer. Alexander, a man of few words, merely motioned toward the 45 now sitting in the garbage can and said, "You want it? You got it. It's all yours—right there."

When he took the record back to the studio for Ricky to hear, Osborn's instincts proved to be right on the money. Nelson loved the song. So much so that he and his band cut it within days, and it soon became his first number-one hit in over three years.

Jerry Fuller had scored big. With the success of "Travelin' Man" for Ricky Nelson, Fuller's stock as a songwriter had risen dramatically. Nelson now wanted to know what else he had song-wise, and Fuller had plenty to offer. He also brought in his old pal Glen Campbell to sing with him on backing vocals for Ricky on every song after "Travelin' Man." Glen got to play his guitar on most of them, too. With help once again from Fuller, a stand-up guy if there ever was one, Campbell had finally achieved his longed-for entrée into the invitation-only world of LA recording studios.

✳

In spite of his initial concerns, Bill Pitman's new role as the teenage Phil Spector's guitar teacher actually went better than he had expected. It wasn't his dream job, but working with the kid was okay.

Each Saturday morning, Pitman would show his earnest young student some standard jazz licks, and then Spector would diligently work on them at his home across town, always returning exactly seven days later to show his progress. Pitman's wife, too, would hang out in the kitchen and make chitchat with Bertha Spector, while teacher and pupil went through their paces just steps away.

But several lessons into the arrangement, Phil Spector showed up one week at his appointed time with something clearly weighing on his mind.

"Bill, I gotta ask you something," Spector said, looking unusually somber.

"What's that?"

"Do you think I have a future as a jazz guitarist?"

Well, there it was. The elephant that had been silently sharing the living room with them from the very first lesson had been acknowledged.

Spector, to his credit, was nothing if not clearheaded and practical about his own prospects. He previously had mentioned to Pitman about his plans to possibly become a court reporter, going so far as to purchase his own stenographic machine and to take a series of courses. A recent job offer had even come his way. So he naturally wanted to know where things stood.

For Pitman, the question created a conflict of emotions. On one hand, he had grown to like Spector. Pitman could see that the serious young man was both hardworking and conscientious—two admirable qualities. But Pitman also detected one fatal flaw in Spector's playing. And he felt he had to be honest.

"No, Phil, in truth, I don't see that for you," Pitman replied. "You're lacking one thing that a musician absolutely has to have. And that's meter. You don't *feel* when one musical phrase ends and another begins."

Spector didn't argue.

"I know I don't," he replied resignedly.

Though perfectly proficient skill-wise, and with a good ear, Phil Spector—for all his intense effort and desire—just never seemed able to grasp where he was in a song.

"I'm sorry," Pitman offered, feeling genuine empathy for the boy. "But I can't teach you that. I don't know anybody who can."

✳

Not long after the terrible circus fire in Hartford, fifteen-year-old Hal Blaine and his family moved to Southern California. His father had developed a serious asthma condition and the family doctor recommended drier air and a reduced amount of pollen as the best course of action. While Hal's parents moved in with his aunt and uncle in the Santa Monica area, he ultimately chose to live with his older sister, Belle, in San Bernardino, about eighty miles to the east of Los Angeles.

It was in San Berdoo, as the locals called it, that Blaine's professional drumming ambitions finally began to take shape. Getting together with some local high school friends, Blaine formed his first band, a little six-piece, part-time combo, and subsequently played his first paying gig at the Chick-A-Bunny restaurant and nightclub in tiny Norco, about a half an hour away. The place wasn't much, but Blaine earned five bucks a night and had his choice of either a free chicken or rabbit dinner. And he loved every minute of it.

After dropping out of high school and serving a two-plus-year hitch in Korea during the late Forties playing drums as the only PFC in an all-officer U.S. Army band, a nineteen-year-old Blaine returned stateside and soon used his G.I. Bill benefits to enroll in the prestigious Roy C. Knapp School of Percussion in Chicago. Blaine knew that to really succeed as a professional drummer he needed to both polish his skills and learn how to read music. Guys who could read drum charts, as well as the rest of the band's music charts, were the ones who were in big demand. Without that ability, the chances of one day playing for a major orchestra led by someone like Count Basie or Benny Goodman were practically nil.

Following graduation, Blaine then spent several years honing his sight-reading skills by playing drums in several Chicago strip joints and then in nightclubs and supper clubs all over the country with a number of small bands. He even found time in the mid-Fifties to squeeze in a short-lived marriage to a beautiful young singer named Vicki Young. But by 1957, with Blaine single once again, he finally made his way back to California for good, settling in for an extended run as the drummer for the Carol Simpson Quartet, a noted jazz combo.

One night, just after finishing a show with Simpson and the band at the celebrity-laden Garden of Allah hotel lounge in Hollywood, Blaine felt a tap on his shoulder. He turned to see a short, stocky Mafioso type standing right behind him.

"Hey, kid, I've been watching you," the wiseguy said, puffing on a cigar. "And I like the way you play. You wanna make some money? I got a band auditioning tomorrow for Capitol Records and they need a drummer."

Hal thought for a moment. Getting some studio work was definitely appealing. That had long been one of his goals. Maybe it would be worth hearing this guy out.

"What kind of music?"

"It's called rockabilly, like rock and roll, but with some country and western thrown in."

Blaine had been listening to some of the latest rock-and-roll records on the radio and didn't think much of them. As far as he could tell, rock and roll was mostly just a bunch of beats and a bass drum. Not nearly as interesting or challenging as playing jazz, his latest love. And he was already in a band.

"Nah, I don't think I'd be interested," Blaine said. "I don't really have much experience with that kind of music."

"Well, would you be interested if I gave you seventy-five bucks just to come in for the audition and then leave?"

Now that was more to Blaine's liking. No strings attached and some quick and easy green to shove in his pocket.

"Okay, I'll do it," he said.

It would be one of the smartest moves the young drummer would ever make. And a funny thing happened to Hal Blaine after barely playing one song with the unknown rockabilly musicians just before their big audition: he became the band's permanent drummer.

After meeting with the young trio of musicians to talk things over and maybe rehearse a little bit, Blaine, much to his surprise, found himself taking an instant liking to them. They were country to the core and at least a decade younger, but he loved their enthusiasm and collective sense of humor. It also didn't hurt that they told Blaine they were in fact auditioning to be the backing band for teen sensation Tommy Sands and desperately needed a good drummer to go on the road with them if they got the gig.

Hal knew that a national tour with a name star like Sands would likely mean a nice pay increase and it also might provide some welcome exposure for his drumming career. The kid was too hot not to score some major network TV appearances along the way, Blaine thought.

Though he wasn't really looking to leave the Carol Simpson Quartet, by the time Blaine finished jamming with the three Texans on an old tune made famous by Hank Williams called "My Bucket's Got a Hole in It," the notion of actually throwing in with them began to take hold.

But before Blaine could give it any further thought, a booming voice rang out from the shadows.

"You're just what we need," a man said. "When can you start?"

Tommy Sands and his manager had been secretly watching the whole time. And they liked what they had heard. The four musicians were a perfect blend.

After an exchange of introductions and a quick round of small talk, the pair got down to business, offering Blaine a deal on the spot: he would start at three hundred dollars a week to be the band's drummer and road manager. He would also get to play on Tommy's recordings at Capitol, something Blaine particularly coveted. That would give him some important studio experience and might also help him make a few good connections. And with many veteran drummers in Hollywood unable or unwilling to play rock and roll, Hal Blaine's timing could not have been more perfect. Working with Sands would provide a road-tested crash course in laying down a solid rock beat, a skill that producers, arrangers, and contractors all over town were increasingly hungry to find.

As they all said their good-byes that day, Tommy Sands's manager, Ted Wick, wanted a decision. Was Blaine on board?

"Let me think it over," Hal said with a smile, knowing full well he had been presented with the opportunity of a lifetime.

"Don't think too long," Wick replied. "You're leaving next week."

With Blaine agreeing by the next day to accept the manager's offer, going on tour with Tommy Sands and his band turned out to be three years' worth of everything that the drummer could have hoped for and more. The quintet toured the world several times over, playing for hoards of screaming teens by night and lounging by the pools of luxury hotels by day. And Blaine did in fact end up on national television multiple times, appearing with Sands on network variety shows hosted by the likes of Red Skelton, Tennessee Ernie Ford, and Garry Moore.

Perhaps more important, while working at Capitol Records Blaine not only played on most of Sands's recordings but also got to know plenty of movers and shakers involved in LA's studio world. These connections directly translated into playing on session dates for other major-label artists, including the Diamonds, the singers Patti Page and Connie Francis, and even Elvis on several of his movie soundtracks, including *Blue Hawaii* and *Girls! Girls! Girls*. Other than occasionally kidding around in the studio, however, Hal Blaine and the rest of the movie musicians interacted sparingly with Elvis on a personal level. The King had his so-called Memphis Mafia on hand for all that. If Presley so much as wanted a Coke, a half dozen of these handpicked hangers-on would leap to grab one for him.

By the beginning of the Sixties, through this growing number of session opportunities, Blaine also got to know a couple of fellow studio musicians named Steve Douglas and Earl Palmer, who were doing most of the rock-and-roll dates around town. Not only did they quickly become Blaine's good friends; they also generously saw fit to recommend his services to producers and contractors wherever they could.

Suddenly Blaine's stick work was in high demand. And the irony of it all didn't escape him. After years of virtual invisibility while providing the rhythm on countless, often-complicated arrangements for all sorts of crooners, Big Bands, and jazz combos, it took playing the drums in a three-chord rockabilly band to finally put him on the map. Hal Blaine was now fast becoming the last thing he could have imagined: a rock-and-roll studio drummer.

✳

Despite the deflating realization that he had no future as a professional jazz guitarist, Phil Spector found it within himself to take the news from Bill Pitman in stride. There were other ways Spector could make a living in music; he was sure of it.

No longer seriously considering the option of becoming a court reporter, the diminutive Spector instead was pushed by his overriding love for music and his overweening personality in another, more suitable career direction. He decided to form his own singing group.

In early 1958, after joining with a couple of his classmates from Fairfax High School, Annette Kleinbard and Marshall Leib, the always-hustling Spector managed to finagle a record deal for the trio (through a friend's neighbor) with a tiny label in Hollywood called Era Records. Naming themselves the Teddy Bears (after the Elvis Presley song from the year before), they worked up an arrangement of a Spector-penned song based on the epitaph carved on his late father Ben's gravestone. To virtually everyone's surprise, the song—"To Know Him Is To Love Him"—ended up becoming a number-one national hit. Still only a senior in high school, Phil Spector had accomplished what seemed to be the impossible. He had metamorphosed from an unknown, struggling jazz guitar student to local rock-and-roll royalty, all within a matter of months.

With the Teddy Bears' promising future unfortunately derailed in less than a year by the release of a series of ill-conceived follow-up singles, their initial chart-topping success did serve one major purpose. It provided Phil Spector with a clear view of *his* future. Yes, he had enjoyed all the singing, writing, and camaraderie that had gone into creating their one and only hit. But what *really* turned Spector's crank had been putting all the individual elements of the song together in the studio. It was like working on a real-life jigsaw puzzle, only he got to control all the pieces. An especially intoxicating proposition for a boy desperate to forge his own identity away from a domineering mother.

Carefully weighing his options, Spector decided he would set his sights on an even loftier occupational prize. No more singing for his supper. No more answering to others. He now wanted the top job. Phil Spector would become a record producer.

Behind the windowless walls of a recording studio, the producer is the one in charge of everything. It is his (or her) absolute domain. From the choosing of the musicians and the engineers to exactly how a song is recorded, the producer runs the show. An obviously powerful position, it also comes with its share of stress. Producers are usually put in place to make the best possible commercially viable recording. When things go right, the monetary rewards can be significant. And the acclaim can establish a career overnight. But when a record with high expectations fails to become a hit, it's the producer who most often winds up being called on the carpet by unhappy label executives.

In mid-1960, through a connection made while singing with the Teddy Bears, Phil Spector, with characteristic industriousness, landed a job as an apprentice producer in New York City with the famed songwriting team of Jerry Leiber and Mike Stoller. The duo, composers of classic hits like "Hound Dog," "Jailhouse Rock," and "Stand by Me," took the twenty-year-old Spector under their wing, where his producing prowess and fanatical devotion to his newly adopted craft soon became apparent.

After a little over a year of tutelage, while manning the productions for major artists like Ruth Brown, LaVern Baker, and Ray Peterson ("Corinna, Corinna," a number-nine hit in early 1961), Spector felt he had squeezed all he could out of his relationship with Leiber and Stoller. Spector had seen firsthand the methods they employed in creating important songs for important artists. How they used multiple percussionists. How they positioned the microphones just so. How they carefully mixed down all the competing sounds at the control board into a cohesive, unique, and compelling finished product. Nothing escaped Spector's hawk-like vision and hearing. Now he just needed to put the second part of his plan into play.

Traveling back to the West Coast, Spector quickly wheedled his way into a partnership with Lester Sill, the same guy who had recommended his services to Leiber and Stoller in the first place. Only this time around, instead of just producing, Spector had a grander vision. He now wanted to have his own record label, too. That way nobody could ever again tell him what to record or what to release. For Sill, the pairing made good sense as well. His forte was record promotion, an extremely important sales-related task for which Spector had shown little natural interest.

Settling on the corporate moniker of Philles Records (the merging of their two first names), the two opened a small office in Hollywood and promptly set about looking to record some hits. One day, in the summer of

1962, while visiting Aaron Schroeder Music Publishing in New York City on a scouting mission to look for new song possibilities, Spector came across a demo recording that made his eyes light up. Written by the popular singer Gene Pitney, the hard-hitting tune, called "He's a Rebel," was all about teenage alienation, a traditionally relevant—and bankable—theme among young record buyers.

From the moment the song started to play, Spector could feel a stirring in his gut. This was it: the surefire pop smash he had been looking for to put his new label on the map for good.

He leaped to his feet.

"I want an exclusive on *that* one!"

✳

Racing back to Los Angeles with a copy of "He's a Rebel" burning a hole in his briefcase, Phil Spector immediately booked time at Gold Star Recording Studios, the same place he had used for his big hit with the Teddy Bears. Spector loved the sound and vibe the studio provided, which he felt had directly contributed to his early success. He also knew he needed to work fast. Great songs don't stay unrecorded for long. And an "exclusive" from a publisher often wasn't worth the handshake it came with. Back in New York, Aaron Schroeder had let slip that another producer by the name of Snuff Garrett had recently shown interest in the song, too. Time was clearly of the essence.

With a sense of urgency, Spector next placed a call to an old friend from Fairfax High School, Steve Douglas. Besides having become one of the most sought-after sax players on the West Coast (after spending several years as one of guitar star Duane Eddy's Rebels), Douglas also found time to moonlight as a freelance contractor, the guy in charge of hiring all the musicians on any given studio date. Whenever a producer or arranger had a new recording project coming up, one of the first calls was to a contractor. From there, the contractor would begin booking the exact number of musicians needed to fit the style of music and the budget.

On many, if not most, rock-and-roll recording dates at that time, only a few instruments were commonly utilized—often just guitar, bass, and drums.

Sometimes a saxophone or piano might be thrown into the mix, too. But keeping a rock-and-roll arrangement clean and simple was part of the whole point. It's what helped give the genre its propulsive quality, its sense of in-your-face immediacy. The proof of the minimalistic formula's success lay evident in the massive number of hits recorded by everyone from Elvis to Buddy Holly to the Everly Brothers.

But Phil Spector saw things differently. He would have none of the status quo. He had other ideas for his latest production. Transcendent ideas. To him, less wasn't more—*more* was more. He told Douglas to get him two bass players, two guitar players, and two sax players, plus a drummer and a pianist. Eight players instead of the usual three or four. It would be rock and roll writ large, Spector-style.

When they all gathered in Studio A at Gold Star, the engineer, Larry Levine, did a double take. He had never seen that many musicians on a rock-and-roll date before. But having worked with Spector in the past, Levine knew enough to go with the flow. To him, the kid was an abrasive, spoiled brat, but Levine never once doubted Spector's talent.

Built in 1950 by David Gold and Stan Ross on the corner of Santa Monica and Vine in what used to be a dental office, Gold Star had become, by the early Sixties, one of the most successful and influential recording studios in the world. Well before the Record Plant in Sausalito, Electric Lady Studios in New York, or Muscle Shoals Sound Studio in Alabama, Gold Star was *the* place to cut a record in America. Especially during the early days of rock and roll, few studios witnessed more history than the scuffed linoleum of Gold Star.

Though a comparatively small structure, with only two undersized tracking rooms, it featured the most highly regarded echo chamber in the music business. And Gold Star's handcrafted audio compressors and microphone preamps were the envy of every engineer in town. "Summertime Blues" by Eddie Cochran had been recorded there. Same with "Tequila" by the Champs and "La Bamba" by Ritchie Valens. Gold Star had a sought-after, hit-making mojo all its own.

As the musicians settled into their metal folding chairs scattered throughout Studio A, Steve Douglas took the opportunity to walk Spector around for some quick introductions. Spector already knew a couple of the guys—Ray Pohlman on electric bass and Howard Roberts on guitar were guys he had worked with before—but the rest were unfamiliar faces.

After Spector said hello to Tommy Tedesco (guitar), Al DeLory (piano), and Jimmy Bond (upright bass), he stopped in front of the drum kit.

"I'm Phil," he said, extending his hand.

A dark-haired, blue-eyed drummer stuck out his hand in return.

"Nice to meet you, Phil. I'm Hal Blaine."

✳

Within weeks of its release, "He's a Rebel" became exactly what Phil Spector had envisioned from the start: a number-one hit. Credited to the Crystals, a New York–based vocal group with whom Spector had been working on and off, the song had actually been sung by a local LA session veteran named Darlene Wright. Blessed with a powerful voice and a charismatic presence, Wright was a natural at singing up-tempo material that required passion and swagger. And she, along with the expanded number of musicians who had performed with her on "He's a Rebel," had allowed Spector to test his orchestral approach to rock and roll, with spectacular results.

Now, like an obsessed alchemist frantically trying to turn base metals into gold, Spector wanted to toss additional instrumental ingredients into his sonic stew, to make an even bigger sound. If more was more, why couldn't a *lot* more be the most? Spector wanted to push his Wagnerian concept to its absolute limits, to make what he began to refer to as "little symphonies for the kids."

In typically unorthodox fashion, the next song on Spector's docket would be, on its face, a most unusual choice. Thinking back to his childhood one day as he fooled around on his guitar, Spector suddenly flashed on a tune he loved from a Disney movie called *Song of the South*. It had won an Academy Award in 1946 for best original song, and, he thought, it would make an even better rock-and-roll record.

Gathering at Gold Star on August 24, 1962, Spector and his engineer, Larry Levine, set about turning "Zip-a-Dee-Doo-Dah" into yet another three-minute rock-and-roll symphony. And in keeping with the boss's explicit instructions, Steve Douglas had gone all out in his contracting efforts this time around. Spector wanted "the same drummer as last time," and Douglas also brought in two other players who were making significant names for themselves in the studios: Carol Kaye and Glen Campbell.

Now, instead of eight pieces like had been used on "He's a Rebel," those present totaled a mind-boggling *twelve*—including three guitarists, three bass players, and three piano players—four times the total number of musicians found on a normal rock-and-roll date. But there was nothing remotely normal about Phil Spector or his methods. Competition and common sense be damned; he wanted the fattest, densest sound he could possibly muster.

As the musicians dutifully labored away over the next three hours rehearsing and refining their respective parts, Spector kept asking Levine to turn up the faders (volume levels) on the mixing board for the microphones used on each of the individual instruments. With his intense focus on every nuance, Spector always liked listening to the music as loud as possible on the three big Altec 603 monitors in the booth. But this time, with so many sounds competing with each other in a low-ceilinged, relatively small twenty-eight-by-thirty-five-foot tracking room, the mélange became too much for the custom-designed board to handle. Levine's meters were pinging into the red zone, indicating a dangerous level of volume overload, causing distortion.

Despite knowing the wrath he would likely incur, Levine took a deep breath and began uniformly turning off each of the faders.

A disbelieving Spector watched in horror.

"What the hell are you *doing*?" he exploded. "I just about had it, man. I just about had the sound."

"I'm sorry, Phil, but the levels were redlining. It was unrecordable."

Spector slumped in his chair, demoralized. His painstaking, hours-long effort at achieving just the right balance between all the instruments—a delicate task far beyond the competency of virtually any other rock-and-roll producer on either coast—had now been completely wiped out.

Without saying anything further, a guilt-ridden Levine did the only thing he could think to do: he began very carefully dialing the faders back up, one by one. Maybe he could somehow salvage things by mimicking Spector's skillfully achieved balances, but at lower overall volume levels.

As the assembled musicians began running through the song one more time, Levine gingerly brought up the levels on the two acoustic guitars. So far, so good. Then, slowly, he raised the volume levels on each of the three basses, followed by the triumvirate of pianos, the sax, and then the drums and percussion. Not bad, he thought—almost there. One more to go.

But just as Levine reached for the final fader, the one that controlled the volume for the lone electric guitar, Spector suddenly shouted, "Stop! That's it. It's perfect."

Levine's hand froze in place.

"What about the electric guitar, Phil? I haven't turned its volume up yet."

"Forget it—don't touch anything. I like the sound the way it is. Let's record it. *Now.*"

With so many instruments crammed into such a small space, the sound from the electric guitar had accidentally leaked into various neighboring microphones, allowing its fuzzed-out tone to artfully blend into the mix like it had all been planned from the start.

As for the tone itself, the guitarist, Billy Strange (always one of Steve Douglas's favorite hires), had decided on his own to pull one of the four 6L6GC output vacuum tubes out of the back of his Fender Twin Reverb amp in order to get the raw sound he felt the song needed. A surprised Spector loved the results. That's why he only wanted to work with the best.

With optimal volume and balance levels finally reset, Levine began rolling tape. On a now-reenergized Phil Spector's cue, the twelve assembled musicians promptly launched into laying down an inspired, slinky, and soulful performance for the ages, sounding like they had been playing together all their lives. The guitars, basses, pianos, drums, and horns expertly melded with the swimming, cavernous echo to create a giant wall of sound. And after the voices of Bobby Sheen, Darlene Wright, and Fanita James were added (dubbed Bob B. Soxx and the Blue Jeans), there was no doubt in anyone's mind as to the specialness of the outcome. Rock and roll had been forever altered.

Semi-randomly chosen though they initially were, Glen Campbell,

Carol Kaye, and Hal Blaine, along with Billy Strange, Bill Pitman (personally requested by Spector), and seven other highly skilled session musicians, had unknowingly created music history—and a career path for themselves. On one level, they had given the twenty-two-year-old wunderkind Phil Spector his second consecutive Top 10 hit, in the process helping to solidify a sound, style, and feel like no other. But on perhaps an even more profound level, their teaming on that one hot August day in 1962 had been carefully noted by most of the other rock-and-roll producers in town. They reasoned that if these particular sidemen were now Spector's secret weapons in cutting his growing list of majestic, operatic smashes, then they wanted in on the action, too. The driven young producer's innovative, interwoven use of just the right musicians in just the right combination had spun gold. And in the music business, imitation has always been the sincerest form of making a profit.

The Little Old Lady
(from Pasadena)

That just blows my mind.
—BRIAN WILSON

By the summer of 1963, Phil Spector was on a roll. With eight more Hot 100 singles to his credit in the first half of the year alone, Spector's carefully crafted, ever-expanding Wall of Sound production process had become a juggernaut. In particular, his work behind the glass for the Crystals on "He's Sure the Boy I Love," "Da Doo Ron Ron (When He Walked Me Home)," and "Then He Kissed Me" generated two more Top 10 smashes and a third that just missed. Spector's power, prestige, and golden touch seemingly had reached its apex. No independent rock-and-roll producer had *ever* released so many hits in such a short period. And his favored vocalists, the Crystals, were fast becoming the biggest girl group in the land.

Yet it would ironically be Spector's first single with a very different trio of female singers that would soon secure his—and the Wrecking Crew's—positions as the most potent underlying combined force in rock and roll.

Standing alone one day along the back wall of Gold Star's Studio A in early July of 1963, Nino Tempo found himself quietly aghast. The handsome, stoutly built singer, sax player, and general aide-de-camp to Phil Spector had been watching a throng of Wrecking Crew musicians some fourteen strong, including by-now-familiar faces such as Hal Blaine, Jimmy Bond, Russell Bridges (aka Leon Russell), Frankie Capp, Steve Douglas, Al De-Lory, Bill Pitman, Ray Pohlman, Don Randi, and Tommy Tedesco, plus several additional horn guys, play the same song over and over for several hours. Growing tired after forty-one takes, some of the players were naturally starting to make an occasional mistake. Not many, but enough so that it stood out to the ever-vigilant Tempo. Musical errors were something that always drove him crazy.

Having previously heard the tune at his house when Spector had stopped by one evening to play it on the piano, Tempo didn't think much of it then, and he thought even less of it now. But all personal preferences aside, at least a song should be played cleanly and correctly before committing it to tape. Of that much Tempo was sure.

"Phil, have you *heard* all the mistakes out there?" Tempo asked, stepping back inside the control booth. "How can you possibly make a record out of this?"

Phil Spector just smiled.

With his bombastic production methods now refined to a level of absolute commercial perfection, Spector knew that within his little kingdom the ends always justified the means, even if the individual elements might seem dissonant to the untrained ear. A few little errors were irrelevant when it came to the big picture.

"Don't pay any attention to what's going on out there," Spector replied. "It's what's coming out of the speakers *in here* that matters."

And he was right.

As Spector's now-trusted engineer, Larry Levine, once again began raising the master volume level on the mono mix of all the tracks, the small room filled with the sounds of the most beautiful backing arrangement Tempo had ever heard. It was nothing like the primitive little composition Spector had haltingly performed on the piano several days earlier. This was altogether *majestic*. There was Blaine, all right, front and center, banging out what would become his signature drum fill: *bom, bom-bom,* bap—*bom, bom-bom,* bap. And the myriad of competing guitar and piano performances by the other players that had all seemed so mistake ridden only minutes before now somehow blended perfectly, creating a sum vastly greater than its parts. Tempo had returned at just the right time. With tape rolling, this, the forty-second take, was clearly the keeper.

By the time the Ronette's vocals were added (featuring Spector's soon-to-be wife, Ronnie Bennett, giving her innocent, seductive all on lead), Nino Tempo stood in awe. This was Spector's finest moment, topping "He's a Rebel" and all the others, no questions asked. In Tempo's mind, this new song, called "Be My Baby," was a true miracle. Perhaps the finest piece of recording he had ever experienced. Spector and his faithful Wrecking Crew charges had outdone themselves.

And Tempo wouldn't be the only one to feel that way. Though the song stalled at number two on the national charts for three straight weeks (bafflingly held off by Jimmy Gilmer and the Fireballs' version of "Sugar Shack," which itself would be supplanted at number one by none other than Nino Tempo and his sister April Stevens with "Deep Purple"), Phil Spector's latest creation had nevertheless hit an aural bull's-eye. Among the public and within the music industry alike, "Be My Baby" was the biggest little symphony of them all.

But for one music producer in particular, "Be My Baby" would come to mean something even more. Its layered, stylistic renderings, all supplied by the Wrecking Crew's crackerjack instrumentation, would soon become a template faithfully emulated by one of the most important figures in rock-and-roll history.

✳

In the early fall of 1963, as a skinny, six-foot-four-inch young record producer leisurely drove along Sunset Boulevard one afternoon in his new aquamarine Pontiac Grand Prix muscle car, a song came on the radio that suddenly made him pull to the side of the road.

"Oh, my God!" he exclaimed to his girlfriend as they skidded to a stop. "This is the best song I've *ever* heard."

Listening intently as he turned up the volume, the twenty-two-year-old immediately seized upon the innovativeness of the production, especially the way the melody line seemed to remain constant while the three main chords kept moving around it. A simple yet ingenious production maneuver.

By the time all two minutes and forty-one seconds of "Be My Baby" by the Ronettes began to fade its way into the next big hit song on "Channel 98 Color Radio" KFWB-AM, the LA area's preeminent Top 40 station, the tension in the car had grown palpable.

"That just blows my mind," an alternately amazed and anguished Brian Wilson said, slapping the steering wheel with both hands. "I could *never* do that."

"Don't worry, baby," his girlfriend replied. "You will. You'll see."

✳

Following his intensely personal roadside encounter with Phil Spector's crowning musical achievement, Brian Wilson did the only thing he could think to do: he immediately bought ten copies of the record. As the producer and co-founder of a rising band called the Beach Boys that had already scored a handful of Top 40 hits of their own, Wilson then proceeded to play "Be My Baby" incessantly, memorizing every note, every sound. With his competitive instincts now energized, he became obsessed.

Once satisfied that he had gleaned every production value he possibly could from the Spector recording, Wilson then called his friend Roger Christian, a lyricist and local disc jockey who held down the 9:00 P.M. to midnight shift on KFWB. Having written songs for the Beach Boys with Christian before ("Shut Down," "Spirit of America," and "Little Deuce Coupe"), Wilson had an idea. This time out he wanted to really go for the gold, to write and record a song that would be every bit as strong as what Spector had been putting out. And not just in terms of the melody and lyrics, either, but the entire production process. If Phil could do it, he could do it.

As the two songwriters worked to finish their collaboration on what would become "Don't Worry Baby" (based on his girlfriend's words of reassurance when he first heard "Be My Baby" in the car), Brian Wilson instinctively knew he had a hit on his hands. Roger Christian could feel it, too.

"It's a damn good song, Brian," he commented.

Now all Wilson had to do was to break his plans to the rest of his band. Though he had for several months brought in various session players on a sporadic, potluck basis to supplement things, the other Beach Boys generally played on the earliest songs, too. But not anymore. If he wanted to raise his game to Spector-like levels, Wilson knew that he would have to go all out. The arrangements would have to become more complex. No more cutting simple little three-chord surf tunes like "Surfin' USA." To accomplish this, he began hiring the same full cast of Wrecking Crew musicians his idol Spector always used. Wilson wanted players with the kind of skills that could help him realize on vinyl the full-blown, multi-layered arsenal of sounds he had floating around in his head. Something that might take rock and roll to a new level, perhaps even eclipsing Spector's vaunted work.

✳

On Christmas Eve, 1964, Glen Campbell received an early and most improbable holiday gift: he became one of the Beach Boys.

With Brian Wilson finally making good on his threat to quit touring with his band in order to concentrate solely on studio work, the rest of the Beach Boys were suddenly in need of a quality road replacement for their leader, someone who could play intricate bass lines while simultaneously singing various high-harmony parts. No easy task for even the best of musicians. But the lads in the striped shirts wouldn't have to look far for an able body.

Having recently worked on a number of prominent studio dates for Wilson with others in the Wrecking Crew ("Be True to Your School," "I Get Around," and "Dance, Dance, Dance" among them), the versatile Campbell perfectly fit the requirements. Clean-cut and handsome, he could play, he could sing, and the boys in the band—Al Jardine, Mike Love, Carl Wilson, and Dennis Wilson—liked him. Perhaps even more important, Campbell already knew most of their songs.

Now, just as he had done with the Champs several years earlier, Glen Campbell had stepped in as part of a separate touring unit for a stealth-like name-brand studio group. But unlike before, this time the producer wanted Campbell to continue playing on the record dates, too, right alongside the rest of the Wrecking Crew. With the lesson of "Be My Baby" still ringing in his ears, Brian Wilson had gradually increased his use of studio players to the point where they now played virtually every instrument. The other Beach Boys then cut the vocals when they came home from touring. And with the change, the hits, growing exponentially more sophisticated by the day, just kept on coming.

Of course, Capitol Records made sure to keep the whole subterfuge well under wraps, never once considering the idea of actually crediting any sidemen on the Beach Boys' record jackets. Just like all the other labels in town that had bands being replaced in the studio by the Wrecking Crew, the notion of that particular secret making its way out to the world was enough to cause apoplexy. Those in power knew that millions of fans might well feel duped if the truth ever leaked. And that would be bad for business. Extremely bad. "What the public doesn't know won't hurt them," one executive was heard to say, evidencing the prevailing sentiment.

For Campbell, joining what was now the most popular American rock-and-roll band proved to be the best of both worlds. It allowed him to stay active on the studio scene with both the Beach Boys and other groups (especially Jan and Dean, who were Wilson's friendly rivals), which was important. That was Campbell's bread and butter, and he needed to keep his name and face out there. But being onstage was a blast, too, and it also paid very well. Not to mention the fact that the Beach Boys traveled first class all the way, nothing like his days with the Champs, when five guys crammed themselves into a worn-out Pontiac after every show and drove until dawn.

Between the two pursuits, Campbell found his income pushing for the first time into the six-figure range, giving him enough cash flow to buy a nice four-bedroom home on Satsuma Street in North Hollywood and lease a brand-new gold Cadillac. From a personal and material perspective, life had gotten very good, very fast, for the in-demand Campbell. Better than he had ever expected. He now had a wife, three children, money in the bank, and a thriving livelihood.

But Campbell also knew that few studio musicians ever broke away and achieved any kind of successful recording careers on their own. Though it could be lucrative, being a sideman virtually guaranteed a future of invisibility and truncated creative freedom. The real joy, he felt, came from singing and playing out front, being the main attraction. Just like he had done back in Albuquerque. And Glen Campbell was determined to one day recapture that feeling.

✳

As sixteen-year-old Donald Altfeld, a recently arrived transfer student from the Rust Belt region of the Midwest, nervously stood in line to register for his first day of classes at University High in West Los Angeles, he couldn't help but marvel at how his existence had suddenly, almost bizarrely, changed.

Like Dorothy summarily being blown into the mythical Land of Oz, Altfeld had just witnessed the contours of his world not only dramatically transform but also seemingly go from black and white to color, practically overnight. From the moment he had stepped onto the school's beautifully manicured campus, everywhere he looked he had seen tricked-out hot rods, billowing palm trees, muscle-bound athletes, and gorgeous blond-haired girls with golden tans, each manifestly more desirable than the last. His life back home in Cleveland—to him a bleak, moldering, and unbearably cold smokestack city—had been nothing like this.

After signing up for several courses, including journalism—his favorite of the bunch—Altfeld set about acclimating himself to his surreal new surroundings. Within days, he managed to wangle a high-profile position as a music columnist for the school newspaper, due in large part to his real-world experience in writing a similar weekly feature for *Dig* magazine, a nationally distributed teen 'zine. His lifelong obsession with album cover credits and record chart rankings had recently paid off, with his uncle (a dentist) helping him get the job through one of his patients. Now, in addition to earning fifty dollars a week as a part-time freelancer with his outside gig, Altfeld would be getting school credit, too, all for doing the thing he loved most in the world—writing about music.

When the issue of the school newspaper containing his first column finally hit the hallway stands, Altfeld rushed to grab a copy. He had picked "Come Go with Me" by the Dell-Vikings as his hit-bound song choice of the week. And he was sure the other students would soon be lining up to praise his oracle-like abilities in predicting the tune's success. That might go a long way toward helping him win some friends inside Uni's intimidating, clique-heavy social scene.

But when Altfeld opened the page to his column, he couldn't believe what he saw. Instead of the record he had carefully chosen—on a tip from his childhood friend Freddie Wieder back in Cleveland, where new 45s usually "broke" on the local charts several weeks before making any noise out west—someone had inserted the song "School Day" by Chuck Berry.

Incensed with the violation of his private domain, Altfeld let out a yelp of frustration and immediately took off looking for the culprit. Nobody was going to change his song pick without his permission. That went to the core of his very being. Besides, who in the school could possibly know as much as he did about the record business? Didn't the other students know he wrote for *Dig*?

When the journalism teacher, Mr. Wingard, simply shrugged and said, "Sorry, Don, it wasn't me," Altfeld figured he had better check with the school's print shop. Maybe they would know what the hell had happened.

As Altfeld marched across campus to the tile-roofed building that housed the newspaper's giant Linotype machine, he was prepared to throw down the gauntlet. All 120 pounds of him. Yes, he might be the new kid in school and smaller than most, but words—his precisely chosen words—were at stake on this one.

Passing through the double-wide doorway leading into the busy print shop, Altfeld approached the first person he saw, a guy with his back to him, hunched over the big press, apparently tinkering with something. As the student worker turned to see who had just come in, he suddenly lost his footing on the slippery floor, did a half pirouette, bounced off the edge of the typesetting machine, and then fell flat on his face, scattering newsprint everywhere.

As Altfeld watched in amazement, his fellow student then just as quickly jumped back to his feet, dusted himself off, and said with a grin, "Hi there— I'm Jan. How can I help you?"

"My name's Don," Altfeld said, duly impressed by the tall, good-looking kid's nimble recovery. "I write for the *Daily Warrior* here and somebody recently changed the name of the record 'pick of the week' in my music column without asking me. Would you happen to know who that was?"

"Well, yes, I do—it was me, actually," Altfeld's ink-covered schoolmate admitted, laughing. "Did you like it?"

"No, I hated it. Don't *ever* do that again."

"All right, all right, no hard feelings. Okay, man? Don't blow a gasket. That was the first and last time. I promise."

Altfeld, though feeling somewhat appeased with the semi-apology, still had his concerns. He didn't know this guy from a bucket of paint. And Altfeld had one more important question on his mind. He had to know the full identity of his perpetrator. It might come in very handy down the line, should there be a repeat offense.

"What's your last name?" Don asked.

"Berry," Jan replied, with a larcenous twinkle in his eye.

"Well, Jan Berry," Altfeld said, smiling, "maybe we'll run into each other again sometime. Under better circumstances, of course."

✳

Outside of their little encounter in the school print shop, there is little chance that Don Altfeld and Jan Berry would have ever met. At least not at Uni High.

Built in 1924, the school had become over the years the preferred educational destination for the children of the rich and famous. And many were classmates of Altfeld and Berry. Frank Sinatra sent his daughter Nancy there. Actor James Brolin (née Craig Bruderlin) held forth in Uni's drama department. Even the real-life Gidget (Kathy Kohner) graced the school's hallways when she wasn't off surfing with her pals at nearby Malibu Point.

With a well-defined and multi-layered social structure, Uni's students tended to hang out with those of like kind. There were the jocks, of course. And the surfers. Plus the hipsters, the thespians, the preppies, and the hardcore academic types. Sometimes a few in each group might overlap, but not often. Jan Berry, however, happened to be one of those exceptions.

Born to a well-to-do family in Bel Air, Berry grew up a child of privilege.

His father, part of Howard Hughes's inner circle at Hughes Aircraft, made sure Jan and his siblings lacked for nothing. Berry also liked living on the edge, and he had an unusually strong competitive streak, something that drove him to become the best he could at everything he tried, legal or not. Berry starred on the football team. He raced street rods with his friends. And he maintained a solid A average in his courses—all the while regularly stealing hubcaps (and sometimes even purses) just for the thrill of it.

But what the undeniably gifted and hell-bent Jan Berry liked more than anything was popular music. Whenever he and Don Altfeld ran across each other at school, the odd couple found themselves chatting more and more frequently about current songs, radio station playlists, and how to go about possibly cutting a hit record of their own. Little by little, without realizing it, the unlikely duo from vastly different ends of the high school social spectrum became the best of friends.

During the spring of his senior year in 1958, Jan Berry formed a singing duo with a fellow classmate named Arnie Ginsburg. One afternoon, they decided to record a simple song in the Berry family's garage on an AMPEX two-track reel-to-reel tape recorder. Written by Ginsburg and called "Jennie Lee," the doo-woppish recording featured Jan and Arnie on vocals, with Don Altfeld banging out the rhythm on a children's metal high chair. With the help of a local producer who loved their rough demo, the trio subsequently reunited at a small studio called Radio Recorders, where Berry and Ginsburg recut their vocals on state-of-the-art equipment. Released by tiny Arwin Records, the song surprised everyone involved by making it into the national Top 10.

Suddenly Jan & Arnie (who would soon change their name to Jan and Dean when Dean Torrence stepped in to replace Ginsburg) had a serious singing career on their hands, with Don Altfeld helping them write many of the songs. And the studio musicians they began to use like Glen Campbell, Carol Kaye, and Hal Blaine, along with several other Wrecking Crew players—including a garrulous second-generation Italian-American guitarist born in the misty shadow of one of the Seven Wonders of the World—would in short order become central figures in helping Jan and Dean evolve into an internationally known rock-and-roll hit-making machine.

*

Living in predominantly blue-collar, rough-and-tumble Niagara Falls, New York, during the mid-Thirties meant many things to many people. For some, it meant going hungry. For others, it meant working two and three jobs just to keep a roof over their heads. For still others, it meant mind-numbing factory work with little chance for advancement. And for virtually everyone, it meant long, frigid winters, punctuated by unbearably humid summers.

But for little Tommy Tedesco of 307 12th Street, life on the American side of the famous falls couldn't have been any sweeter. Because for Tedesco, it meant becoming the best hustler in the neighborhood.

With the swift and deep Niagara River providing a cheap, abundant source of electrical power as it dumped its contents over three massive sets of falls, a variety of industries began to dot the town's landscape during the late nineteenth century. First came Occidental Petroleum, with its chemical might. Then the Shredded Wheat factory arrived on the scene, with workers toiling long into the night feeding wet, cooked grain through giant grooved rollers, helping to fill America's cereal bowls the next morning. Carborundum, too, set up shop, producing large quantities of heat-resistant silicon carbide to be used in the electronics, automotive, and diamond-cutting industries. Factories meant jobs, and most men were grateful for the opportunity.

But for a boy with a natural aversion to manual labor the same factory jobs that employed his father, uncles, cousins, and brother—and put food on his family's table each night—were something to be avoided at all costs. In fact, any kind of job was anathema to the eleven-year-old Tommy Tedesco.

"Tommy, why don't you go down to Mrs. O'Shea's restaurant on Fall Street and ask for a job washing dishes?" his mother inquired early one summer day.

"I'm too young. They won't hire me," Tommy replied, hoping that his mother would let the subject slide. "Besides, I wanna play baseball with my friends."

"You can play baseball another time. Go down there today and tell her I sent you," she directed.

Tedesco knew it was pointless to argue. Italian mothers were not used to taking no for an answer. Especially his.

"Yes, ma'am," he said.

Later that afternoon, as a dejected Tedesco slowly made his way down to the small, slightly run-down restaurant near downtown Niagara Falls, he kept wondering how he was going to get out of working there—or any-place else, for that matter. The busy restaurant catered to those in need of a quick lunch during the workday or an inexpensive place to take their dates on a Saturday night. And Tedesco knew that the kind of foot traffic they generated probably meant a whole lot of filthy dishes were already stacking up with his name on them.

After a warm greeting by Mrs. O'Shea ("How's your mama doing? She's a *wonderful* woman, you know"), the lead dishwasher handed Tommy a stained, tattered apron and told him to get busy scraping whatever food he could off the plates and utensils before dropping them into a giant sink for washing.

"Don't break anything, either," he growled.

On about the sixth dish, as an increasingly depressed Tedesco contem-plated making a run for it out the back door, he suddenly had a brainstorm. Maybe I really *am* too young to be doing this, he thought. Is it even legal to hire eleven-year-olds?

Early the next morning, Tommy fairly skipped as he headed down to the local Board of Labor office. Time to put the plan in play.

"Excuse me, ma'am," he said as he stood on his tiptoes to see over the long wooden counter. "My name is Thomas Tedesco and I'd like to get some working papers."

A thin, gray-haired woman peered suspiciously over her reading glasses at the young face in front of her.

"Working papers?" she asked. "How old are you?"

"I just turned eleven."

"You're too young to work," she said firmly. "In Niagara County you need to be at least fourteen."

"What'll I tell my employer, then?"

"Your *employer*?" the woman gasped. "What's their number? I need to call them right now. You're not to go back there."

Hallelujah! The plan had worked. Good-bye, dirty dishes. Hello, baseball, sunshine, and a life of leisure. Sorry, Ma…

An eleven-year-old hustler was on his way.

✳

A wholly unexpected thing happened to Tommy Tedesco on the way to turning fifteen. He discovered the guitar. Or perhaps it discovered him. Either way, the kid actually had some talent and it showed. He also developed a seriousness about practicing that ran counter to his usual preference for avoiding any endeavor that took physical exertion.

As his guitar-playing skills improved, it slowly began to dawn on the tenth-grader that something as simple as a piece of wood with six wire strings attached just might be his salvation from a probable lifetime spent in close proximity to the most horrific four-letter word he knew in the English language—"work."

Deciding to see if he could actually make some money from his new avocation, Tedesco put together a trio with his high school pals Angelo La Porta (accordion) and Ralph Vescio (bass). Tedesco then banged on practically every club door in the greater Niagara Falls area, begging the owners for a chance. "Please, mister, give us a try. You won't be sorry," he would say. "If you don't like our act after the first show, you don't even have to pay us."

Using the charm and chutzpah that came so naturally to him, Tedesco finally secured the fledgling trio's first paying job at Cutt's Hotel Delaware in nearby Tonawanda, where they were to receive the princely sum of twenty-five dollars per night, split three ways. They worked six nights per week for the first two weeks and thought for sure they had hit the big time. The crowd loved them, the manager loved them, and it looked like fat city for the foreseeable future.

But at the beginning of the third week, some unexpected news came their way: the hotel had burned to the ground the night before. No more gig. No more money.

Despite this devastating setback, for Tedesco it also provided the clearest of revelations. You really *can* make money by being a musician, he realized soon after the fire. This guitar-playing thing was the best hustle yet. No heavy lifting or boring shit to do.

From then on, Tommy became so serious about learning to play the guitar that nothing else mattered. He practiced day and night, sometimes all the way until he had to leave for school the next morning. Sometimes even until his fingers bled. It was going to be his way out of Niagara Falls and away from the slow death of factory work. It had to be.

✳

By the early Sixties, just as rock and roll was beginning to take permanent root as the dominant form of popular music in America, Tommy Tedesco finally fulfilled his cherished dream. Through single-mindedness and, yes, through the dint of hard work—there was *that* word again—he had managed to turn himself into one of the most sought-after guitarists around. His impeccable acoustic and electric playing could be found on everything from the Academy Award–nominated *Spartacus* soundtrack to most of Spector's singles to the groundbreaking *Twilight Zone* series on CBS, with hundreds of other important rock-and-roll, jazz, film, and TV credits in between. There was no style the heavyset guitar virtuoso with the outré personality couldn't make his own, no music notation he couldn't read. Every producer in town wanted him, especially those who cut rock-and-roll records. But it hadn't always been that way for Tedesco.

Having moved from the frozen tundra of Upstate New York to sunny Southern California with his beautiful young wife, Carmie, back in 1953 in order to jump-start his career and get away from the specter of the factories, Tedesco had at first taken any paying date he could get his hands on. Starting at little known LA-area clubs like the Buggy Whip, Peacock Lane, and the South Pacific, he had sometimes earned all of ten dollars per night for his guitar work. Not much money, but it quickly taught him the value of a buck and about fair treatment. Nothing made the Niagara Falls transplant bristle faster than when he or any other musician was treated poorly or ended up being stiffed on the payout. If Tedesco's blue-collar background had taught him anything about life, it was about treating people the right way—fair and square. Accordingly, Tommy Tedesco became a very big believer in the local musician's union.

If a guitarist or anyone else wanted to play music professionally in Los Angeles, he or she had to become a member of the American Federation of Musicians. Period. In exchange, the AFM, like most strong unions of the day, sought to establish fair wage standards and acceptable treatment for its members in the workplace. All the main music recording studios, movie and TV studios, and live concert venues were "union shops," agreeing to only use union musicians and to pay the stipulated rates set forth by Local 47, the AFM's LA County branch (located on Vine Street in Hollywood). In return, the union provided a large roster of dependable, skilled musicians of every stripe, from string players to vibraphonists to guitar virtuosos and everything in between. Virtually any type of player a producer, arranger, or bandleader might need for a recording date or a live gig could be readily obtained with a phone call.

But the union also ran a tight ship; fail to pay for a session and a producer or studio might be put on probation or even cut off for good. Eight roving reps made sure of that. They didn't take kindly to scabs, either. Taking money under the table was strictly prohibited. Caught, and a member could be fined. Or, worse yet, expelled.

Local 47 also took a dim view regarding undocumented overtime. If a particular three-hour recording date (the contractual minimum) went so much as one paltry second past the specified time, the contractor was expected to notate the session log accordingly for every union member present. Overtime was overtime, no exceptions. And especially at some of the bigger, busier studios, such as Capitol, Columbia, and United/Western, it was not uncommon to have a union rep hunt down a session date and "magically" appear just as it wound up, stopwatch in hand.

Though they were the scourges of parsimonious producers everywhere, Local 47's stealthy squad of gumshoes did their jobs, and they did them well. Their presence, or, more often, the simple fear of their *possible* presence, saved many a powerless musician from being exploited by being short-changed. When playing an instrument is someone's sole way of earning a living—as with those in the Wrecking Crew—getting into a personal beef with a producer over wages is a sure way to never be rehired. Better to keep your mouth shut, your fingers on the fret board, and let the union handle all the dirty work.

But one day, on a studio date in early 1964 with Jan and Dean, Tommy Tedesco, who had become a Wrecking Crew fixture, decided he could neither hold his tongue nor defer matters to the union, no matter the consequences.

During the session at Western's Studio 3 (the only place Jan and Dean liked to record), the producer's secretary happened to stop by for a few minutes to discuss some business. With a short break in the action having been called, Tedesco took the chance to say hello to her and to also mention in passing that he had not yet received fifty dollars that the duo still owed him from his last recording date. To his dismay, however, the secretary completely ignored him, as if he had never even spoken.

Rather than getting uptight and turning the perceived disrespect into some kind of regrettable verbal confrontation, however, Tedesco simply put his guitar down and quietly announced to Jan, Dean, and their producer, Lou Adler, that he would not play any further until he was paid. Within minutes, the cash appeared as requested, and Tedesco continued with the session. His point having been made, he then proceeded to use the money to take all the rest of the on-hand members of the Wrecking Crew out to dinner. For Tedesco, it was less about the dough and always about the principle.

During this same time, Jan and Dean were also searching for what they hoped would become their next big single. The two teen idols had charted eight different Top 20 hits over the previous several years, including "Surf City" (co-written with Jan's friend Brian Wilson), which made it all the way to number one. Their manager and producer, Lou Adler, wanted them to strike again while the public still had interest. Having a shrewd view of the music business, Adler (and Berry) knew how fickle the record-buying public could be. The surf and car music crazes could only last so long. The Beach Boys had, for the most part, already moved on. But Jan and Dean, along with the Wrecking Crew, still had one last souped-up jalopy to roll off the line.

*

Out for a leisurely drive in his brand-new Corvette late one evening in early March of 1964, Don Altfeld surprisingly found himself well past his usual zone of comfort. He had somehow driven about a half an hour east of his home in West LA, all the way to Colorado Boulevard in Pasadena.

As Altfeld cruised along the traditional path of the annual Tournament of Roses Parade, checking out the sights and sounds of the historic Old Town area, the notion of a little old lady speeding down the road in a yellow tricked-out '32 Ford "deuce" coupe hot rod mysteriously flashed across his mind. Maybe it was a random thought. Or maybe it was rooted in something the comedian Jack Benny liked to say on his TV show during a regular used-car skit where a "little old lady from Pasadena" invariably had been the previous owner of the cream-puff vehicle for sale. Whatever the source, Altfeld couldn't get the vivid, cartoonish image out of his head.

After running the unusual idea by Lou Adler the next day ("Go for it," he said), Altfeld, along with an enthusiastic Jan Berry, immediately began crafting a musical tale about a fictional granny with a lead foot. Bringing the ubiquitous Roger Christian on board to add authenticity to some of the car-specific lyrics, the trio soon had what they decided to call "The Little Old Lady (from Pasadena)" ready to record.

Following a phone call from Jan Berry, Hal Blaine, the usual contractor for Jan and Dean, rounded up Berry's requested retinue of Wrecking Crew regulars: Russell Bridges (who would soon change his professional name to Leon Russell) on piano; Jimmy Bond and Ray Pohlman on bass; Tommy Tedesco, Billy Strange, and Bill Pitman on guitar; Earl Palmer and Hal himself on drums; and Tommy Morgan on harmonica.

As they converged upon the studio at a little before 2:00 P.M. on March 21, 1964, Berry, Adler, and their engineer, Bones Howe, knew that time was going to be especially tight. For budgetary reasons, they needed to cut five songs in a standard three-hour session, which would be a real push. A normal Jan and Dean session, even on the high end, consisted of *maybe* three. Berry was notorious for taking forever in the studio. But by virtue of an edict handed down from Liberty Records, the expense of overtime was now absolutely out of the question.

After a time-consuming, on-the-clock rehearsal, mainly spent with Blaine and Palmer carefully choreographing their double-drum patterns (Berry liked to have them play every hit and every fill in perfect unison for a bigger sound), the musicians were finally ready.

Launching into the first song, called "'A' Deuce Goer," the Wrecking Crew blew through the music in just one take. So far, so good. Next up was "Malibu Beach," followed by "Little School Girl," and then "Go-Go-Go." Everything was going well. The quadruplet of typical Jan and Dean–style album-filler songs was coming out clean and tight, just like Berry and Adler had hoped.

But with only ten minutes left on the date, they still hadn't touched the oddball yet promising song about the old lady and her car. The only one of the bunch that might be worth releasing as a single. And as bad luck would have it, one of the union reps happened to be lurking nearby, watching the high-profile session like a hawk, making sure that any overtime would be duly reported on the session log.

After they quickly regrouped following a false start due to a tape machine malfunction, there were now only three minutes left, barely enough time to get the song in the can. Nerves were on edge. The second take would have to be it.

However, with a singular crack of their synchronized snares, Hal Blaine and Earl Palmer set the world right for one and all. Using only Jan Berry's scratch vocal track as their guide, they instantly moved to push the other Wrecking Crew players into an inspired effort, surging along with them in laying down a perfectly executed, rollicking instrumental track, hitting the last notes precisely as the second hand hit the twelve. The union man could now go home; Granny had crossed the finish line right on time.

It was not only a spotless performance by the best sidemen in Los Angeles, but it saved Berry and Adler from running afoul of the tight-fisted execs at the record label. It also helped Jan and Dean earn one last Top 5 hit.

But by this time in 1964, for the Wrecking Crew it was all in a day's work. Playing fast and flawlessly under pressure was their hallmark. They made life easier for those around them. It was why they were in such demand, why harried producers all over town were often willing to pay them double, even triple scale to assume the roles of the real bands in the studio. Whatever it took, just as long as the record-buying public didn't find out.

5

What'd I Say

Segregation now, segregation tomorrow, segregation forever.
—George Wallace

Those who played as part of the Wrecking Crew often came to their positions of prominence and demand through more than just skill and ambition. With competition fierce, they also sometimes needed a sprinkling of fairy dust along the way, to luck into playing for the right star at the right time. A sideman's reputation could be built in a hurry with a big-time name attached to his résumé. Especially if the name happened to be that of Ray Charles.

At a well-to-do children's camp in Malibu, California, during the summer of 1956—the same year that Memphis-based rock and roller Elvis Presley first realized the power of his musical calling by blowing the collective minds of millions of American teens with his racy, raucous "Hound Dog" and slinky, soulful "Heartbreak Hotel"—fifteen-year-old Don Peake, a shy math and science high school honors student, also discovered *his* life's calling. Except, uncharacteristically for Peake, it had absolutely nothing to do with solving quadratic equations or studying the molecular structures of hydrocarbons.

While not thrilled with the idea of going off to some camp he'd barely heard of—for the whole summer no less—Peake, always the dutiful son, did what his parents wanted. Maintaining a commitment to the Jewish faith was important to them and they wanted him to follow suit. Camp Hess Kramer specialized in creating an immersive religious and cultural environment with frequent prayer, kosher meals, and many, if not most, songs sung in Hebrew. A different world, for sure, but one that fostered a strong sense of identity and self-esteem.

In Southern California, when the warm Santa Ana winds are blowing just right, whipping with their dry, deceptive fury from east to west over the mountains and deserts, the slightest sounds can often travel great distances, sometimes right to the ocean's edge. And so it was one afternoon for Don Peake as he walked across Hess Kramer's large, open beachfront compound on his way to lunch. An unusual series of harp-like tones wafting through the air suddenly caught the youngster's ear, stopping him in his tracks. What could they be?

With his curiosity getting the better of him—not to mention an acute case of boredom—Peake decided to check things out. Eating could wait.

Following the mysterious music to its source in a nearby wooded area, Peake came across a group of older boys he'd noticed around camp before. Huddled in a small circle, they seemed to be taking turns strumming something odd that looked like a tiny guitar. A *very* tiny guitar.

"Hey, guys, what are you playing?"

"A ukulele. Arthur Godfrey plays one on his show every week."

Peake stood transfixed. The small, wooden, figure-eight-shaped instrument with the four nylon strings was like nothing he had ever seen. Certainly not where he came from. *Talent Scouts,* Arthur Godfrey's hugely popular show on CBS in the late Fifties—or, for that matter, any other "frivolous" TV program—wasn't usually on the viewing schedule in the decidedly intellectual Peake household.

As the other boys continued to strum away with amateurish abandon, Peake remained fascinated. Not so much with the sound but with the fingering required on the miniature fret board. The deft, precise movement—the *exactitude* of it all—was almost mathematical. Peake liked things that added up. He also liked working with his hands. And this strange little instrument with the high-pitched tones magically fit the bill on both counts. He was hooked.

With his usual industriousness, Don Peake began practicing the ukulele day and night. At first he borrowed the one at camp from the other kids, who had quickly grown tired of playing with it. Then he got one of his own back home.

Returning to high school that fall in Los Angeles, Peake made a natural progression to playing the guitar. Stringed instruments were now his thing, his abiding passion. And the acoustic guitar was clearly a step up from a ukulele in terms of function, status, and style. Six strings instead of four, far more frets, and a much bigger, better sound. You sure didn't see Bill Haley or Chuck Berry strumming a uke.

Quickly teaching himself three simple chords, Peake worked up his courage and volunteered to accompany a fellow student while she sang "Black Is the Color of My True Love's Hair" on a local TV show called *Spotlight on Youth*. Thrilled with the experience, a couple of other times he even tentatively stepped forward to play a few tunes on his guitar during the school's morning "nutrition break." Nothing fancy, but all performances nonetheless, a way to show off. And it felt good.

With Peake's sudden, if modest, public exposure also came an unexpected yet welcomed bonus: girls. They were now actually *noticing* him for the first time, even hinting about going out on dates. Seriously heady stuff for an introvert whose main instrument until then had been his trusty wooden slide rule. The notion of perhaps someday playing music as a career option began to ever so subtly creep its way into his imagination.

Don Peake's parents, however, very much wanted their only son to be practical, like them. They urged him to consider going into the family business, a thriving upscale retail establishment called William Peake Men's Clothing, located in downtown Los Angeles. That had a guaranteed future, some security. Having scraped their way through the Great Depression, they knew just how tough things could really be out on the streets. A young man needed a solid profession to rely on. The life of a professional musician was foolishness, a meshuga way to earn a living.

With their old-world views firmly in place, Peake's mother and father had never been encouraging about his musical aspirations anyway. And they especially loathed rock and roll, a genre far too primitive for their cosmopolitan tastes. They much preferred composers like Chopin, Mozart, and Rachmaninoff. The only music they ever allowed Don to listen to in the house, at least when they knew about it, was classical.

But Peake had a mind of his own. He had already worked in the clothing store during summers as a kid, enough time to know that he didn't want to spend the rest of his life folding shirts and chalking inseams. Maybe, just maybe, there was some way to merge his love for all things mechanical with his passion for music.

One hot afternoon in the summer of 1959, just after his high school graduation, Don Peake heard his parents' doorbell ringing several times in rapid succession.

Looking out the dining room window to see who on earth it could be making all the noise, he saw one of his best friends, Stan Hall, standing on the front porch, clutching something under his arm. Opening the door, Peake stepped aside as Hall practically leaped inside the large, well-kept home.

"Stan, what's the rush, man?"

Wasting no time, and with a big smile on his face, the visitor answered by quickly pulling out a 45 rpm record.

"Donny, here—put this on."

"What is it?"

"Just play it," Hall instructed. "You'll see."

With his parents fortunately away from home for a couple of hours, Peake did as he was told, carefully loading the seven-inch vinyl disc onto the family's record player. By now he was used to Stan's exuberance over the often mundane.

But what happened next would change Don Peake's life forever.

As soon as he heard the deep, buzzy tones of a Wurlitzer electric piano begin delivering an impossibly raw, blues-inflected, boogie-woogie-style series of notes, the hair on the back of Peake's neck stood up.

"Oh, my God!" he exclaimed. "What is *that?*"

"That, my friend, is Ray Charles."

Exploding onto the national seen in 1959 with his risqué, hip-shaking

"What'd I Say," the Georgia-born Charles caused a minor sensation among American teens, both black and white. The song's genesis came courtesy of a show he had played one evening in Brownsville, Pennsylvania. While running short on material, Charles had begun vamping on his keyboard to fill some time, in the process initiating an impromptu call-and-response with his backup singers, a female quartet called the Raelettes.

"Listen," he told them. "I'm going to fool around and y'all just follow me."

Each time Charles would moan out an "oh" or an "aah," the Raelettes would respond in kind, with an ever-increasing sense of urgency. Sending the crowd further into a dancing, pulsating frenzy with each chorus, the sex-drenched message of it all was impossible to miss. Not one to ordinarily try out new song ideas on his audience, Charles nonetheless immediately recognized that he was on to something big.

After adding some formal lyrics to go along with all the ohing and aahing, Charles managed to squeeze out a quick break from the road to cut the song in a hastily arranged session at a New York City studio, where both he and his record label (Atlantic) felt sure they had a hit on their hands. And they were right. "What'd I Say" shot to number six on the national pop charts, despite being initially banned by dozens of stations around the country. It also became Charles's first gold record.

For Don Peake, "What'd I Say" was a stone-cold epiphany, the revelation of a lifetime. The song had spoken to him like no other. What the ukulele had started Ray Charles had now finished. *Emphatically.* There could be no turning back, no more second-guessing about what he might want to do with the rest of his life. Peake instinctively knew at that moment that he had been presented with the blueprint for his musical destiny.

But what Peake couldn't have known that day, however, was that Ray Charles—a blind R & B musician from the Deep South whom he had never even heard of just ten minutes before—would soon, quite literally, save his very life.

✳

Within seconds of walking into the Rag Doll nightclub in North Hollywood, nineteen-year-old Don Peake knew he had made a big mistake. Having recently returned to his parents' home after a six-month stint in the U.S. Coast Guard, Peake still very much had guitar playing on his mind. While enrolled at Los Angeles City College in early 1960, he had heard about an open audition over at a place in the San Fernando Valley for a singer named Jackie Lee Cochran and decided to give it a try. The rough-hewn, Georgia-born Cochran—known among his fans as Jack the Cat—was looking for a guitarist to fill out his small-time rockabilly band during their two-week gig at the club. With a recent single on the tiny Jaguar record label called "I Wanna See You" stirring up a bit of local airplay, Cochran had unexpectedly found himself in the position of needing a replacement rhythm guitar player, someone who could step in and help him capitalize on his hard-won momentum. And Don Peake very much wanted to be that guy.

But as Peake waited his turn in line in the club's run-down lobby, he watched one guitar-toting hopeful after another come and go. And he started to sweat. If all these guys couldn't cut it, what chance did he have? Why was he even here? After all, Peake had no experience, knew all of five chords, and could play exactly one song. Not the sort of foundation normally associated with obtaining a paying job as a guitarist.

Just as Peake was about to turn around and join the growing parade of rejected guitar players streaming out the front door, Cochran's manager suddenly motioned him inside.

"Okay, kid—you're on. Do you know 'Be-Bop-a-Lula'?"

Don Peake couldn't believe his luck. Out of all the songs in the world this guy could have possibly asked for, he had chosen the one Peake actually *knew*.

"Do I," he blurted.

As he excitedly plugged in his guitar and amp, Peake called out, "Key of A," and he and the band launched into a fevered version of the old Gene Vincent and His Blue Caps hit that rocked the room like a hurricane. With Peake having already played the tune dozens of times on his own in front of several friends (and girls) he wanted to impress, his well-practiced three-chord rhythm playing was spot-on. And it got him the job.

During his short run in Cochran's band, Don Peake learned more about playing the guitar than he ever thought possible. After he nervously faked his way through the first evening's show, Peake's more experienced band-mates immediately took him aside and showed him the chords needed to correctly play all the songs on the set list. And though Cochran could have easily fired Peake for his obvious lack of skills (and for misleading every-one to begin with), he and his band instead generously chipped in to send Peake over to the Clara Joyce Sherman School of Music on La Brea Boule-vard in Hollywood for a quick batch of daytime guitar lessons. It was here, too, that Peake learned to read music, a skill that would prove to be a valu-able and distinguishing asset down the line.

Later in 1960, following the Cochran gig, an increasingly confident Peake gradually fell in with a bunch of ambitious young musicians who regularly jammed late into the night at a local nightspot called Sun Valley Rancho. From there, Peake joined up with an R & B outfit playing at a pop-ular club in Van Nuys (also in the San Fernando Valley) called the Cross-bow. Going by the name of Lance and the Dynamics, they were fronted by Elvis Presley's movie stand-in and good friend, Lance LeGault. A particu-larly tight blues-oriented band, they specialized in performing a wide range of Ray Charles songs, something near and dear to Peake's heart ever since he had first heard "What'd I Say" in his parents' living room.

Don Peake was now not only starting to make some decent cash; he was also playing the music he loved. And he was rapidly gaining a reputation around town as a rock-solid rhythm player who could lay down a groove fat enough to land a plane on.

By mid-1961, on the heels of a surprise phone call from his old pal Mar-shall Leib (Phil Spector's former co-singer in the Teddy Bears), Don Peake suddenly, stunningly, found himself ensconced as the new lead guitarist for one of the best-known bands in the country: the Everly Brothers.

Though Phil and Don Everly—the singers behind classics like "Bye Bye Love," "Wake Up Little Susie," and "Cathy's Clown"—were just past their hit-making prime, they still had a very big following around the world, especially in the UK. And that's exactly where they wanted Peake to travel with them first.

Playing the Odeon Theatre circuit throughout England with the Everly Brothers from 1961 to 1963 proved to be Don Peake's professional coming-out party. With heavyweight supporting acts like Bo Diddley, Little Richard, and the Rolling Stones regularly on the bill, Peake soaked up every ounce of musical wisdom he could. And in the process he became known as a guitar player's guitar player, impressing the likes of both Keith Richards and Eric Clapton with his technique and deep knowledge of the blues. Even the Beatles, who hadn't made it big in the United States yet, could be found on more than one occasion standing backstage, watching Peake and the Everly Brothers perform.

But in the music business, all good things too often come to an early, disheartening end. By the middle of 1963, with Don Everly experiencing a nervous breakdown compounded by unregulated prescription drug use, Peake's run on lead guitar for the famed duo came to an abrupt close. The Everly Brothers were no more.

Back in Los Angeles, and looking for work, Don Peake discovered to his surprise that his newfound reputation as a skilled lead player had preceded him. He joined Local 47, the musician's union, and promptly found session work through a well-connected arranger named Jimmie Haskell, who employed him whenever he could. Peake's studio career was on its way.

One day, in early 1964, as Don Peake made his way down the main hall toward the back door after another session for Haskell at Gold Star, he heard a familiar voice call his name from behind.

"Hey, Don, hold on a minute."

It was Arthur G. Wright, a black session guitar player mostly known for cutting sides for soul and blues acts. He was standing next to the studio's one and only pay phone.

"What's up, Arthur?" Peake said, turning around.

"You need to talk to this guy," Wright replied, holding out the receiver.

"Who is it?"

"It's Ray Charles's manager, man. Ray needs a guitar player right away, and I'm booked."

Peake paused. Ray Charles was his idol, of course, and one of the biggest, most highly respected entertainers in the world. By that time in 1964, Charles had twenty Top 40 hits to his credit and countless more on the R & B and even the country charts. The guy was practically an industry unto himself. He also had, to Peake's knowledge, a 100 percent black band.

"But, Arthur, I'm white."

"Take the call, Don."

Peake did as he was told, grabbing the phone from Wright.

"Hello?"

"Don, this is Joe Adams. I'm Ray Charles's manager. We've heard some good things about you. Can you come down here right now to the corner of Washington and Western for an audition at Ray's studio?"

Peake hesitated.

"But, Joe, I'm white," he finally said, still unsure as to whether Adams and his famous client were actually aware of his ethnicity. Brother Ray *was* blind, after all.

"But can you *play?*"

"Yes."

"Then get yourself down here."

✳

On January 21, 1963, George Wallace, the newly elected governor of Alabama, made the citizens of his fair state a solemn promise. Standing in front of the state capitol on the very spot where Jefferson Davis had declared an independent Southern confederacy just over one hundred years before, Wallace ominously proclaimed during his inaugural address that "in the name of the greatest people that ever trod this earth, I draw the line in the dust and toss the gauntlet before the feet of tyranny and I say: segregation now, segregation tomorrow, segregation forever."

Making national headlines, the defiance and barely concealed vitriol contained in the speech served to further inflame an already racially charged atmosphere in the South. It also helped anoint Alabama, a roiling cauldron of church bombings, bus boycotts, and lynchings, as the virtual ground zero of the civil rights movement. A place where blacks were clearly to avoid mixing in any meaningful way with whites. Or else.

Having successfully passed his audition with Ray Charles in early 1964 by wowing the room—and the hard-to-impress man himself—with his encyclopedic knowledge of the singing star's catalog of songs (courtesy of the time spent with Lance LeGault at the Crossbow), Don Peake had become the one and only white guy in a very hot all-black band of almost twenty. But unlike many other white musicians trying to make it in the mostly black jazz and R & B world of 1964, Peake experienced none of what was often referred to as Crow Jim (the opposite of Jim Crow)—a kind of reverse discrimination where whites were considered to have no civil rights. For many black jazzers of the era, their music represented a sacred, shared heritage and a private language—something often expressed in the adamant refusal to hire whites. Peake, however, with his genial nature and gift for playing like it came from deep within his soul, easily won over his fellow group members. White though he might be, the new kid was no ofay.

After a couple of weeks of rehearsals and a few shows in Los Angeles at major venues like the Shrine Auditorium and the Santa Monica Civic Auditorium, it was time for the Ray Charles Orchestra to head out on tour and make some money.

First stop: Montgomery, Alabama.

Flying along in the comfort of Ray Charles's private Martin 404 twin-engine prop plane (purchased from Eastern Airlines), Don Peake gazed out the window at the golden wheat fields of the nation's heartland gently rolling by. Having heard, of course, about all the racial turmoil in the South, he wondered what he should expect. Footage of the often-violent clashes between protestors and police had been all over the evening news for some time. And he had never been part of an all-black band before. But maybe it would be no big deal. Having toured extensively with the Everly Brothers, Peake figured that star status would surely win out if any problems arose. The likelihood of anybody messing with a guy as important as his new boss had to be extremely slim.

After landing in Montgomery at Dannelly Field in the late afternoon, band and crew quickly loaded themselves and their gear into a waiting Greyhound-style sightseeing bus and headed north toward the center of town. The show would begin in a scant two hours and there was little time to waste.

As they neared the main entrance to Garrett Coliseum, the city's largest concert venue, Don Peake's jaw dropped and his heart sank, both at the same time. Passing by outside his window, in what seemed like some kind of perverse, slow-motion, neorealist-style post-war film about life behind the Iron Curtain, were row after threatening row of razor-sharp barbed wire strung across an endless procession of poles, completely encircling the building and its grounds. Heavily armed state troopers were also standing in groups around the perimeter. And, in case anybody missed the point of the whole display, a large red Confederate flag flapped prominently in the breeze atop a tall, gleaming, floodlit pole.

Uh-oh, this can't be good, Peake thought.

But before he or anyone else on board could further process the frightening scene, the band's bus slowed to a stop. As the front door of the huge, now-silent vehicle hissed open, several grim-faced, shotgun-carrying state troopers immediately climbed inside. As they spoke with the driver in a series of hushed tones, it became apparent they had something—or more likely *someone*—on their minds.

"What do they want?" Ray Charles asked his tour manager, Jeff Brown, who was sitting nearby. As a famous black entertainer, Charles was a high-profile target and had every reason for concern. He had grown up in the South and had experienced the evil and unpredictability of racism firsthand.

Straining to hear the conversation going down in the front of the bus, Brown finally deciphered exactly why Ray and his band had been stopped.

"They want the white boy," Brown said.

✳

Word had apparently traveled with speed uncommon on the day that Don Peake and the Ray Charles Orchestra had flown into Alabama. The assembled state troopers had been told that Charles was carrying a white musician in his entourage. They had also been told that Governor Wallace had decreed that there would be no white people allowed at the Ray Charles concert in Montgomery that night, either audience or band. The black population could have their little show, fine. But by the grace of the good Lord—*and* the boot heel of the law—there would be no mixing.

Glen Campbell ready to play as part of the Wrecking Crew in the studio at Western Recorders, mid-Sixties. *Courtesy of Michael Ochs Archives/Getty Images*

Carol Kaye swings it on her P-Bass, late Sixties. *Courtesy of Michael Ochs Archives/Getty Images*

Hal Blaine lays down the beat at Western Recorders, mid-Sixties. *Courtesy of Hal Blaine*

Virtuoso guitarist Tommy Tedesco with his Fender Telecaster in the studio, mid-Sixties. *Courtesy of Denny Tedesco*

Carol Kaye and Bill Pitman on guitar at Gold Star, circa 1963. *Courtesy of GAB Archive/ Redferns*

Drumming great Earl Palmer in a pensive moment in the studio, mid-Sixties. *Courtesy of Michael Ochs Archives/Getty Images*

Phil Spector and Sonny Bono shakin' it with the Wrecking Crew at Gold Star during the recording of the legendary holiday album *A Christmas Gift for You from Philles Records*, 1963. *Courtesy of Ray Avery/Getty Images*

The brain trust: from left to right, Larry Levine, Phil Spector, Nino Tempo, and Bertha Spector (Phil's omnipresent mother) in the control booth at Gold Star watching the Wrecking Crew play, circa 1963. *Courtesy of Ray Avery/Getty Images*

And then there were three: from left to right, Don Randi, Leon Russell, and Al DeLory play the keyboards on one of Spector's Wall of Sound dates at Gold Star, circa 1963. *Courtesy of Ray Avery/Michael Ochs Archives/Getty Images*

From left to right: Edgar Willis, Don Peake, and Jeff Brown of the Ray Charles Orchestra, 1964, just before the fateful trip to Alabama. *Courtesy of Shirley Brown/Michael Lydon*

Larry Knechtel at the Hammond organ, with Al Casey (left) and Barney Kessel (right) on guitar behind him. Unknown player on string bass in back, circa 1964. *Courtesy of Lonnie Knechtel*

Bones Howe (bottom) and Jan Berry (middle) mix a Jan and Dean session in the booth as the Wrecking Crew plays out in the studio, 1963. The assistant engineer, Henry Lewy, is at the top. *Courtesy of Bones Howe*

CBS Columbia Square at 6121 Sunset Boulevard, where the Wrecking Crew cut "Mr. Tambourine Man" for the Byrds, "Woman, Woman" for Gary Puckett and the Union Gap, and "Bridge Over Troubled Water" for Simon & Garfunkel, among many other classic hits. The studios were located in the back of the courtyard behind the trees. In 2009, the Los Angeles City Council designated the now-empty modernist-style building as a historic-cultural monument. *Courtesy of Gary Minnaert*

Looking west on Sunset Boulevard in 1965 toward Vine Street. Wallichs Music City is in the foreground on the corner (the place that Brian Wilson talked into opening up on a Sunday in order to get Billy Strange the 12-string electric guitar he played on "Sloop John B"). Just behind Wallichs is RCA Records's West Coast office and studios, where the Wrecking Crew recorded many times over for the Monkees, Harry Nilsson, and others—even Lorne Greene from *Bonanza*! *Author's Collection*

Behind closed doors: the entrance to the world-famous Gold Star on Santa Monica Boulevard, as it looked in the Seventies. *Courtesy of Dave Gold/Stan Ross/Kent Crowley*

Ray Pohlman (circa 1970), the original number-one call rock-and-roll electric bassist among the Wrecking Crew, abruptly left for a couple of years in the mid-Sixties to become the musical director for ABC's teen-themed concert series *Shindig!* The well-liked Pohlman was also a fine guitarist and backup singer. *Courtesy of Guy Pohlman*

Producer Lou Adler sits in the control booth inside Western 3 during a Mamas & the Papas recording session in 1966. Adler's uncanny ear for what radio stations would go for, along with Papa John Phillips's songwriting, the group's exquisite singing, and the Wrecking Crew's spot-on playing, made their combined efforts an unbeatable creative and commercial force. *Courtesy of Lou Adler*

Chuck Berghofer, pictured here in the early Seventies on an electric bass, was better known as one of the Wrecking Crew's main string bass players. Berghofer played the famous, signature descending bass run on "These Boots Are Made for Walkin'" by Nancy Sinatra. *Courtesy of Chuck Berghofer*

Everybody loves Dino! The Reprise recording session at United Recorders for the song "Houston" in 1965, with, from left to right, Glen Campbell, the producer, Jimmy Bowen, Dean Martin, and the arranger, Billy Strange. Hal Blaine's famous blue sparkle Ludwig drum kit is just visible in the bottom right corner. *Courtesy of Billy Strange*

Engineer Bones Howe sitting in on the drums during the recording of "Where Were You When I Needed You" by the Grass Roots, 1966. *Courtesy of Bones Howe*

A recording date for the groundbreaking *Pet Sounds* album, with, from left to right, Brian Wilson, Lyle Ritz, and the drummer/percussionist, Jim Gordon, early 1966.
Courtesy of Lyle Ritz

Creed Bratton (aka Chuck Ertmoed) of the Grass Roots singing in the studio, 1967. *Courtesy of Creed Bratton*

The Versatiles, better known as the 5th Dimension, with their beloved producer, Bones Howe (glasses), and multi-Grammy-winning songwriter Jimmy Webb (far right) in Western 3 during the sessions for *The Magic Garden* album, 1967. *Courtesy of Bones Howe*

Hal Blaine, going tie-dyed this time around, tells one of his trademark jokes to start a session in Western 3, circa 1968. *Courtesy of Bones Howe*

Joe Osborn holding the 1960 Fender Jazz bass that he played on countless rock-and-roll masterpieces such as "MacArthur Park," "Aquarius," and "Bridge Over Troubled Water." Osborn never changed the strings once during his entire tenure as part of the Wrecking Crew. *Courtesy of Michael Ochs Archives/Getty Images*

Mason Williams (right), composer of the Grammy-winning "Classical Gas," confers with Tiny Tim (left) and Tommy Smothers backstage, 1969. *Courtesy of Mason Williams*

Grammy time: from left to right, Rod McKuen, Mason Williams, José Feliciano, and Glen Campbell cradling their trophies at the big 1969 awards ceremony. *Courtesy of Mason Williams*

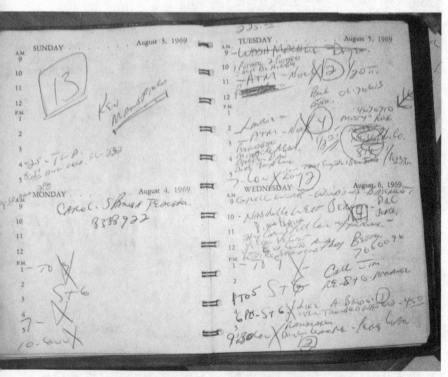

A couple of pages from Hal Blaine's session diary, showing his work for Simon & Garfunkel on their legendary *Bridge Over Troubled Water* album in August 1969. The entries are notated as "S&G." *Courtesy of Hal Blaine*

Michel Rubini (right), along with Sonny and Cher, during his later tenure as the musical director for their hit television series, *The Sonny & Cher Comedy Hour*, early Seventies. *Courtesy of Michel Rubini*

Just two good ol' Arkansas boys: friends and fellow guitarists Glen Campbell (left) and Louie Shelton pose in the studio around the time of Campbell's breakout success in 1969 on *The Glen Campbell Goodtime Hour* on CBS. Shelton was just getting hot as part of the Wrecking Crew as Campbell was leaving for good. *Courtesy of Louie Shelton*

Mark Lindsay, solo star and the lead singer of Paul Revere & the Raiders, confers with session guitarist Louie Shelton inside Studio A within the CBS Columbia Square facilities in late 1969. Shelton would be back in December 1970, along with Hal Blaine and Carol Kaye, to help Lindsay cut "Indian Reservation." *Courtesy of Louie Shelton*

Gary Coleman plays percussion in the studio, early Seventies. *Courtesy of Gary Coleman*

The transition continues: guitarist Richard Bennett, Wrecking Crewer Al Casey's youthful protégé, jams in the studio in 1973 with Joe Osborn (far left) and Gary Coleman (wearing shades behind Osborn). Bennett, one of the young guns then coming on strong, also worked as Neil Diamond's principal guitarist for seventeen years. Since 1994, he has continued in the same capacity for Mark Knopfler. *Courtesy of Richard Bennett*

The famous stamp that Hal Blaine used on the pages of his drum charts in order to remember his place. The unique imprint also seemed to find its way onto other surfaces in recording studios all over town. *Courtesy of Hal Blaine*

HAL BLAINE
STRIKES AGAIN !!

The changing of the guard: from left to right, Michael Omartian, Johnny Rivers, Jerry Allison, Jim Gordon, Joe Sidore (engineer), Joe Osborn, Dean Parks, and Larry Carlton during the 1972 recording of Rivers's *L.A. Reggae* album, which featured Larry Knechtel (not pictured) playing the classic piano part on "Rockin' Pneumonia and the Boogie Woogie Flu." Omartian, Parks, and Carlton were among the new breed of sidemen that gradually began to replace the Wrecking Crew. *Courtesy of Johnny Rivers*

The check that Michel Rubini returned to Phil Spector after the final, aborted recording date at Studio 56 in 1992. Rubini felt the payment was undeserved. An appreciative Spector promptly sent it back to the keyboardist with a friendly note written in red that said, "Thanks, Michel. Happy Holidays! See you soon —Warmest Regards, Phil." The two would never work together again. *Courtesy of Michel Rubini*

As the troopers began to menacingly shine their flashlights up and down the aisle of the stranded bus, looking for the purportedly Caucasian interloper, Ray Charles had to think fast. He wasn't going to allow anyone to take one of his band members away.

"Tell them he's Spanish," Charles whispered to Jeff Brown. "Maybe the crackers will go for it."

Peake, sitting just behind them and scared out of his mind, took the hint. He knew he would likely never be seen again if those lawmen took him away. That's how things worked in the Deep South when you crossed the color line.

Lowering his head, Peake inched down in his seat and tried his best to look and act the part of a non-English-speaking guitar player, mumbling a bunch of random Spanish-sounding gibberish that he vaguely recalled from a class he once took in high school.

After Brown passed the word along that there was indeed a Spanish band member aboard, the state troopers huddled in the front. After about a minute of discussion, they suddenly stepped off the bus and motioned it down the ramp toward the stage entrance. Twenty different sets of lungs exhaled as one. Alabama's finest had bought the story.

In their limited, bigoted knowledge of the world, the governor's garrison of gendarmes had incorrectly assumed that being Spanish and being white were mutually exclusive. Just like Ray Charles thought they might.

For his part, Peake could not have been more relieved. Or more grateful. Ray Charles's gamble on the ignorance of the locals had just saved Peake's life. While quickly performing their show that night, a still-scared Peake (now wearing brown makeup, no less) understandably declined to stand up and play his customary guitar solo during his big spotlight moment. He and the band then left the state of Alabama as fast as they could.

Though the Montgomery incident certainly had been the most harrowing encounter of his young life, Don Peake found through it all that he very much liked playing in the Ray Charles Orchestra. It tested his skills, it satisfied him musically, and it further burnished his growing reputation as a premier guitarist. Not to mention that it brought him full circle from that intoxicating day five years before at his parents' place when he first heard

"What'd I Say." Now he got to play it every night onstage with the legend himself. What were the chances of *that* ever happening? Peake felt as if he had received an all-expenses-paid scholarship to attend the "Ray Charles School of Music."

It was also a level of prominence that would lead Peake, by the mid-Sixties, toward a gradual integration into the exclusive ranks of the Wrecking Crew, where he would become a first-call choice for Spector, Wilson, and just about every other important rock-and-roll producer in Los Angeles (including continued on-and-off work for Charles). Everyone knew that if you could play for the Genius of Soul, you could play for anybody. And Don Peake could play.

6

I Got You, Babe

Phil, I think we need to change the sound.
—SONNY BONO

Looking out through the grimy window of his run-down Hollywood office, twenty-seven-year-old Salvatore Bono knew he needed a change. With a dead-end job at a company called Record Merchandising, an independent record distributor catering to stores of all sizes, the short, dark-haired, affable promotions man spent his workweek endlessly schlepping copies of mostly lackluster 45s to local radio stations, trying to somehow squeeze out a little airtime for them. And he just wasn't very good at it.

In the early Sixties, disc jockeys at Top 40 radio stations in major markets around the country were the undisputed, exalted—sometimes practically deified—gatekeepers of all that passed by the ears of their faithful listeners. By sheer cult of personality, they ruled the airwaves with a dizzying gift for all things gab, their on-air patter a seamless blend of charisma, cleverness, and relentlessly good cheer.

Behind the scenes, the air talent also had a big say (second only to a station's program director and/or music director) as to which songs were to be played. And it was the job of the indie promotions men to sway the opinions of the various jocks and directors in any way possible. Treat them nice and magic could happen. Buying dinners, giving gifts, even sliding the occasional wad of cash into an open palm, were all typical tools of the promo trade. Whatever it took to get a new release noticed, just as long as nobody got caught. Payola *was* illegal after all. Winnowed to its core, the promotions racket had little to do with merit and everything to do with the schmooze.

But Salvatore Bono—known to his friends and family as Sonny—simply couldn't get used to being a shill for other people's music. His heart just wasn't in it. More often than not, he tossed his daily allotment of 45s into a large, steel waste receptacle behind his office and instead hotfooted it over to Hollywood Lanes, the music industry's unofficial hangout. It was there at the bowling alley that he picked up the latest scuttlebutt about what was happening behind studio doors and who was getting hot on the charts. More than anything, he wanted to join the ranks of those on the other side of the control room glass—to become a writer and a producer, to make his *own* hit records.

Just like his idol, Phil Spector.

By the middle of 1963, Sonny Bono had taken all he could. His career in the doldrums, it was time to finally *do* something with his life, to make his mark. It was time to get in touch with Spector.

After running things by a mutual friend, songwriter and arranger Jack Nitzsche, Bono weighed out what he wanted to say. Spector was the most important rock-and-roll producer in the country. That much was clear. Bono also knew that watching things up close and in person, like how to make a great record, was the only way he would ever really learn to do it for himself. But first he needed to somehow get his foot in the door, to show why he would be an indispensable addition to the empire.

Taking a deep breath and crossing himself for luck, Bono nervously dialed the producer's office number.

"Yes, I'd like to speak to Phil Spector, please," he said.

"Who may I ask is calling?" a female voice responded.

"Sonny Bono."

"Please hold."

And Bono did hold. For what became five minutes, and then ten. He began to wonder if he had been permanently shuffled off to telephone purgatory. Spector had never heard of Bono and had absolutely no reason to even take his call. He knew that. But he also refused to hang up. This was his dream and he wasn't going to give in until he caught the break he was looking for.

Finally, after what seemed an eternity, a thin, nasal, bored-sounding voice came on the line.

"Yeah?"

It was *him*, the man himself.

In an explosion of words, Sonny Bono told Spector about his promo background at Record Merchandising and that Jack Nitzsche had encouraged him to call. Bono also told Spector in no uncertain terms *why* he had called.

"Mr. Spector, I want to work for you. Just you. And I'll work for any amount of money, for any amount of time."

The directness of the solicitation seemed to catch the self-absorbed producer slightly off guard.

"So, what is it that you want to do for me?" Spector asked dryly.

What Bono really wanted, of course, was to receive an immediate, in-depth tutorial straight from the master on how to cut a number-one record. But Bono couldn't very well say that. Everybody in town wanted to know how the secretive Spector did what he did. For now, a more palatable-sounding proposition would have to do.

"I want to be your West Coast promotions man at Philles Records," Bono boldly announced. "Your label is too big and too important to keep using the outside indie guys. I think you need someone who will work for you alone."

After a brief pause, Spector mumbled, "Yeah, I like the idea."

Bono was halfway home.

Following several more minutes of expertly executed persuasion, laced with heavy doses of flattery, promises, and a natural-born earnestness, the deal was set. Spector hired Bono sight unseen.

With one gutsy phone call, Sonny Bono, a high school dropout and former meat delivery boy, had conjured a position out of thin air with the hottest record label in town. Now it would just be a matter of putting phase two of his grand plan into play.

✳

Just as he had hoped, Sonny Bono did indeed become more than just Phil Spector's West Coast promotions man. He also became Spector's favorite go-to grunt, the guy who ran out for coffee when ordered to do so or who willingly climbed out of bed in the middle of the night to join the boss for coleslaw at a twenty-four-hour diner. The producer's whims were his command.

Like clockwork, too, Bono was there in the studio whenever Spector had a recording session scheduled, watching over the producer's shoulder, absorbing everything, helping as needed. Sometimes just to keep Bono busy and out of his thinning hair Spector would ask Hal Blaine to give Sonny a tambourine or some other innocuous percussion instrument, anything to keep the guy from hovering all the time—though this gambit sometimes backfired on Spector, with the rhythmically challenged Bono seemingly incapable of playing at the same tempo as the rest of the musicians.

As he tried his best one day to vigorously lay down some funky castanet sounds during the fade on the twenty-fifth take of "Be My Baby," Bono's feeble, spastic attempt was finally too much even for the generally patient Spector to ignore.

"Sonny, consider yourself jive, all right?" the producer said, his voice honeyed with sarcasm, as he and the rest of the Wrecking Crew broke into knowing laughter. Bono was nobody's threat to become the next great bebopper.

But despite Sonny Bono's struggle to find his inner groove, he was always a dutiful manservant to Spector. And Bono's eagle eye, especially during the mammoth series of sessions in the late summer of 1963 for Spector's landmark holiday-themed album, *A Christmas Gift for You from Philles Records,* helped him reap the real reward he was after. It gave him the mental road map he needed in order to feel confident about producing his own songs. He was now sure he could do it. Maybe he couldn't play an instrument, maybe he couldn't sing very well, either, but he *had* learned from the best in the business about how to put the right elements together in the right order. How to make a hit record. All Bono needed now was the right opportunity.

*

By the end of 1964, Sonny Bono sensed that the foundation of Phil Spector's Wall of Sound formula was starting to crack. Though the producer was on the cusp of creating several Top 10 hits for a duo of blue-eyed soul singers called the Righteous Brothers (with various members of the Wrecking Crew on all the instruments), the rest of his Philles acts were by this time struggling to even make the Top 40. The era of the girl groups was clearly on the wane. And unfortunately for Bono, he made the mistake of telling Spector as much.

As per Bono's custom as the head of West Coast promotions, one December morning he decided to take the newest release by the Ronettes over to KFWB in Hollywood. The men behind the mics there usually loved getting a copy of Spector's latest and greatest creation before their archrivals at KRLA even knew it existed. The station had flipped over "Then He Kissed Me" and "Be My Baby," helping in no small part to turn those songs into major hits.

But not this time around. As the disc jockey listened to the song "Walkin' in the Rain," he noticeably grimaced, telling Bono that, in his opinion, the big Spector sound just didn't impress anybody anymore. Tastes were changing; the recent influx of powerhouse British bands like the Beatles, the Rolling Stones, and the Dave Clark Five had seen to that. A new style of rock and roll had taken hold.

"Have you heard what Lennon and McCartney are doing?" the DJ asked.

With a heavy heart, Bono knew the radio guy was right. The charts didn't lie. The Brits were now setting the pace. As Bono left the station and slowly walked over to a nearby phone booth on Hollywood Boulevard, a sudden wave of trepidation washed over him. He had to call the office and somehow break the news to Spector. The man in charge always wanted an immediate update on the latest song pitch. And he didn't take rejection well.

But in relaying the story to him about what had just happened, Bono made one fatal error in judgment. Instead of simply reporting exactly what the disc jockey had said and nothing more, Bono tried to soften the blow by adding, "Phil, I think we need to change the sound."

That was all Spector needed to hear. No one talked to him that way. At least no one who had any realistic expectation of remaining in Spector's life. He was a genius after all. The press and other musicians had said so. And now one of his underlings had the gall to question his production methods?

But Spector didn't debate with Bono. Spector didn't scream at him, either. In fact, he didn't say anything. All Bono heard was the endless whoosh of midday traffic passing by. And as he waited through the lengthy, intense silence on the other end of the line, he instinctively knew that he was out. As in gone for good. Excised from the fold. For Bono had just committed the most heinous, unpardonable sin of them all. He had seen the elfin emperor without his clothes.

With a finality borne of one ill-worded transgression, it was now time for Sonny Bono to stake a musical claim of his own. To use the skills he had developed while standing so steadfastly in Spector's imposing shadow. It wouldn't be easy, but there was no other choice. Bono's exodus had probably been inevitable anyway. No one really ever lasted long in Spectorville.

Taking stock of his prospects in light of his new free agency, Bono thought he saw some potential in recording vocals with his girlfriend. She was a beautiful raven-haired teenager eleven years his junior who possessed a powerful vibrato and definite star-like presence. Perhaps they could forge a career together as some kind of a singing duo. It had been done before. And strong female vocalists, especially those like Petula Clark, Jackie De-Shannon, and Dusty Springfield, were getting very popular. A trend to capitalize on for sure. At least it might be a way to keep the wolf from the door.

*

During the late spring of 1965, as Sonny Bono sat at the kitchen table late one evening inside his small Benedict Canyon house, he began to wonder where he had gone wrong. Having recently moved into the home with his eighteen-year-old girlfriend-cum-common-law wife, Cherilyn LaPierre (she had "married" them herself with an exchange of cheap souvenir rings in their old apartment's bathroom one day), the would-be tunesmith and producer desperately wanted to write a hit song. Bono had seen his old boss

Phil Spector do it countless times. For that matter, it seemed like everybody Bono knew in the music business was finding some kind of success, writing and otherwise.

Following his abrupt and disheartening departure from Philles Records, the ambitious Bono had been nothing if not active. His first order of business had been to create a singing duo with Cher (as her friends and family referred to her) called Caesar & Cleo. The shaggy-haired, fur vest–wearing pair cut a few self-funded demos, with several members of the Wrecking Crew agreeing to help out their old friend Sonny by accepting fifteen bucks a head in cash under the table. The well-connected Bono also managed to score a distribution deal for his new recordings with Reprise Records. One of the singles, "Baby Don't Go," even made a respectable showing on the local LA record charts in late 1964. That was enough to get the duo some live work in small clubs throughout the area, which, in turn, was just enough to pay the rent on their tiny bungalow. But nothing was breaking for them nationally. And that was where the real money and fame were to be found.

With all this on his mind, Bono eased back in his chair and let out a long sigh. No point in trying to sleep on a night like this. Leaning forward again, he absently began scribbling down a bunch of seemingly unrelated snatches of song lyric ideas on a discarded sheet of thin cardboard that had been part of the latest delivery from the local laundry. The exercise was more of a habit than anything else. Something he liked to do to blow off steam. Nothing important had yet come from it.

But the more he wrote that night, however, the more Sonny Bono felt that, for once, he might actually be on to something. He found himself in a mode of emotional free association, unexpectedly tapping into the honesty of his domestic situation, with the feeling that although he and Cher had yet to make it big and had very little to show for themselves in terms of material possessions, at least they always had each other.

After finishing about half the lyrics, the suddenly energized Bono raced downstairs to the banged-up fifty-dollar upright piano he kept in the garage for just such songwriting purposes. Maybe he knew only a handful of chords and couldn't even play those very well, but they would have to do. In a burst of inspiration, the words and music flowed through Bono's mind and fingertips like never before. Plunking away with all he had, he managed to complete the full song in less than an hour.

As Bono excitedly played and sang his new creation for Cher, she gleefully grabbed the piece of cardboard with all the lyrics and declared, "I'm saving this forever." The two singing hopefuls instinctively knew that this was the hit they had been waiting for.

✳

Within days of Sonny Bono's late-night songwriting breakthrough, at his request a dozen-plus Wrecking Crew musicians piled into Gold Star's tiny Studio A. As the session got under way, it quickly became clear to everyone that Bono was right: his new composition, called "I Got You Babe," was indeed no ordinary song.

But as had become characteristic of a Bono-produced session—à la his role model Phil Spector—getting to the final recorded take on any given song was a lengthy, painstaking process. And "I Got You Babe" was no different. As the musicians played their respective parts over and over while Bono slowly worked his way through creating a mix that he thought radio might go for, the drudgery ultimately became too much to bear for one of the guitarists. A mild-mannered and highly respected regular by the name of Barney Kessel felt compelled to speak up.

"Oh, Sonny," Kessel called out during a break in the action.

"Uh, yes, Barney?" a surprised Bono replied over the talk-back mic from the control booth.

"If the doctor told me I had only two weeks left to live, I'd rather spend them with you. Because each moment is like an eternity."

Taking the off-the-wall comment at face value, the guileless Bono seemed pleased with the sudden showing of brotherly love from one of his favorite guitarists.

"Gee, thanks, Barney," he said.

Between the normally taciturn Kessel's wry observance and the ever-slow-on-the-uptake Bono, it was all too much for the Wrecking Crew to handle. They burst into laughter.

But by the time "I Got You Babe" finally made it into the can at the end of the three-hour session, the merriment had turned to awe. The song was an obvious smash.

Taking advantage of his time spent as a smooth-talking promo man, Bono quickly cut an acetate demo of the song—now credited to Sonny & Cher—and rushed it down to a new, red-hot Top 40 radio station on Melrose Avenue called KHJ, offering it to them as an exclusive. Hungry to get the jump on his two main competitors, KFWB and KRLA, the program director, Ron Jacobs, snapped up the recording and put it into regular rotation. The phone lines immediately lit up, with "I Got You Babe" soon vaulting to the top of the local, then national, and even the UK charts. Sonny & Cher had achieved a rare rock-and-roll feat: an across-the-board transatlantic number-one hit.

After years of dreaming, plotting, and hustling, Sonny Bono—with plenty of in-studio help from the Wrecking Crew—finally had made it to the pinnacle of his profession. A lofty lair where esteemed names like Spector, Wilson, Jagger, Lennon, and McCartney were considered to be the gold standard. And though he felt like a bit of a fake when being mentioned along with them by the press, Bono's vision had nonetheless been realized. He *had* made the big time. Now it would just be a matter of finding some way to stay there.

Mr. Tambourine Man

Don't be nervous, kid. Just take a deep breath.
—HAL BLAINE

On January 20, 1965, at the same time that Lyndon Baines Johnson stood before America delivering his inaugural address underneath the U.S. Capitol's East Portico for his second term in office as the nation's thirty-sixth president, Jim McGuinn, a little-known folk guitarist, nervously slid into *his* place of honor on a simple metal folding chair inside a giant, windowless recording studio on Sunset Boulevard.

But unlike the highly anticipated speech going down three thousand miles to the east—during which Johnson waxed rhapsodic about his belief in the divine mandate of his controversial Great Society program—the newcomer McGuinn had absolutely no reason to think that anything remotely historic was about to happen on his end of the line. Rather, McGuinn's biggest concern on that winter Wednesday morning was just making sure he didn't somehow make a fool out of himself.

Several months earlier, like so many other aspiring musicians, the twenty-two-year-old Chicago native and recent LA transplant had gone to see the Beatles' film debut in *A Hard Day's Night*. It was McGuinn's first real chance to see the group up close, to dissect what they did and how they did it. And it would be an event he would never forget.

At the precise moment the movie had begun, as George Harrison, the Beatles' lead guitarist, delivered one mighty downward strum on his Rickenbacker 360/12 twelve-string electric guitar, Jim McGuinn had felt a surge of adrenaline go through his body. The pulsating, chiming sound of the guitar filled both the theater and his imagination. "A Hard Day's Night" was now in play, and McGuinn, for all his musical experience, had never seen or heard anything like it. If one simple Fadd9 chord can be said to have changed a man's life, it occurred in that room, on that day.

Soon thereafter, the still-mesmerized McGuinn boldly traded in his acoustic twelve-string guitar and his five-string banjo—the tools of his livelihood—and bought the same semi-hollow-body Rickenbacker guitar model that Harrison had brandished up on the big screen. From its polished rosewood fret board and lacquered maple body to its two single-coil, high-gain pickups, McGuinn immediately fell in love with everything about his new Rick. The way it felt in his hands, the unique bell-like tonal quality. Now he could finally fully express himself as an artist, particularly in regard to exploring the more advanced jazz textures of those like John Coltrane and others.

Practicing for eight hours a day on his new axe, McGuinn quickly became far more than proficient. He taught himself a variety of complicated jazz and blues scales, even incorporating banjo-style picking patterns along the way. And he especially loved taking a potluck approach toward mixing and matching various elements of folk and rock, creating a musical Mulligan stew distinctly his own.

During this same period, Jim McGuinn also co-founded the Byrds, a folk-based quintet that had formed out of the Troubadour nightclub on Santa Monica Boulevard (where he had played many solo gigs). Through a lucky break, they had recently received the help of jazz trumpeter Miles Davis in securing a much-coveted recording contract with Columbia Records (Davis's label). The big catch, though, was that the five folkies with the rock-and-roll pretentions would be allowed to cut just one single. If it performed well on the charts—and, more important, at retail—the group would be permitted to record another. If not, they would be dropped.

With so much riding on the one-off recording, the pressure was on for both the Byrds and Columbia's management. The label still had not made any sort of real commitment to rock and roll (Paul Revere & the Raiders' first album wouldn't come out until later in the year), and they were cautious about investing too much time or money in a genre they felt could still very well prove to be a fad. This would be an important test.

Understandably interested in hedging their bet, Columbia promptly assigned an ever-so-mellow flaxen-haired twenty-two-year-old by the name of Terry Melcher—the youngest, hippest West Coast staff producer they had on the payroll—to see what he could achieve with the Byrds in the studio. Melcher's successful background as a writer, producer, and singer with his own surf/car rock outfits like Bruce & Terry and the Rip Chords ("Hey, Little Cobra"—a number-four hit in 1964, featuring Hal Blaine, Glen Campbell, and several other Wrecking Crew regulars) made him just about the only person at the label who had any actual experience with rock and roll. It also didn't hurt his in-house status and clout that his mother, the singer and actress Doris Day, was Columbia's biggest recording star.

Soon deciding on an as-yet-unreleased song by Bob Dylan called "Mr. Tambourine Man" to be the most promising vehicle through which to showcase their complex vocal harmonies, the Byrds primed themselves to hit the studio at Columbia and make the most out of their lone recording opportunity. Time to break out the instruments, they figured, and show the world what they could do. This was their time to shine. But, instead, the band found themselves on the receiving end of a rude, music business–style wake-up call: with one exception, Terry Melcher made it plain that he planned to use the Wrecking Crew in each of their places.

Having been an acoustic guitar–playing sideman for several years in New York for seasoned folk acts like the Limeliters, the Chad Mitchell Trio, and Judy Collins, Jim McGuinn (who would soon change his first name to Roger) already knew his way around a recording studio. And his years of practice and dedication had helped him evolve into a strong player, someone capable of studio-quality work. With this in mind, Melcher had no issue with using McGuinn's services. In fact, he welcomed it: the Ricken-backer gave the Byrds a much-needed signature sound.

But the young producer had a very *big* problem with the other four members of the band. In his view, they were utterly incapable of playing their own instruments at a professional level. He had caught a couple of their rehearsals, immediately realizing that they were, in essence, a bunch of beginners. And Columbia wasn't in the habit of doling out music lessons or allowing hours of precious studio time to be wasted while amateurs learned their craft.

In addition, Melcher had been heavily influenced by his friend Brian Wilson's now-almost-exclusive use of the Wrecking Crew in the studio, a gambit that had immeasurably increased the creative depth and efficiency of the Beach Boys' recorded work. With time being money and with his growing reputation at stake, Melcher wanted the same arsenal of pros at his disposal. It was essential that he put out the best possible product in the shortest amount of time.

One way or the other, the members of the Byrds would just have to deal with it.

✳

As Hal Blaine casually walked into Columbia Records' Studio A at a little before 10:00 A.M. on the day of the recording for "Mr. Tambourine Man," he first popped his head into the control booth to say hello to Terry Melcher. Having worked together several times before, they had a good rapport. And young though Melcher might have been, Blaine considered him to be an important up-and-coming talent. In turn, Melcher always thought of Blaine as the finest studio drummer in town.

"Gonna really need your help today, Hal," Melcher said from his seat behind the large mixing console. "The label's watching this one."

"Ready when you are," Blaine said with a smile.

Stepping back out into Studio A's main tracking room—a huge, now-converted 1940s-era radio broadcast theater formerly known as the Columbia Playhouse, once capable of holding an audience of over a thousand—Blaine entered to greet an array of familiar faces scattered about, all in various stages of warming up on their instruments. Guys he worked with practically every day of the week like Jerry Cole and Bill Pitman on guitar, Russell Bridges (aka Leon Russell) on piano, and Larry Knechtel on electric bass. It sometimes seemed like Blaine saw them more than he saw his own wife (he had recently married a beautiful young woman named Lydia, his third try at matrimony).

While putting his stick bag next to his set of blue sparkle Ludwig drums, Blaine also happened to notice a young face he had never seen before. Someone holding an electric twelve-string guitar in his lap, clearly appearing apprehensive.

Walking over, the always-welcoming Blaine extended his hand to the worried-looking guitar player.

"I'm Hal," he said warmly. "You with the band?"

A startled Jim McGuinn looked up at the figure standing before him. No one else in the place had even bothered to acknowledge his existence.

"Yes," McGuinn replied tentatively while returning the drummer's handshake. "I'm the lead guitar player. My name's Jim."

In reality, however, Jim McGuinn already knew who Hal Blaine was. McGuinn knew who the rest of the Wrecking Crew musicians were, too. He had long been in awe of Phil Spector's productions, and McGuinn was well aware of who had played what on those heralded Gold Star sessions. Having bought most of the big Wall of Sound singles like "Be My Baby" and "Da Doo Ron Ron (When He Walked Me Home)," the studious McGuinn had privately spent many hours meticulously picking them apart, instrument by instrument, while they blared through his hi-fi.

No, McGuinn needed no introductions. These cats were his idols. They were the best in the business. And now he was actually sitting in the same room with them, about to cut a record. He felt both honored and daunted. It didn't get any more intense than this.

Sensing McGuinn's continued unease, Blaine offered a quick piece of advice.

"Don't be nervous, kid. Just take a deep breath."

And then, flashing his trademark double-thumbs-up as he headed back toward his drums, Blaine added, "You'll be fine."

✳

Having seen his share of jittery young musicians over the years, the well-seasoned Hal Blaine proved to be as solid as his unwavering sense of time in his assessment of Jim McGuinn. The Byrds' guitarist *was* fine in the studio that day over at Columbia. In fact, he was more than fine.

With McGuinn's nervousness fortunately fading as soon as the red "recording" light came on, his Bach-inspired intro and outro riffs on "Mr. Tambourine Man" provided the perfect set of jangling bookends to a tight two-and-a-half-minute tune. Combined with Blaine's expertly executed drum licks, Jerry Cole's syncopated guitar "chinks" (borrowed directly from his own work on the Beach Boys' "Don't Worry Baby"), and Larry Knechtel's memorable sliding bass line, the whole production was spot-on.

Melcher was happy. McGuinn was happy. The Columbia execs were happy. Everyone seemed happy.

Everyone, that is, except for four-fifths of the Byrds.

In particular, the band's drummer, Michael Clarke, was flat-out angry. Though he had spent precious little time to that point playing on an actual drum kit (strapped for cash, he mostly had been practicing on a jury-rigged set of cardboard boxes), it never interfered with Clarke's firm opinion of his own place and position within the flock. Novice or not, he had no taste for being relegated to a bench role. This was a *band*, man. And he was their drummer. Or hadn't anybody gotten the memo?

After the release of the "Mr. Tambourine Man" single in mid-April, with Columbia starting to get a good feeling about the record's commercial prospects, the Byrds were invited back into the studio to cut what would become the rest of their first album, appropriately titled *Mr. Tambourine Man.* While having reluctantly agreed in the interim to allow the other four members to now also play their own instruments (through heavy pressure from the band's management), Melcher still found the occasional need to bring in Hal Blaine to "sweeten" some of the percussion. Having a rock-solid rhythm track was vital for any song—it was the foundation upon which everything else was built. But the unrelenting Michael Clarke saw Blaine's presence in a different light.

"We don't need another drummer in here," a still-resentful Clarke said to Melcher one afternoon as they and the rest of the band listened in the booth to a song on which Blaine had contributed. "It should just be the five of us. I can handle all the playing. I've been doing it onstage every night at Ciro's, you know."

Here we go again, thought the producer.

"We've already been through this, Michael," Melcher said evenly, trying his best to remain patient. "Playing live is very different from what is needed in the studio. In some ways, I just don't think you're quite there yet."

"Bullshit," Clarke replied.

That finally tore it. Clarke never did know when to quit. And Melcher had taken all he could of the rookie drummer's constant complaining.

"Listen," said Melcher, his voice rising as he spun around in his chair. "You need to sit down and shut the fuck up right now. Or leave this studio. Your choice. *Got* it?"

A silence fell over the small room.

Melcher obviously meant business. And with their one-shot record deal for a big-time label all that stood between the Byrds and the street, it was not the best time to push personal agendas. For now, anyway.

Clarke grudgingly took a seat.

But the producer and the drummer would each soon be able to claim a measure of vindication. Exceeding all expectations, the title track, featuring the Wrecking Crew, raced to number one on the singles charts. And the album itself, with the full band laboriously playing their own instruments on ten out of the twelve tracks, trucked in at number six.

Even more meaningful, their successful debut established the Byrds as one of the founding fathers of a new genre of popular music called folk rock. With a skillful blend of vocal harmonies, social messages, and a unique combination of acoustic and electric instrumentation, the band hadn't just become successful; they had become seminal. McGuinn had made social history on the same day as LBJ after all.

In short, by mid-1965 the Byrds had helped take popular music from "I wanna hold your hand" to "I wanna change the world" in one fell swoop. Their success instantly, and ironically, also served to further marginalize the now increasingly dated-sounding, over-the-top rock and roll put forth by Phil Spector—the very person Jim McGuinn had studied so closely in his earlier days. Yet the determined Spector was in no way ready to go down without a fight. To hell with folk rock. The brilliant musical auteur had one more creative card up his sleeve, one last way to deal himself back onto the top of the charts. And, as always, he would need the Wrecking Crew by his side to help him pull it off.

River Deep, Mountain High

See you around, Phil. Take care.
—Michel Rubini

During the late fall of 1945, just after the end of World War II, inside an expensive home located along the shimmering waters of the Pacific Ocean just north of Los Angeles, a precocious curly-haired toddler with large expressive eyes sat frozen in place, staring. Having pressed his young face between two narrow wooden stairway balusters high above his family's elegantly appointed living room, the three-year-old watched intently from his secret perch as two men, who seemed to be very far below, made the most beautiful sounds he had ever heard.

One of those playing was the boy's father, a world-famous classical violinist by the name of Jan Rubini; the other was his longtime piano accompanist. And as the two musicians diligently rehearsed for an upcoming concert tour, the only thing running through the young child's mind was wondering how soon he could be just like them.

For some people, becoming a musician is a rational, well-planned vocational decision. Much like becoming a doctor or a firefighter or an accountant, it is a deliberate career choice that evolves through considerable thought and planning. For others, the desire to spend a life in the musical arts is a feeling unexpectedly thrust upon them by the vagaries of fate. Like choosing to become a guitarist after watching the Beatles' first appearance on *The Ed Sullivan Show* or suddenly realizing the ability to sing while sitting with friends around a campfire.

Though for a select few, however, the idea of becoming a musician is never viewed as some kind of occupational option. It is simply an automatic extension of who they are: the fortunate recipients of highly specific familial DNA. And so with a celebrated concert figure for a father and a principal with the Royal Conservatory of Music in London for a grandfather—not to mention many other similarly employed forebears—little Michel Rubini, late of Old Malibu Road, didn't *become* a musician; he was born one.

But birthright or no, making the most out of an innate musical talent still takes practice. Plenty of practice. And it was no different for Rubini. His parents cut him no slack, requiring that he sit before the piano—his instrument of choice—for a minimum of one hour before *and* after school, every day. He faithfully did as he was told, too, even while he heard the other kids in the neighborhood through the open windows having the times of their lives playing baseball, riding bikes, and just generally goofing off.

From the works of Chopin, Mozart, and Schumann to every classical composer in between, Rubini quickly excelled at playing anything and everything put in front of him. So much so that by the age of fourteen he became his father's regular piano accompanist during a string of prestigious performances around the country. An unheard-of experience for someone so young, and a career-making opportunity to be envied.

But Michel Rubini, for all his seeming good fortune, hated every single minute of it.

Sometime before, while running errands with his mother one day in nearby Santa Monica, Rubini had gone into the local record shop to buy a song he had heard on the radio, a new release called "Hearts of Stone" by the Jewels. He loved everything about the little R & B number. The simplicity. The power. And, especially, the *feel*. It was nothing like the usual vanilla-sounding stuff coming over the airwaves. Singers like Tony Bennett, Perry Como, and Eddie Fisher—the top stars of the day—were fine in small doses. But they sorely lacked any kind of soul. On the other hand, "Hearts of Stone" stirred more emotion inside of Rubini than ten piano concertos stacked on top of each other. It was also the perfect example of the kind of music his father despised most.

"Don't let your dad know you bought that," his mother warned as they drove northward on the Pacific Coast Highway toward home.

However, within days, Rubini's father did find out about the record and soon thereafter, many more just like it. He tried his best to put an end to what he perceived to be his son's wayward musical ways, but it was too late. Michel Rubini was completely, hopelessly hooked. The kid had stumbled onto a kind of music that spoke to him. And he wasn't going back. He began to realize that he no longer wanted to become a concert pianist, either.

By the time Rubini began attending Hollywood High School in 1956, his parents, after years of marital discord, finally called it quits. He at first lived with his mother in Studio City, but her subsequent decision to relocate to New Jersey pushed him into moving over to his father's Beverly Hills home instead. It wasn't that he liked him better. Mostly Rubini just didn't want to live on the East Coast. It seemed so desperately far removed from where the real action was. He wanted to stay near the thriving popular music scene in Los Angeles, hoping that somehow, someday, he might find a way to become a part of it.

In what evolved into a shockingly unsupervised and lonely existence for someone so young, Rubini largely ended up living solo in the lavish Beverly Hills mansion, answering to no one. Meanwhile, his virtuoso father spent the bulk of his time either on tour, staying with various lady friends, or living separately in his Malibu beach pad.

On several occasions, when the elder Rubini chose to rent out the house, Michel was forced to live in the maid's sleeping quarters over the garage at the back of the property. Other times, whenever the latest set of tenants didn't want the landlord's son hanging around, Rubini would glumly gather his belongings and move down to an old trailer his father kept in a mobile home park near the corner of Washington and La Cienega Boulevards. Not the kind of glamorous life most would imagine for a child of apparent privilege. Michel Rubini was essentially a Fifties version of a latchkey kid, except in his case it was a 24/7 proposition. A circumstance about which the California Department of Social Services, had they known, surely would have investigated.

To compound matters, Rubini was also on the receiving end of a daily barrage of schoolyard bullying. With his curly hair, girl-like first name, and prominent piano-playing skills, he became an easy mark among the more Neanderthal members of the student body. The taunts often turned physical, too, with Rubini gamely fighting back, ably inflicting his fair share of return punishment. Usually outnumbered, however, most of the time he just plain got the snot kicked out of him, his nose being broken too many times to even bother counting. With little incentive to continue showing up for his regularly scheduled beat-down sessions, Rubini's school attendance suffered accordingly.

With him having no family, no friends, no rules, and a gigantic target of ridicule pasted squarely on his back, Michel Rubini's young life was in a fast-moving downward spiral. Something had to give. He was inches from turning into a juvenile delinquent, maybe worse. Just about the only thing the troubled teenage pianist hadn't experienced was spending any time in jail—yet.

✳

Walking down the street one afternoon in a residential area of Beverly Hills with his eleven-year-old brother in tow (who had come for a visit), Rubini started to feel an old familiar itch. It had been a while, but the high school sophomore-to-be knew the sensation all too well. He had first experienced it while briefly living with his mother and little brother over in the Valley before the two of them moved back east. And, unfortunately, there was no ointment or other medication Rubini could take as a remedy.

No, the only way to successfully scratch this particular kind of itch was to steal a car.

In the heart of the Fifties, the small city of Beverly Hills represented to many the epitome of immense wealth and genteel living. From movie, TV, and music stars to captains of industry, the well-heeled inhabitants enjoyed not only an idyllic, sequestered existence but also one of surprising innocence. So innocent, in fact, that many trusting locals routinely left their expensive automobiles unlocked in the driveway or on the street, some with the key still in the ignition.

For anyone with the nerve and the inclination, a smorgasbord of alluring, luxurious theft opportunities awaited. Let's see, shall it be a Jaguar today? Or perhaps a Bentley? How about a Cadillac Eldorado convertible? With no hot-wiring required, it was as simple as turning over the engine and then driving off. Almost.

With Michel Rubini eventually spying an unattended ride that was to his youthful liking—a brand-new, top-of-the-line, bright red Chrysler Imperial Crown ("The brilliant Chrysler...for those accustomed to the finest!")—he swung into action. Time to scratch that itch.

Stopping along the sidewalk next to the parked vehicle, Rubini first casually glanced up and down the block. No need to have some angry owner start chasing after him. That would be bad.

With nobody in sight, however, the boy quickly stepped toward the curb, bent down, and peered through the passenger side window. Just as he had hoped: a set of keys, glinting in the sun, sat dangling from the ignition. Exhibiting the confident air of someone who had done it all before, Rubini then strode around to the driver's side and opened the unlocked door. So far, so good.

Swiftly sliding behind the wheel, with one quick turn of his wrist Rubini brought the mighty 392-cubic-inch FirePower V8 hemi engine roaring to life. Pulling the PowerFlite automatic transmission into gear, he then reached across the front seat to shove open the other door for his brother, and the two siblings sailed off down the street.

But under the watchful eye of the no-nonsense Beverly Hills police chief, Clinton H. Anderson, successful car thievery was a little more problematic than it might have appeared to the average practitioner. Or at least to Michel Rubini.

With keeping crime to a minimum being a particular point of pride in their squeaky-clean jurisdiction, the cops in Beverly Hills were constantly on the lookout for anything suspicious. And the Chrysler being driven by Rubini definitely qualified. As it zoomed by a parked patrol unit, the officer inside did a double take. To his amazement, all he saw flying past his window were two very small heads in one very big car. He flipped on his lights.

After being arrested and taken to police headquarters inside City Hall on Rexford Drive, Rubini half-expected to spend time in jail. Underage though he was, he had been caught red-handed and he knew it. But instead of being shown to a cell, the teenager to his surprise ended up in an interrogation room sitting across a table from, of all people, Chief Anderson.

"Mr. Rubini, I know that you're on probation for stealing cars in North Hollywood," he began sternly. "And if I were to tell them that you had now done the same thing here in Beverly Hills, you'd be going to prison camp."

Rubini swallowed hard. Having heard the stories, he wanted no part of something like that.

"But I talked to the owner of the car and he's not going to press charges against you. He's a friend of mine."

The chief paused, looking straight at the boy.

"So, this is what I'm going to do," he continued. "I'm putting you on probation here in Beverly Hills. And you're going to write me a letter once a week—every week—for the next two years, telling me everything that you're doing. And if it does not coincide with the reports I get from my officers, then you *will* be going to jail."

Rising from his chair, Anderson then leaned in close to Rubini's face, making sure his message came through loud and clear.

"If you do anything—*anything*—I will know about it," he intoned. "You now have two strikes against you. Don't get a third."

✳

In what at first seemed to be yet one more desperate act by an unhappy kid who was on his way to almost certain incarceration, being busted by the Beverly Hills police turned out to be the best thing that ever happened to Michel Rubini. Thanks to a decent cop who scared the daylights out of him, Rubini learned his lesson. Just as he had been instructed, he faithfully wrote a letter every week for two years regarding his whereabouts. And he privately vowed to funnel his boundless energy and talent into creating a professional music career. It was the one thing he knew for sure that he could do. His brief crime spree was dead and buried, a function of silly youthful indiscretion.

By 1961, having finally graduated from the awful torment of high school, Rubini began taking a series of weekly piano lessons from a legendary jazzer named Harry Fields. Rubini also started frequenting some of LA's black jazz venues, places like the Black Orchid and the It Club. With an eye toward one day possibly joining their ranks, he wanted to watch the best of the best do their thing. In particular, keyboardists like Les McCann (piano) and Richard "Groove" Holmes (organ) could alternately make Rubini cry and blow his mind with the depth and beauty of their playing.

Over the next couple of years, while still occasionally working as his father's accompanist, Rubini spent many hours a day honing his technique on the piano. He wanted to start building a name for himself in the clubs, just like so many of his bebop heroes had done. Even with the notoriously poor pay, he figured that jazz was the milieu for him.

But life had other plans for Michel Rubini.

One night, after impulsively stepping in to play the Hammond organ onstage for a shorthanded surf band in a small club on the Sunset Strip, Rubini surprised himself afterward by agreeing to become their regular tour organist. He had no rock-and-roll experience, of course, but the simple three-chord music was hardly a challenge. And with time on his hands and looking to make some quick cash, he thought it would be a lark. How long could it last, anyway?

Produced by a guy named Joe Saraceno, the group was called the Marketts, and they were constructed exactly like the Champs and the Beach Boys before them: one version stayed out on the road, while studio pros—namely, the Wrecking Crew—cut all the records back home. For Saraceno, like so many other producers, it was all about expediency and keeping costs to a minimum. Already successful with releases by various phantom bands he had produced, including the Routers ("Let's Go" and "Sting Ray"), the shrewd Saraceno had his lucrative formula down to a science.

But with word soon being passed along from the road about the organ-playing Rubini's even more out-of-this-world abilities on piano, Saraceno decided to give the kid a listen for himself. He was always on the lookout for strong keyboard talent to bolster his various studio projects.

After meeting with Saraceno and providing him with the requested run-through of his skills, an astounded Rubini was offered a job on the spot.

"Listen," said Saraceno. "If you want to, you can come in and play on a recording session we've got coming up. I'll let you play on one of the sides."

"Yes, sir, that'd be great," Rubini enthusiastically responded.

Saraceno clearly wanted to take him on a test drive before committing to anything further. But that was okay. Rubini felt he could play alongside anybody, and he had also heard that studio work, reportedly tough to get, paid well, too. The whole thing sounded like a gas.

But from the moment of his first official recording date for Saraceno, when Rubini sat down inside Liberty Records' in-house recording studio next to the imposing likes of Glen Campbell, Carol Kaye, Hal Blaine, and several other Wrecking Crew heavyweights, the twenty-one-year-old knew he had found his calling. He loved it. And the producer loved him back.

Rubini could sight-read like nobody's business. He could play by ear. And he could improvise when needed, playing any kind of style. He was also fast and usually flawless. Rubini had everything in his musical toolbox a rock-and-roll producer could want.

Saraceno soon began using Rubini on just about everything he cut, including the Markett's Top 5 instrumental smash, "Out of Limits." Big-time arrangers like Ernie Freeman and Gene Page, along with a rising young producer named Jimmy Bowen, also brought Michel Rubini in. He was quickly becoming *the* hot new must-hire inside the cloistered world of LA recording studios, an important addition to the Wrecking Crew's hit-making ranks.

And that's why Phil Spector had to have him, too.

By early 1966, with his last bankable Philles act, the Righteous Brothers, having recently made a very public (and litigious) jump over to MGM/Verve Records, the once-dominant Phil Spector was suddenly left with no one important to produce. With his previously unrivaled position in the music industry's fickle pecking order rapidly slipping away, Spector was desperate to regain his former glory. He decided that his only option was to go for broke. He would need to pull out all the stops and create the master-piece of all masterpieces. Something so monumental that it would instantly reestablish his status as the biggest producer of them all. And he thought he knew just who should sing it for him: Tina Turner.

With a frenetic, charismatic stage presence and arguably the most pow-erful set of female pipes in the business, Tina Turner was a musical force of nature. As the lead singer next to her guitar-playing husband in the Ike and Tina Turner Revue, a gospel-tinged funk and soul act, she was the estrogen-fueled R & B equivalent of James Brown—and then some. Particularly when it came to her ability to squeeze every gut-wrenching ounce of pathos and believability out of a set of lyrics, the undeniably potent Turner didn't so much sing a song; she *became* it.

Figuring the marriage of Tina Turner's voice and his Wall of Sound production technique (with the Wrecking Crew playing the instruments, of course) to be the ultimate musical union, Spector poured every bit of his ingenuity and creativity into staging what he hoped would be his finest three minutes plus of vinyl. He even co-wrote a power ballad called "River Deep, Mountain High" specifically for the project with his longtime col-laborators Ellie Greenwich and Jeff Barry. It seemed like the halcyon days of the early Sixties were on the verge of a triumphant return. The pieces were nicely lining up.

After Spector somehow shoehorned a handpicked throng of over twenty top musicians into Gold Star's tiny Studio A, and with Turner laying down a magnificent, fevered vocal performance, the final mix of "River Deep, Mountain High" had all the apparent makings of a huge success, perhaps the most significant symphonic statement of his career.

But it was not to be.

KRLA, which had been given the local exclusive, was lukewarm about it from the start. Other important radio stations, like WMCA in New York and WDRC in Hartford, flatly deemed the overwrought production to be way too much, a bunch of noise. It sounded out-of-synch with anything else on the air. Top 40 radio was an ever-changing animal, just like Sonny Bono had tried to explain to Spector, back when he still worked for him.

Even several of those in the Wrecking Crew who had listened afterward to the tape playback were disappointed. Turner's raw, goosebump-inducing performance, practically a sexual experience for them to be a part of when they cut the song live with her, now sounded washed out with the excessive amount of echo Spector had slathered all over it in the booth.

But the esteemed producer thought he knew better than everyone else, and now he had a flamingly public failure on his hands to show for it. The song, meant to be his crowning achievement, instead barely crept its way into the Hot 100, lodged at an anemic number eighty-eight for just one week, and then dropped off altogether.

By the early summer of 1966, around the time that "River Deep, Mountain High" finally sank beneath the waves, Michel Rubini retrieved a message one day from Arlyn's Answering Service (the telephone exchange most of the musicians used) saying that Phil Spector wanted him to play on an upcoming studio date. Having become one of the producer's favorites, Rubini gave the call little thought, other than to log the day and time into his schedule book. He knew that the big, ill-fated single on which he had played hadn't done well. And he knew that Spector had been counting on its success. But more releases than not failed to make it. That was just a fact of life in the music business.

When Rubini entered Gold Star for the recording session a few days later, it seemed like business as usual to him. The same batch of Wrecking Crew players, with whom he was now firmly entrenched, were all there, as was the usual engineer, Larry Levine.

After Spector's arranger, Jack Nitzsche, gave everyone their chord charts and told them basically what was needed, they began rehearsing the song. As always, the collective members of the Wrecking Crew expected the mercurial producer to interrupt them countless times along the way as the more complex layers of the material began to fully take shape in his mind.

But on this night, nothing. Not a peep. No words were spoken to them for almost three straight hours, practically the entire length of the session. The silence was eerie, not to mention unprecedented. And none of what they had been working on had been recorded, either. Committing everything to tape, listening to the playback, and then repeating the process ad infinitum was the Spector way. His *only* way. Something was clearly wrong.

As the session neared its end, the mystified musicians finally heard a voice over the speaker say, "Okay, thanks everybody. That's it for tonight. The session's over."

Over? They hadn't even done one complete take yet. But, as usual, there was no time to sit around and chat about the strangeness of the evening or about anything else. For many of them, if not most, another session at another studio immediately awaited.

As the musicians all began to file out, Rubini lagged behind. He had become a friend of the producer's and was frankly worried. The absolute lack of communication was way out of character, even by the enigmatic Spector's standards.

Happening to notice the producer through the control booth glass sitting alone in a corner, Rubini decided he had better check things out.

"Phil, is everything okay? What happened?" Rubini gently inquired as he stepped inside the small room.

Spector made no answer. Instead, he just stared blankly into space in the general direction of the studio's oversized set of playback monitors.

"Phil? *Phil?*"

Still no answer.

Finally, without shifting his heavy-lidded, trance-like gaze, Spector faintly mumbled, "Uh, yeah, yeah, everything's fine."

But everything wasn't fine. Rubini could see that. He had never witnessed anyone, let alone Spector, in such a weirdly catatonic state. And it wasn't drugs, either. Rubini had seen enough of that in the clubs to know the difference.

As the pianist debated about what to do next, the door opened again. It was Larry Levine, back from taking down some of the expensive mics out in the studio.

"Larry, what's going on?" Rubini whispered, now genuinely alarmed.

"Something's not right. Phil's having a problem, that's all. Don't worry about it," Levine quietly replied. "We'll take care of him. You go on home."

Like the fictional actress Norma Desmond's sad, misguided attempt at a comeback in the classic film *Sunset Boulevard,* Spector's time also had passed. He hadn't made the Top 40 charts in more than half a year, an eternity in his world. Having hidden behind a well-practiced façade of indifference for some time, the man who had given life to the Wrecking Crew so long before now seemed to Rubini to have finally had some kind of breakdown, very possibly relating to the "River Deep" failure. And he felt genuine sympathy for the producer. Growing up with a famous musician for a father had provided the young pianist with a front-row seat to what the unrelenting pressures of trying to keep a toehold in the business could do to a person. Especially someone as gifted and sensitive as Spector.

As Michel Rubini headed for the door, he stopped for a moment, turned, and softly said, "See you around, Phil. Take care."

9

Eve of Destruction

Steve, what did you do with the ... tape?
—LOU ADLER

If one person in the history of popular music could ever be compared to Leonardo da Vinci in terms of his breadth of accomplishments, it would have to be a chain-smoking, electronics-obsessed ex–Boy Scout from Danville, Illinois, by the name of Bill Putnam.

Born in 1920, the unusually gifted Putnam was nothing if not a whirlwind of activity. Growing up in a middle-class household during the Great Depression, if he wasn't building crystal sets from scratch he was fixing people's tube radios. By high school, he had managed to create an intricate homemade neighborhood telegraph system that was far beyond the scope of his peers. After an honorable discharge from the Army at the end of World War II, Putnam's unabated fascination with all things sound and audio led him to a critical decision: he would permanently focus his career on the development of new recording techniques and new technical equipment, specifically in regard to high-end studio use.

Soon thereafter, with the help of two partners and twenty grand in seed money, Putnam built Universal Recording in Chicago, one of America's first independent (i.e., not owned by a record label) recording studios and an eventual landmark. Thanks to his stellar work there behind the mixing console—which, naturally, he also hand-built—luminaries such as Sarah Vaughan, Patti Page, and Duke Ellington raved to anyone who would listen about his rare abilities. At the same time, the obsessively tinkering Putnam, with his trademark cigarette forever in hand, devised a number of ground-breaking in-studio innovations, including the first use of tape repeat, the first drum booth, the first use of artificial reverb, the first multiple-voice recording technique, and one of the first uses of eight-track recording. In addition, he designed every inch of the acoustic wall and ceiling treatments, occasionally wrote songs, and even tuned the pianos when needed.

In 1958, at the repeated urging of Frank Sinatra, Bing Crosby, Quincy Jones, and several other major music figures—all now chums, as well as clients—Putnam boldly sold his interest in the thriving Universal Recording and moved to the West Coast. There he founded a new company called United Recording on Sunset Boulevard in Hollywood and promptly set about building the finest studio of its kind.

Located inside a massive old movie soundstage once owned by a predecessor of Columbia Pictures, the refurbished structure was a sight and sound to behold. The perfectionist Putnam had painstakingly put together his dream layout, consisting of two giant custom-designed studio tracking rooms (plus one smaller one)—all with immaculate acoustics—plus a dedicated mixdown room, three mastering rooms, and a small record-manufacturing plant. There was even a large stereo echo chamber attached to the roof of the edifice for use by all the studios. And with the addition of many of the West Coast's best audio engineers, guys like Eddie Brackett, Chuck Britz, Winston Wong, Phil Kaye, Captain Nemo, Wally Heider, Lee Herschberg, and Bones Howe (who was the only freelancer among the bunch), it didn't take long for United to become the busiest independent recording studio in town, acing out both Radio Recorders and Gold Star for top honors.

But Putnam wasn't finished. He also acquired the former Radio Center Theater across the parking lot from United, turning it into Western Recorders, where it instantly became the favored haunt of younger acts like the Beach Boys, Jan and Dean, and Johnny Rivers. Now Putnam had all of his stylistic bases covered, with the name-brand crooners and the big-time orchestras generally choosing to work in one building (United's Studio A or Studio B) and the rock and rollers mostly opting for the more intimate atmosphere of the other building (usually Western's smaller Studio 3).

By the mid-Sixties, Bill Putnam's United/Western colossus was putting out more hits than any other studio in town, independent or label owned. It was also about to become the recording home for a flurry of some of the most important songs in popular music history. And one of those on the list—with its stark, unabashedly anti-establishment message—would come courtesy of the combined efforts of Lou Adler, two of his young songwriter/producers, and, as usual, several members of the Wrecking Crew.

*

Growing up in Brooklyn during the Forties and early Fifties, Steve Lipkin realized from an early age one singularly defining characteristic about himself: he desperately wanted to be in the music business. Having attended a live show at Radio City Music Hall that had left him reeling with joy, Lipkin came away from the experience with the abiding notion of becoming either a disc jockey or a songwriter. With no readily apparent gift for either singing or playing an instrument, the twin arts of spinning records and writing songs seemed like the most plausible ways to make a living.

Moving to Los Angeles with his family in 1954, Lipkin soon immersed himself in that city's thriving new rock-and-roll culture. Like so many others before him who would one day make a career in the field of music (including Herb Alpert, Jerry Stoller, and the opera singer Jerome Hines), Lipkin attended Fairfax High School, quickly becoming friendly with a number of aspiring songwriters and musicians there, such as Phil Spector, Marshall Leib, and Annette Kleinbard (aka Carol Connors) of the Teddy Bears.

Ever consumed with putting pen to paper and sounds to vinyl, in 1961, at the age of nineteen, Lipkin (now known professionally as Steve Barri) ended up recording a demo of one of his compositions with Connors and her sister on co-lead vocals called "When Two People (Are in Love)." Though the beautiful little ballad garnered but a small amount of local airplay, it did manage to catch the ear of Lou Adler, who heard it one day on KFWB. Adler, at the time the head of A & R for Colpix Records (a subsidiary of Columbia Pictures), got in touch with Barri and told him he wanted to put the song out nationally. Though the higher-ups at the label ultimately nixed his plan, Adler hired Barri instead as a staff writer for Screen Gems Music Publishing, a sister company. It would prove to be one of the smartest moves Adler ever made.

At the same time, a kid named Philip Schlein, who had a remarkably similar background to that of Barri, also dreamed of a career in music. Born in New York in 1945, Schlein moved with his family to Los Angeles just before entering the seventh grade, where he immediately began to make *his* musical mark. An unusually skilled guitarist for his age, the intelligent, dark-haired boy had an equal facility for writing songs and singing, putting him far ahead of most of his peers. Though his parents were not the least bit encouraging about his all-consuming fascination with music, Schlein never let it hold him back.

Both resourceful and determined, at the age of twelve Schlein took the bus one day to an open audition he had heard about at a place called Aladdin Records on West Pico Boulevard. When the dust settled after a long afternoon of waiting around with over a hundred others who were much older, Schlein miraculously found himself as the one candidate chosen to record a song for the little R & B label called "I Don't Care If the Sun Don't Shine." Though the final product never made it onto the charts, the enthralling experience of actually being inside a recording studio solidified his interest in becoming a professional musician.

By the time he turned seventeen, Schlein (now known professionally as P. F. Sloan) had developed enough of a reputation as a songwriter for various local recording acts to also catch the attention of Lou Adler at Screen Gems. Always looking for new talent, Adler hired Sloan and immediately paired him with Steve Barri, thinking that the two might work well together.

Adler, who wore many simultaneous hats, also acted as the manager and producer for Jan and Dean. And he liked what he heard from the newly formed duo of Barri and Sloan, enough so that they began writing surf songs for Jan and Dean on a regular basis. By the time Adler broke away from

Colpix/Screen Gems and formed Dunhill Records and Trousdale Music Publishing with partners Jay Lasker, Bobby Roberts, and Pierre Cossette in 1964, the tandem of Barri and Sloan were natural additions. And it wouldn't take them long to make their mark.

Working late one night at his parents' dining room table, nineteen-year-old P. F. Sloan (known as Phil to most) found himself tapping into an inspiration for a song that seemed to flow directly from some kind of inner voice. It was a plea of desperation to God about a number of social issues that Sloan found simply unbearable, including the general hypocrisy of hatred, the continuing racial disharmony between blacks and whites, and the utter injustice of sending young American males off to war in Vietnam when they weren't even allowed to vote. Calling the tune "Eve of Destruction," Sloan subsequently joined forces with Steve Barri to put a few finishing touches on the melody and structure.

Ultimately hiring a gravelly voiced former singer with the New Christy Minstrels named Barry McGuire to record it—along with Wrecking Crewers Hal Blaine (drums, tympani), Larry Knechtel (bass), and Don Randi (piano), plus Sloan on acoustic guitar—Barri still had his doubts, however.

"It's kind of a depressing song, Phil. I don't know if it's right for Barry," he said.

With the song's apocalyptic lyrics and equally ominous sonic quality, it was not exactly the ideal choice for pop radio in late 1965. Folk rock, of course, had already hit the airwaves earlier in the year with the arrival of the Byrds, among others. Message songs were not new. But "Eve of Destruction" was something else altogether. It was flat-out *dark*. No one at Dunhill, especially Adler, figured it for anything more than an album cut, maybe the flip side of a 45, at best. There were other, more promising songs to work on anyway.

✳

Following Barry McGuire's recording session, Steve Barri took a tape copy of "Eve of Destruction" home from the studio overnight so that he could play it the next morning when he got to the office. Arriving around 9:00 A.M., Barri immediately spooled up the unusual-sounding song on his reel-to-reel deck and let it rip. He wanted to assess its possibilities one more time.

From the office next door, Barri then heard a loud voice say over the top of the music during mid-play, "What is that?" The question had come from Jay Lasker, the president of Dunhill.

"It's gonna be the B-side of Barry McGuire's next single," the young producer and songwriter replied.

"Let me have the tape, Steve. I want to take it into my office and listen to it."

Thinking nothing of it, Barri handed the tape to Lasker and went about his business. Around three hours later, just before heading out for another recording session, Barri suddenly noticed a bunch of yelling coming from one of the offices down the hall. He then heard his name being called. As Barri entered the room, he saw a red-faced Lou Adler ready to wring someone's neck, possibly his.

"Steve, what did you do with the 'Eve of Destruction' tape?" Adler bellowed.

"I gave it to Jay."

"Well, there has to be another one, then."

"Why?"

"Because I just heard it on KFWB in my car."

Unbeknownst to either of them, Lasker had given the tape to one of the promotions men to run down to the station. He wanted to know firsthand whether radio would even *consider* playing such a controversial record. Instead of rejecting it, however, as Lasker had feared, the program director, William J. Wheatley, loved it. He immediately made a copy of the tape and put it on the air within minutes. Which normally would have been good news. Except that Adler did not feel that the song was finished. In his opinion, McGuire very much needed to rerecord his lead vocal. Unfamiliar with the lyrics, he had sung them in an oddly halting fashion, even letting out an audible, anguished-sounding "ahhh" at one point while trying to buy time as he attempted to decipher the tiny handwriting on the paper in front of him. That was not the kind of thing Lou Adler wanted on the air. It was patently unprofessional.

But KFWB wouldn't budge. "We don't want to pull it," Wheatley said. "It's now our most-requested song since 'I Want to Hold Your Hand.' You can finish it up and get us a new one. But we're gonna keep playing this version in the meantime."

Realizing that they were staring at a smash, the Dunhill execs backed off. They never did ask McGuire to go back in the studio. His rough vocal attempt turned out to give the production the perfect air of authenticity. P. F. Sloan's heartfelt protest composition subsequently went all the way to the top of the national charts, giving Dunhill its first number-one hit. But there would be one more unexpected gift soon to come from the unusual song. The Wrecking Crew were unknowingly on the cusp of beginning work with four of McGuire's best friends, who would also be recording for Dunhill. An unknown, sweet-singing, bohemian quartet called the Mamas & the Papas.

✳

When Barry McGuire first heard his old friends Denny Doherty, Cass Elliot, John Phillips, and Michelle Phillips sing their latest material, he knew they had something special. Having moved to Los Angeles after performing in a variety of small clubs in New York City and the Virgin Islands, the down-on-their-luck quartet were desperately looking for a record deal. They were inches from becoming destitute. And with a huge current hit on the charts in "Eve of Destruction," the affable McGuire was their main music biz contact.

Stopping by the foursome's tiny shared apartment one day for a listen, the rising Dunhill star told them just what they were hoping to hear.

"You guys sound really good," McGuire enthused as they all passed around a joint. "Why don't you come down and sing for my producer, Lou Adler?"

A few days later, when McGuire and his four pals all trooped into Western Recorders, the first to hear them sing were the staff producers Barri and Sloan. And they were bowled over. Barri immediately got on the phone to Adler at the nearby Dunhill offices on South Beverly Drive.

"Lou, you have *got* to come down here to Western Three and see these people," he said.

After Adler arrived, he, along with the engineer Bones Howe, then took the group down the hall into an empty studio tracking room and asked them to sing what they had. After they turned in a soaring, goose bump–inducing four-part harmony vocal on one of Phillips's compositions called "California Dreamin'," Adler dryly said over the talk-back, "You got any more?"

More? Hell, yes, we have more, the quartet's lead tenor, Doherty, thought. They might be poor and they might look kind of funky, but they *knew* one thing for sure: they could sing like nobody's business. The four then launched into "Straight Shooter," "Go Where You Want to Go," and a newer tune called "Monday, Monday."

Secretly delighted but playing his cards close to the vest, Adler casually told them afterward, "I think maybe we can do business." He then slipped them a hundred bucks and told them to come back the next day. The Mamas & the Papas had their record deal.

After signing them to contracts, Adler then assigned the four to the duties of singing backup for McGuire on his second album. As the recording progressed, however, it became clear who the real singing stars were. Taking John and Michelle Phillips out into the hall during one recording session where McGuire was recording his own version of "California Dreamin'," Adler said, "We're not giving this song to Barry. I know we told him we would, but we're not. I want this to be *your* single."

John Phillips then asked his friend McGuire if the Mamas & the Papas could release it as their first single, rather than putting McGuire's name on it. "Sure, John," he said generously, if a bit disappointed. "It's your tune, man; you wrote it."

Soon wiping McGuire's lead vocal off the instrumental track already created by the Wrecking Crew—specifically the work of Hal Blaine on drums, Joe Osborn on bass (the same guy who several years earlier had fished "Travelin' Man" out of the trash), and Larry Knechtel on keyboards, with Phil Sloan sitting in on acoustic guitar—Adler had the four singers come in to lay down their vocals. Bones Howe set up everything to mimic the way the group naturally stood when singing together, with the men and women facing each other, close in. A pair of RCA DX-77 mics were then strategically hung overhead. On cue, the well-practiced foursome once again put forth a bravura performance on the tune, with the beautiful arcing blend of their voices magically achieving what sounded almost like a fifth level of harmony, something they privately referred to as "Harvey." With Howe having the additional inspiration to craftily insert a flute solo in the middle during the bridge (played by his friend the noted jazz man Bud Shank), the song was complete. Now the only challenge would be finding some way to get airplay.

✳

At exactly 3:00 P.M. on April 27, 1965, from inside a drab, nondescript, bunker-like building at 5155 Melrose Avenue—directly across the street from the legendary Lucy's El Adobe Café and less than a block from Paramount Pictures—the following words were spoken into a microphone, forever changing the landscape of Top 40 radio in Los Angeles:

"Ladies and gentlemen, presenting *The Real Don Steele Show*...with a sneak preview of the all-new Boss Radio on...KHJ, Los Angeles."

With an all-star disc jockey lineup, more music per hour, a faster pace, and the inviolate mantra of "no dead air," a new kind of radio had materialized in a rush of masterful publicity. The brainchild of three industry veterans, Gene Chenault, Bill Drake, and Ron Jacobs, within six months of its launch 93 KHJ's electric, larger-than-life format had earned the third-highest overall ratings in town.

Suddenly the game had changed for the record labels, too. By early 1966, with KFWB and KRLA lagging behind, KHJ had become the new power broker in terms of getting all-important airplay. For a pop song to become a hit, it needed to somehow make its way onto their tightly scripted playlist, zealously guarded by both Jacobs and his next-in-command, the station's music director, Betty Breneman.

Needing to find some way to break "California Dreamin'" in the second-largest radio market in the country in terms of metro population—and arguably *the* most important in terms of trend setting—Lou Adler knew that all roads led through KHJ. The question was how to get them to go for a folkie-style song performed by two women and two men about missing California. There were plenty of male and female solo singers on the radio, and girl groups, too. But there were few, if any, music acts that had two of each gender. That was something new.

By this time, having produced artists like Sam Cooke, Jan and Dean, and Johnny Rivers, Adler had developed a reputation as a real player in the business. And he traveled in the most exclusive rock-and-roll circles, counting among his good friends people like the Rolling Stones' manager, Andrew Loog Oldham. The two were first introduced backstage at the groundbreaking T.A.M.I. Show at the Santa Monica Civic Auditorium in October 1964, where Mick, Keith, and the rest of the Stones appeared as the headline act along with an astounding star-studded underbill featuring the Beach Boys, the Supremes, James Brown & the Famous Flames, Marvin Gaye, Billy J. Kramer with the Dakotas, Leslie Gore, the Miracles, Gerry and the Pacemakers, and Chuck Berry, plus the Adler-managed Jan and Dean as hosts. The two-day T.A.M.I. Show (short for Teenage Awards Music International, a totally made-up name) had been designed from the start as a vehicle to become rock and roll's first live concert film, something that teenagers could see in a local movie house in Anytown, USA, and actually *feel* like they were there in person.

With so much riding on the line budget-wise, the event's director, Steve Binder, made sure that he left nothing to chance in terms of the quality of the music production. Binder went right to the source, bringing in Phil Spector's arranger, Jack Nitzsche, to handle all the conducting duties, who then promptly turned around and hired a bunch of Spector's Wrecking Crew favorites like Hal Blaine, Jimmy Bond, Glen Campbell, Plas Johnson, Lyle Ritz, Leon Russell, and Tommy Tedesco to play all the incidental music and to become the house band behind the acts (other than for the Stones, Pacemakers, Dakotas, and Fabulous Flames, who played their own instruments). Though it ultimately achieved only so-so box office returns upon its release a couple of months later, the T.A.M.I. Show did serve to set the creative and technical template for live concert films to come. It also allowed some of the Wrecking Crew guys, though uncredited as always, to have a little fun showcasing their skills onstage for a change during a rare couple of days away from the studios.

A little over a year after the big concert, in January of 1966, Adler, with his pal Oldham in tow during a subsequent Stones visit to Los Angeles, decided that it was finally time to make his first pilgrimage to the hallowed halls of KHJ. They were now the Southland's undisputed Top 40 radio gatekeepers and the Mamas & the Papas sorely needed some airtime.

As Ron Jacobs worked in his office just past the front reception area of the radio station, Betty Breneman poked her head inside his doorway. "Lou Adler from Dunhill Records just stopped by," she said. "He wants a few minutes with you." Adler, by then, had gone next door to wait with Oldham at Nickodell Restaurant, a small, dimly lit diner/bar with red vinyl booths and a perpetual smell of Scotch and Lysol.

"He's going to sit there all day until he can see you," she warned, despite knowing that Jacobs had a firm policy about never meeting with promo men from the labels. But Adler was different, she figured. He was a big-time guy. And they *were* a new station.

"I don't give a fuck," said the brusque, driven Jacobs, who was also considered a brilliant programmer. "I'm busy."

"Ron, just let them come in for five minutes," Breneman continued. "You can meet them in the back in the library."

Against his better judgment, Jacobs gave in. He liked and respected Breneman enough to break his own rule. "Okay. Five minutes. That's it," he said firmly.

With Breneman then ushering Adler and Oldham into the station's small production library, the Dunhill exec got down to business. "This is the first release from our new artists the Mamas and the Papas," he said, handing a 45 to Jacobs, who then placed it on one of several turntables.

As the song began to play, Adler glanced over at the program director, hoping for some kind of positive sign. He got anything but.

"You mean that you've been waiting all day drinking or doing whatever next door at Nickodell's to play me *this* MOR shit?" Jacobs said as the two-minute-forty-two-second tune ended. "This song just ain't happening." A disappointed Adler left without getting his "add."

But an interesting thing happened with "California Dreamin'." Over the next several weeks, some of the staff at KHJ started getting word back from various minor-league stations, those in smaller markets like San Bernardino and San Diego, that it was taking off, getting lots of requests. A firm believer in cold, hard data, Jacobs could see that the song had legs after all. Despite his dislike for it, Jacobs grudgingly added "California Dreamin'" to the KHJ playlist, where it promptly went to number one. Adler, the Mamas & the Papas, and the Wrecking Crew all had their hit. And for the next couple of years, the nation would have a new favorite band.

Strangers in the Night

Okay, ladies. We're going to start recording now.
—DEAN MARTIN

One afternoon in the fall of 1963, twenty-five-year-old producing hopeful Jimmy Bowen heard his telephone ring. Sharing a magnificent Frank Lloyd Wright–designed home just off Sunset Boulevard with the teen idol Frankie Avalon, Bowen figured it was probably just another of the many girls who called the house day and night, always looking for the handsome, pompadoured singer. "Is Frankie there?" "When will Frankie be back?"

As the Texas-raised Bowen picked up the receiver and drawled out a "hello," all he heard on the other end was the sound of somebody whispering. Of course, there was nothing unusual about that, either. The relentlessly enterprising female callers were known to try any tactic they could think of to get through to their heartthrob.

Bowen even knew a little something about that kind of thing himself. In the late Fifties, he had been a member of the Rhythm Orchids, the backing band for the rockabilly singer Buddy Knox. Together, the quartet had generated several Top 40 hits on Roulette Records, including the number-one smash "Party Doll." Their turn in the spotlight, however brief, had come with its own fair share of amorous attention from adoring adolescent bobby-soxers.

But this time around it wasn't one of Avalon's girlfriends phoning. No, this was quite obviously a man, and the guy was trying to tell Bowen something on the QT.

"Hey," the hushed voice said, pausing. "I got you the job."

Bowen quickly recognized the owner of the whisper. It was a friend and business associate named Murray Wolf, and there was no question as to the meaning of his statement. With a major inside connection in his pocket, Wolf had been angling for Bowen to get the coveted position of running the A & R department for Reprise Records, an easy-listening label now looking to update its artist roster and overall sound to appeal to a more youthful market.

"That's great," a surprised and delighted Bowen replied. He knew it was a rare opportunity, especially for someone his age.

Before Bowen could catch his breath or even say "thank you," however, Wolf, now back to speaking at normal volume, told him to hang on the line for a minute. The high-powered founder of Reprise was on his way to the phone and he wanted to say something to his new hire.

"James," came the sonorous, unmistakable voice of a man who had once been the biggest teen idol of them all. "Glad to have you aboard."

Click.

The Chairman of the Board—Mr. Francis Albert Sinatra—had spoken.

* * * *

By the early Sixties, Dean Martin's recording career was sagging. With his last Top 40 hit single, "Volare," coming out back in 1958, the international star desperately needed something to break his way. Though he had appeared in many movies over the years, with a couple of his late Fifties performances in films like *Some Came Running* and *Rio Bravo* earning critical acclaim, his inimitable way with a song was always Martin's main calling card among the public. Everything else he did fed off that.

At the same time, Jimmy Bowen wanted to find a first big act to produce at Reprise. With Martin having signed a recording contract there in 1962 at the urging of his close friend Frank Sinatra, the man born Dino Crocetti in Steubenville, Ohio, seemed like a perfect leadoff choice for the ambitious young producer. Bowen instinctively knew that he could make an album for Martin that had some radio-friendly hits on it for a change. In his opinion, the singer just needed to be presented the right way, to be brought into the modern era. And Bowen felt he had the perfect song with which to do it.

Dean Martin's longtime pianist, Ken Lane, had been fooling around with a little tune on the piano for almost twenty years, something he had written called "Everybody Loves Somebody." It had a pretty melody and a great hook, both of which caught Jimmy Bowen's ear one day in the studio. "If I can cut that with a big orchestra," Bowen said to Martin, "I can get that record on the radio for you."

True to his word, after calling in twenty-plus musicians to United Recorders for a date on April 16, 1964, Bowen got the version of the song he wanted and more. The lush yet punchy production promptly became Dean Martin's first number-one hit in almost ten years, instantly reviving his moribund musical fortunes, right in the heart of Beatlemania, no less.

Among the musicians playing on "Everybody Loves Somebody" was Hal Blaine. Bowen wanted the recording to have some serious R & B–style bottom end to go with the pop melody and all the strings on top. Bringing in Blaine was a no-brainer in that regard. Like many in the Wrecking Crew, Blaine occasionally stepped away from his usual steady diet of rock-and-roll dates to join with assorted non–Wrecking Crew musicians on other projects. Bowen was fully aware of Blaine's diverse and successful background in playing for artists like Patti Page, Connie Francis, and the great Count Basie, each of whom had an inimitable, decidedly non-rock-and-roll style yet expected anyone drumming for them to be able to cook with some serious gas.

For Blaine, working with Dean Martin was another in a seemingly endless series of eye-opening music business experiences. Every star had his or her unique style, and the smooth, glib Martin was no exception.

One day while in the studio to record what would become one of Martin's better-known songs, a country-flavored tune called "Houston," Blaine looked on in amazement as the veteran crooner handled an audience of fifty or more mostly females like a monkey handles coconuts.

"Okay, ladies," Martin said in his rich, easy baritone as he ambled over to their seating area. "We're going to start recording now. It's time to make some records. So I want you all to sit back and relax. But remember, we have to be *very* quiet. No talking, no nothing."

Martin gave them a wink and then held an index finger up to his lips for emphasis as the gathered guests chuckled in delight.

But just after the carefree star began singing during the first take, sure enough, a couple of the women started talking. "So, Shirley, I don't know if you're going on Thursday, but..."

Eddie Brackett, the engineer, immediately stopped the tape.

"Hold it, folks," he said over the speaker from the control booth. "We're going to have to do another one. Some voices were leaking into the mics."

As Blaine and the rest of the musicians waited and watched with smiles on their faces, Martin then strolled back over to the small audience and kicked his incomparable charm up another notch.

"Ladies, *please*," he said in mock admonishment, with an obvious twinkle in his eye. "We simply can't have any talking."

But just to drive his point home in a way that only he could, the effortlessly engaging Martin then slid himself onto one unsuspecting middle-aged woman's lap, gently cooing in her ear, "You do understand, don't you, dear?" With that, he kissed her on the cheek, rose, and sauntered back across the room to his music stand.

Mission accomplished. With the throng now hopelessly mesmerized by Dino's dazzling display of savoir faire, the recording was completed without further interruption.

Aside from the entertaining theatrics of the day, however, Hal Blaine had a very serious idea about how he might be able to make "Houston" even better. Blaine, like most of those in the Wrecking Crew, considered that to be one of their primary roles. They weren't hired to merely play. Lots of people could do that. They were brought in because they were the best of the best, able to not only execute quickly and at the highest of levels but also, perhaps especially, provide invaluable input along the way. In essence, they were all mini-arrangers, constantly working on their own parts in order to improve a song's overall chances of becoming a hit.

"Jimmy, do me a favor," Blaine said to Bowen after the session had concluded. "Let me overdub an extra little percussion thing whenever you have a moment. It's something that I'm hearing."

Bowen, as astute as they came, didn't have to be asked twice. When a guy of Blaine's skill and reputation said he had an idea, the producer knew enough to just step out of the way and reap the benefits.

"Sure, go for it," Bowen said.

Noticing that the production seemed like it was kind of flat, Blaine grabbed one of the many glass ashtrays scattered throughout the studio (most of the musicians were smokers) and tapped its contents into the trash. Then, while standing before a live mic, he asked the engineer, Brackett, to roll tape. As the first throaty notes of a heavily reverberating hollow-body electric guitar began to ring out, Blaine started hitting the ashtray with his wooden drumstick, playing ever so slightly behind the beat. It provided the perfect Western-style, crystalline counterpoint to Martin's languid vocal work, almost like that of a blacksmith striking an anvil with his hammer. With this one simple bit of well-placed creativity, Hal Blaine instantly helped turn the song into yet another Dean Martin Top 40 hit record.

✳

After about a five-month run with the road version of the Beach Boys, Glen Campbell had decided it was time to call it a wrap. Though he liked all the guys in the band and enjoyed playing their music, he just wasn't a surf-rock type of musician at heart. Session work, along with playing and singing on his own demo recordings, seemed to him to be a better use of his time. He wanted to keep his focus on the big prize, and staying near the studios was an important part of that. Campbell never wavered in his dogged determination to one day become a star in his own right.

One day in the spring of 1966, Campbell got a call from Donnie "Dirt" Lanier, the boyhood chum, former Rhythm Orchid, and current contractor for Campbell's old pal Jimmy Bowen. Lanier wanted to know if the former Beach Boy could do a 6:00 P.M. session over at United Recorders on the eleventh of April. "Jimmy wants you to play some rhythm guitar," Lanier said.

Campbell and Bowen, two down-home country boys from the Mid-South, had come up the LA ranks together in the early Sixties while working as apprentice songwriters for a brief period at a publishing company called American Music. Though the duo never wrote anything particularly noteworthy during their short stint, their friendship became a keeper. Golf, cigars, and the occasional snort of Jack Daniel's Tennessee Whiskey were but a few of their common interests. Now with Bowen an important producer and the head A & R man at Reprise Records, he liked to use his old buddy Campbell's incredible picking skills whenever he could. And this time out, the scheduled date was a whopper.

During the previous summer, Frank Sinatra, who had been closely watching his employee Bowen's success in revitalizing Dean Martin's singing career, had decided that he wanted in on the action, too. "What would you do for me as a producer to get me hits?" he had asked.

Bowen's solution was to surround Sinatra's golden voice with a dramatically more modern backing sound, particularly regarding the rhythm section. The producer promptly brought in a bunch of his regulars, installing Hal Blaine as the main drummer, while adding other Wrecking Crewers like Chuck Berghofer on stand-up bass and Emil Richards on percussion. Bowen wanted some rock-and-roll-style heft on board, just like he had done with Martin. Something to return the almost-forty-nine-year-old Sinatra to relevancy among contemporary radio listeners now accustomed to the likes of the Beatles, the Rolling Stones, and the Beach Boys. Popular music had changed, and Sinatra was going to have to change with it.

With Bowen's first production effort—a song called "Softly, As I Leave You"—putting Sinatra back in the Top 30 for the first time in four years, it also came with added pressure. Ol' Blue Eyes now wanted more.

For their all-important follow-up release Bowen knew he had to really come through. The song had to be chosen with the utmost care. Now that he had tasted success, Frank was not going to be pleased with anything less than making the Top 10 this time out. And it wasn't good when the chief was unhappy.

Trying to keep their shared momentum going, Bowen came up with the novel idea of marrying the melody from an instrumental piece of soundtrack music he had heard from the movie *A Man Could Get Killed* to a set of newly commissioned lyrics. The result yielded just the kind of beautiful, distinctive song that he thought Sinatra could outright own from note one.

Coming into the studio for the big recording session, Glen Campbell had no idea what to expect. He found himself as nervous as a long-tailed cat in a room full of rocking chairs. Playing for Frank Sinatra was serious business. Granted, it was every musician's dream, a milestone worthy of one day telling the grandchildren about. And Campbell was in no way intimidated; he knew he was good. But it was also not the kind of date during which a mistake was to be made. Sinatra, a well-known perfectionist, would never tolerate that.

Fortunately, Campbell was in excellent company. He was one of four Wrecking Crew guitarists on hand for the occasion, including stalwarts Al Casey, Bill Pitman, and Tommy Tedesco. The blend of their sounds along with a vast number of string and horn instruments would almost certainly minimize the chance of any one of them standing out too prominently in case of an errant note.

Better yet for Campbell, the recording engineer, Eddie Brackett, had decided to position the guitar players immediately adjacent to Sinatra's vocal booth, with Campbell being the closest. The soon-to-be thirty-year-old Arkansan was practically giddy over the seating arrangement. Here he was, on his first studio date playing for the most revered performer in the history of popular music, and he would get to watch the man do his thing from a mere six feet away, the best seat in the house.

Another Wrecking Crew musician on hand that evening was Michel Rubini. He had been playing a variety of session dates on piano and harpsichord for Jimmy Bowen for the better part of a year, and the producer had recently elevated his status to the position of assistant producer at Reprise. It was a glorified gofer job much of the time, but it did have its good points. Aside from the drudgery of screening the piles of demo tapes that came flooding in the door each day from artistic hopefuls the world over, Rubini also was allowed his first real crack at producing a few things himself, working with the teenage Dino, Desi & Billy, among other acts. And, of course, given his unrivaled prowess on the ivories, whenever a major-league session came up like the one with Sinatra, Bowen made sure that Rubini was right there with him.

As the musicians took their places at precisely 6:00 P.M., Bowen came into the huge studio tracking room and announced to everyone, "After we rehearse, we're going to do one song for Frank tonight, and then one song after that for Dean." Nobody needed any last names.

To spend so much of Reprise's money on so many musicians for one three-hour session meant that Bowen wanted to squeeze as much out of it as he possibly could. With Sinatra notorious for being willing to only do one or two takes of any given song, Bowen figured there should be plenty of time to slide in a tune for Dean Martin during the back side of hour three.

For the next two hours, the musicians rehearsed like never before, making sure everything about their performances was pitch perfect. With Bowen finally calling a ten-minute break at a little before 8:00 P.M., a fleet of assistant engineers immediately flooded into the studio, making sure that every microphone was still in place and every metal folding chair was still squeak free. No chances could be taken on a night as important as this.

As everyone settled back into position after hurriedly grabbing a cup of coffee and/or hitting the head, the back door of the studio suddenly swung open. A hush quickly fell over the large room. The artist known to millions of fans as simply the Voice was entering the house.

In marched an entourage befitting that of a major foreign dignitary, a single-file procession of over twenty immaculately dressed individuals, the men in dark, custom-tailored suits and the women in expensive evening dresses, jewels, and furs. They were an assortment of friends, family, and flunkies, all clearly on their best behavior and all there to watch Frank. About the fourth from the front of the snaking line of humanity came Sinatra himself, walking just behind his usual contingent of menacing-looking bodyguards.

Jimmy Bowen immediately stepped out to greet his boss, as did the date's arranger, Ernie Freeman.

"Hello, boys," said Sinatra. "Ready to make a record?"

As the threesome held a short, private chat away from everyone else while looking over the music charts, Sinatra's longtime personal music director and pianist, Bill Miller, came into the studio. Assuming that he was to play the piano on the session, just as he had done for Sinatra during the past fifteen years, Miller walked over to Michel Rubini, who was already seated behind the Steinway concert grand on the far side of the room. Miller tapped him on the shoulder.

"Excuse me," Miller said politely. "I'll need to take your place."

A startled Rubini at first didn't know what to think. Bowen had specifically told him that he was to play the main piano part on the song. But it now looked like Sinatra had his own guy. And who was Rubini to argue, anyway? He knew that he was way too far down the Reprise food chain to even merit a say in such matters.

"Oh, sure," Rubini said cordially, getting up. "No problem."

With nowhere else to go, he decided to head into the booth. As Bowen's assistant producer, Rubini figured that would be the best place to watch the proceedings and to help out if needed.

As Rubini silently eased into an area along the back wall of the small room, Bowen, intensely focused and now seated in position behind the large mixing console, seemed to sense someone's unwanted presence behind him. He turned to see who it was.

"What the hell are you doing in here, Rubini?" the harried producer said, looking both surprised and irritated. "You're supposed to be out at the piano. We're just about to roll tape. You're not producing tonight."

"Yes, I know. But there's a guy out there who told me not to play. He kicked me off the piano."

"What?"

Bowen looked like he had just swallowed a dose of the same nasty castor oil his mother used to force down his throat as a kid. His carefully scripted recording session, the most important of his career, was about to unravel. Rubini already knew the piano part cold, and it was central to the song. There was no time to show someone else how to play it. To compound matters, Sinatra, not the most patient of men, was waiting at the microphone.

"I'll take care of this," Bowen said, jumping to his feet. "C'mon."

As Bowen and Rubini strode across the studio's vintage post-war-style asphalt tile floor toward the piano, Bowen knew he was going to have to think of something fast. His job hung in the balance.

"Bill, good to see you again," the producer said, extending his hand. "This is Michel. I think you two have already met."

Miller nodded.

"I know you're Frank's piano player," Bowen continued, "and I've admired your work for years. But I've rehearsed a special part with Michel here that's not on the sheet music. I don't have time to show you now what we need."

Bowen, of course, was making it all up on the fly. There was no special part for Rubini to play. But Bowen had to find a way for Miller to save face. For if he didn't, Miller's boss would lose face as well. And Frank Sinatra never took kindly to looking bad in front of others.

"So, Bill, if you don't mind, please come in the booth and help me with the song in there."

Whether Miller knew what was really going on no one could be sure. Nevertheless, the gentlemanly, elegant fifty-one-year-old pianist arose and graciously agreed to accompany Bowen out of the room. As they walked away, Sinatra, who had been watching the whole exchange from nearby, looked askance at Rubini. He seemed to be saying, "Okay, pal, I have no idea who you are. You *better* be good."

But the abrupt switch, as important as it seemed at the moment, would soon turn out to be the least of Frank Sinatra's worries.

With Michel Rubini now safely back in front of the keys and Jimmy Bowen ensconced in the control room with his engineers (and Bill Miller), all systems were finally a go. As the concertmaster, Sid Sharp, lowered his baton in one swift motion, the thirty-piece string and horn section, along with the Wrecking Crew's ace rhythm section led by Hal Blaine on drums, burst forth into a sweet-sounding ten-second instrumental intro, followed by the entrance of Sinatra's resonant light baritone voice.

At first, all was bliss. Ernie Freeman's spectacular arrangement had all the earmarks of creating the smash recording they had all envisioned. The instrumentation sparkled like a pair of diamond earrings on a moonlit night. Sinatra's world-weary yet romantic bel canto vocal interpretation proved to be the very essence of longing and, ultimately, joy. But as the song smoothly sailed along toward its conclusion, with the musicians playing several bars over the last thirty seconds during what had been written as the fade, something didn't sit right with Sinatra. Used to cold endings on most of his songs, he suddenly had no lyrics left to sing while the music continued.

"What the hell am I supposed to do when the orchestra keeps on playing?" the unhappy crooner said to Bowen as the young producer stepped out into the studio at the end of the take.

"Well, Frank," said Bowen, once again forced to think on his feet, "just scat your way out. You're the king of that."

So Sinatra gamely gave it a try as the musicians ran through the number a second time. But instead of rolling out an improvised series of made-up words and sounds that would appropriately fit the melody and feel of the song, all the singer offered was a pedestrian parade of "tra-la-la's."

Bowen, now trying to be *very* diplomatic, said from the control booth at the end, "Okay, Frank, that was good. Now, how about if we try that once more? Do it a little differently this time."

Growing impatient and keenly aware of the large audience looking on (there were close to a hundred VIP guests seated in the huge studio), Sinatra, consummate pro that he was, decided that enough was enough. With cigarette in hand and a take-no-prisoners attitude etched on his face, he came through on the third take with an inspired flurry of "dooby-dooby-doos" that took the song's fade to an entirely different level.

Bowen, for one, was both exultant and relieved. He knew that he had pushed his boss to the limit.

"Okay, that's it. We got it," the producer said over his mic as the entire studio broke into applause.

With that, Frank Sinatra immediately walked over and said "thanks" to the production staff and a few others, nodded to the musicians, and then headed for the door, with his posse of personal guests falling into formation behind him with military-like precision.

For Glen Campbell, the events of the intense three-hour date left him dazed. During each of the takes, he had found that he just couldn't keep his eyes off of Sinatra. More so, each time he had looked at the singer it seemed like Sinatra was looking right back at him. Campbell felt honored, assuming that the vocalist must have been admiring his exceptionally fine guitar skills.

Afterward, Campbell had also noticed Bowen and Sinatra discussing something while looking his way from across the studio. With his curiosity getting the better of him, the guitarist just had to know what had gone down.

"Bowen," he said, catching up with his friend in the booth. "Was Mr. Sinatra talking about me out there tonight?"

"Yep."

Campbell grinned in anticipation. He was certain that he was about to receive the compliment of a lifetime.

"Well, what did he say?"

"Frank said he wanted to know who the fag guitar player was that kept staring at him."

After a beat, they both burst into laughter.

But having put all the musicians on a quick break before beginning the recording session for Dean Martin, the producer had far more important things on his mind than Glen Campbell's uneasy man-to-man eye contact with Sinatra. Bowen wanted to know what his assistants thought about the unusual scat tag at the end of the third take. Was it too far out, too corny, to be commercial? He needed to know now. Acetate copies of the recording had to start shipping via the airlines to major-market radio stations around the country that very night in order to beat out a just-released version of the same song by another artist.

"So, what do you think?" Bowen asked after Michel Rubini, who had joined him in the booth, finished listening to the playback.

"Well," Rubini said, deciding to lay it on the line, "people are either going to laugh you out of town or they're going to turn on to it. One or the other."

Bowen's gut told him it was the latter. Different was good. Top 40 rewarded different. So he went with it. And the producer was maybe even more right than he knew: "Strangers in the Night" would soon knock the Beatles' "Paperback Writer" right out of the number-one spot on the pop charts. It would also go on to win the Grammy Award for record of the year, in the process becoming one of Frank Sinatra's best-known recordings.

For Hal Blaine, who had employed a modified version of his famous "Be My Baby" drumming pattern during the session, "Strangers in the Night" would become his second-straight record of the year. He had also laid down the beat on Herb Alpert's Grammy-winning "A Taste of Honey" the year before (along with a mix of Wrecking Crew players and straight jazz players), where his *boom-boom-boom-boom* count off on the bass drum had become that song's signature element. Life was good and getting better all the time for the drummer.

But in less than twelve hours following the unequaled exhilaration of playing for the one-and-only Frank Sinatra, Hal Blaine's fast-moving world would come skidding to a stop. One of the biggest stars in rock and roll—and Blaine's close friend—would tragically find himself lying near death.

Good Vibrations

Brian, I don't even own an electric twelve-string guitar.

—BILLY STRANGE

During the early afternoon on April 12, 1966, still in a state of euphoria following the big "Strangers in the Night" recording session from the night before with Frank Sinatra, Hal Blaine received a message in the recording studio that instantly turned his world upside down. His good friend, the singer Jan Berry, was dead.

Quickly moving into action, Blaine made a series of frantic phone calls to find out what had happened. He just couldn't believe it. The two had talked only days before, going over some details about the upcoming TV series they would soon all be starring in called *On the Road with Jan and Dean.* ABC had picked up the pilot for a full season and Blaine was to play the duo's comedic sidekick, a slightly dim-witted character by the name of Clobber. With the highly intelligent and energetic Berry also attending medical school while simultaneously balancing his demanding recording and acting careers, Blaine often acted as his study partner, too, quizzing him on subjects like anatomy and physiology.

Finally reaching Lou Adler, Blaine found out to his relief that the report of Berry's death had been slightly exaggerated. Yes, there had been a car accident. A bad one. But Berry was still alive. Barely. Traveling at almost eighty miles an hour down a residential side street, the singer had slammed his fiberglass Corvette Stingray into the back of a parked truck, ironically just blocks from the stretch of Sunset Boulevard that Jan and Dean had immortalized only a couple of years before in their hit song "Dead Man's Curve." Berry was now in critical condition at UCLA Medical Center with severe head injuries, undergoing brain surgery.

As the weeks passed following the crash, Jan Berry remained in a perpetual vegetative state. Many people, including Blaine, didn't think Berry would make it. Then, one day, word came that he had opened his eyes. He was emerging from the coma. From then on, with hope at hand, Blaine, along with those like Lou Adler and Don Peake—who had become one of the most important guitarists in the Wrecking Crew following his harrowing ordeal in Alabama with Ray Charles two years before—all began to make regular visits to their friend Berry's bedside. Blaine, in particular, made it a point to stop by every weekend. Though Berry had a blank stare and was still unresponsive in terms of speaking or moving his limbs, his doctors felt it important for visitors to carry on one-way conversations with him anyway. The doctors were sure that he could hear.

One Sunday, as Blaine finished running down the usual music-related events of his busy week, he bent down close to Berry and said, like always, "Well, see you next time, pal." Only this time, unexpectedly, Berry feebly reached up with one of his arms and pulled Blaine near. It was Berry's first physical movement since the accident. Blaine, with heart pounding, raced into the hallway to get Berry's family. "Jan just moved," he said, and they all burst into tears.

But the limits of Jan Berry's recovery would soon become evident. After several months of intensive physical therapy, he did learn to walk again, albeit with a severe limp. He also regained some, but not all, of his memory. Perhaps the biggest issue was his voice. Berry only partially regained the ability to speak and, for all practical purposes, could no longer sing.

With his career quite obviously over, Jan Berry had now joined Phil Spector on the rock-and-roll sidelines. Two of the most important hit-making forces in Sixties music—and regular Wrecking Crew employers—were gone from the scene. And within little more than a year, yet another titan would be joining their ranks: Brian Wilson.

✳

By the early Sixties, the perpetually busy Carol Kaye found herself at a personal and professional crossroads.

On the home front, after some careful contemplation Kaye made the decision to convert to Judaism. Raised a Baptist, she had married a prominent Jewish businessman named David Firestone in 1961 and had become fascinated with his family's religious and cultural traditions. She dutifully learned to cook kreplach soup and tzimmes, celebrated Hanukah instead of Christmas, and became skilled at making a Seder meal. Kaye eventually had a bat mitzvah ceremony, too, and was given the biblical name of Ruth.

Though the marriage would fail by 1964, Kaye retained her affection for the Jewish faith, even as she unsuccessfully attempted to return to Christianity. She especially related to the Judaic commandments to pursue justice and to welcome the stranger. The overall tone of acceptance gave her a feeling of home, like she belonged. It also, she felt, provided her with a more tolerant heart, helping her to become a better musician.

On the professional side of things, it surprised the guitarist Kaye one day when a producer at Capitol Records suddenly asked her if she minded sitting in on the Fender electric bass instead. The regular bass player had failed to show for a scheduled recording date and they were in a bind. With her well-known background as an expert guitar player, it made sense for them to utilize her services. It wasn't really much of a stretch for someone of her caliber to pick up the instrument, with the strings on a bass (E, A, D, and G) being the same as the bottom four on a guitar, only an octave lower.

What intrigued Kaye, however, was how much she enjoyed doing it. Not just her role in providing some much-needed rhythmic muscle but also the *feel* of the bass. It just felt right in her hands. And, as a practical matter, she realized that if she made the switch a permanent career choice, she would no longer have to drag three or more different kinds of guitars into the studios several times a day in order to suit each producer's fancy. One simple

Fender Precision Bass (colloquially known as a P-Bass) would do the trick nicely. After giving it some thought, she was sold.

With rock and roll now exploding all around her in the studios, Kaye picked the right instrument at the right time. Every song being recorded, whether by a three-piece combo or a full-on Spector-style "rockestra," needed at least one electric bass player to hold down the bottom end, to anchor the all-important harmonic framework. In addition, with the usual first-call rock-and-roll Wrecking Crew bassist, Ray Pohlman, finding himself occupied as the new musical director on the TV series *Shindig!* there suddenly existed a pressing need for someone to step in and pick up many of his high-profile accounts.

There were also a whole lot more guitar players floating around town than there were bass specialists. With visions of one day becoming breakout stars, it seemed like everybody wanted to be a guitarist, a front man. That's where all the glory was—along with plenty of competition to match. The electric bass, however, wasn't seen as being very sexy. To the uninitiated, it was considered to be a workmanlike, supporting instrument that merely helped keep the beat. But in the inventive, capable hands of someone who knew how to lay down a major groove while throwing in a walking bass line for good measure—like the savvy jazz veteran Kaye—the electric bass often made all the difference in bringing a song to life.

By early 1965, Brian Wilson, like many of his fellow rock-and-roll producers, had been primarily using Pohlman on electric bass in the studio for several years. But that all changed once Wilson learned that Kaye was now available for gigs as a bass player, too. She had already played guitar for him on many of the Beach Boys' records, and he liked having her as a part of his creative team.

For the Wrecking Crew in general, playing for the always-quirky Wilson proved to be fun, vexing, perplexing, and breathtaking, often all at the same time. There was nobody like him. On any given day the Beach Boys' charismatic young leader could be alternately charming and distant, confident yet insecure, or thoughtful but self-absorbed. And always—*always*—brilliant.

One afternoon, as Glen Campbell, Carol Kaye, Hal Blaine, and several other musicians sat in the main tracking room of Western's Studio 3 laying down the instrumental parts for what would soon become "Help Me, Rhonda"—a future number-one hit for the Beach Boys—Brian Wilson stood in the window of the control booth, holding a telephone receiver up to one of the monitors.

Normally this wouldn't have been a problem. Producers often talked on the phone, nothing unusual about that. They also commonly asked side-men to do several run-throughs of a new tune in order to gain familiarity with the basic structure before the real recording began. Only this time, instead of having the musicians do two or three quick passes, Wilson kept the Wrecking Crew blowing their chops on the same take for what seemed like ten minutes.

Several of the players in the room that day didn't appear to notice or mind, so lost were they in their work. A few, however, did notice and did mind, particularly Carol Kaye. She began to silently seethe as she watched the fingertips on her left hand start to bleed from their repeated, unrelenting use on the extra-high, heavy-gauge strings of her bass. The hard-won calluses—like her mood—were at their breaking point.

It also didn't help matters during the three-hour date that Brian Wilson's father had dropped in. Murry Wilson, a pugnacious, iron-fisted, old-school taskmaster with a glass eye and a sharp tongue, had pretensions of being the group's real producer. Though he had no such official title, it never stopped him from trying to assert his authority anyway. And nobody could get under Brian Wilson's skin more quickly or effectively than his old man. The elder Wilson was, in Hal Blaine's view, a real pain in the ass. The members of the Wrecking Crew had all seen plenty of arguments between father and son before, and, unfortunately, today was no different.

"Do you want me to leave, Brian?" Murry Wilson asked at one point, his anger rising.

"No, I just want you to let him sing it," Brian said with exasperation, referring to fellow band member Al Jardine, who was diligently working on a rough (scratch) lead vocal while the rest of the Beach Boys practiced their multi-part harmonies alongside him (the song's final vocals, as per their custom, would be cut separately on a subsequent non–Wrecking Crew recording date).

After several more takes, the heated verbal sparring between the two Wilsons finally boiled over, driving everything to an unceremonious halt. Within full earshot of the Wrecking Crew and a number of visitors sitting in the control booth, Brian Wilson could simply take no more, bellowing, "Oh shit. He's driving me nuts!"

Shortly thereafter, with a suitably martyred Murry Wilson still jawing away as he headed for the studio door with his wife ("The kid got a big success and he thinks he owns the business"), the session thankfully, mercifully wound to a conclusion. With the engineer, Chuck Britz, telling everyone, "That's it for today," the musicians breathed a collective sigh of relief and rapidly began packing their gear in order to make it to the next gig, a process they called "dovetailing."

Hal Blaine, for one, took all the drama and strangeness of the day with his usual equanimity. The pay, for him at double scale because of the great demand for his services, was too good to even think about relinquishing. Plus, he and Brian were close; in some ways, Blaine was like a second father to the sensitive young recording star, sometimes offering advice, always willing to listen.

With the studio beginning to empty, Blaine grabbed his leather stick bag (a gift from Aussie drumming legend Billy Hyde), along with his ever-present stash of crossword puzzles, and made for the exit. Time to play for the next client.

But Carol Kaye was still angry. As she carefully placed her Fender electric bass inside its satin-lined case and snapped the locks shut, she decided she just couldn't let this one go. No, this was a matter of respect. They were all pros and Wilson needed to treat them like it. Leaving the musicians to grind out their parts to the point of physical pain was not cool.

As she passed by the control booth window on her way out, Kaye did the unthinkable. While looking directly at the young producer, she gave him the finger.

A shocked Wilson could do nothing but stare. Surely no hired-hand musician had ever had the temerity to flip off the great and powerful Brian Wilson, at least with any expectation in mind of being asked back the next day.

But to Wilson's credit, that's exactly what happened. Kaye's bird-flipping message had apparently hit home, for no mention was ever made of the incident and the session players were never again subjected to any sort of disrespect in the studio on a Beach Boys date.

Score one for the Wrecking Crew, courtesy of the only female in the bunch.

*

By the mid-Sixties, the Wrecking Crew had become an indispensable part of one Beach Boys hit after another on songs like "California Girls," "Little Deuce Coupe," and "Fun, Fun, Fun." And because these sessions were always painstaking affairs in terms of Brian Wilson's creative yet agonizing producing style, the musicians—union members all—tended to rack up some hefty hourly wages along the way. Good old Local 47 made sure of that.

But despite the handsome pay that came with being a highly sought-after professional studio player, to many in the outside world being a musician—even one as skilled as those in the Wrecking Crew—was looked upon as the equivalent of being some kind of a carnival worker. Or less. The looks and comments said it all.

One sunny afternoon, as the Wrecking Crew broke for lunch from yet another Beach Boys session, Leon Russell, one of the piano players that day, took the opportunity to nose his brand-new Cadillac sedan out of the studio's back parking lot. He apparently had somewhere important to go during their short break from working on yet another Wilson-penned hit-to-be.

As a midwestern transplant from extremely modest origins, Russell had begun developing a real name around town in the early Sixties by virtue of his stellar work on a string of high-profile session dates, including many with Phil Spector. Banging the keys on million-sellers like "This Diamond Ring" (for producer Snuff Garrett) and "You've Lost That Lovin' Feeling" (for Spector), Russell had also started earning the first real money he'd ever known. And he didn't mind exhibiting a little bit of conspicuous car consumption—Oklahoma-style—in the process. Given that the eccentric keyboard virtuoso also had long, prematurely graying hair sticking out from underneath a large cowboy hat often perched on his head, he didn't necessarily look the part of the owner of an expensive new luxury automobile.

At least not to the motorcycle cop who had followed Russell back to Gold Star.

As the drama unfolded, it naturally caught the attention of some of the Wrecking Crew, who were just returning from various dining destinations. Several stood transfixed. Was this a drug bust?

Within seconds, the answer became clear. As Russell limped inside the building as quickly as he could on his game leg (he had been born with a malformation of the bones in his head, causing slight paralysis on one side), he then made a beeline straight for his music stand in Studio A. There, much to his relief, sat his wallet, right where he'd prayed it would be. In his haste to take a quick lunchtime spin in his fancy new ride, Russell had forgotten to bring along his driver's license. Not good, especially when the police in the area were known to have a special fondness for randomly pulling over what they referred to as "longhairs."

This was 1965 and hair, drugs, and protests were just starting to become a concern to local law enforcement officials. And, as it turned out, for good reason. In less than a year the Sunset Strip youth scene would explode into a series of full-scale riots by throngs of teens refusing to obey curfew laws following a late-night run-in with police at what became known as ground zero: a tiny, triangular nightclub called Pandora's Box located at the intersection of Crescent Heights and Sunset. These events ultimately achieved musical immortality in Buffalo Springfield's hit song "For What It's Worth," which, naturally, was mixed just down the street at Gold Star.

In the meantime, the cop had followed Leon into the studio.

"Okay, Mr. Russell, since you have no previous record, I'm only going to issue you a warning this time," the by-the-book cop finally said after carefully examining Leon's documentation. "But you need to obey the law. Driving without a license is a misdemeanor in California. If convicted, the penalty can include incarceration."

A shaken Russell could only nod, silently imagining what horrors the county jail's inmate population might have had in store for a scrawny little piano player like him. But as the young patrolman started to leave, something made him stop. As he turned back toward the rest of the musicians—now gathered in the studio alongside their instruments—his eyes narrowed in obvious disapproval.

"Why the hell don't you people get real jobs?" he suddenly said, shaking his head in disgust. "None of you can be making more than twenty bucks a day."

And, with that, one of LA's finest walked out, shutting the studio door firmly behind him.

At first, no one made a sound. And then, on cue, the whole studio burst into a roar of laughter, from Wilson and the engineers right on down to every last one of the Wrecking Crew players in attendance that day. The joke was on the cop.

These musicians without any "real" jobs were, in many cases, making over four hundred dollars a day, which just happened to be about the same as Lyndon Baines Johnson, the President of the United States, was currently earning. And it was also undoubtedly far more than the going rate for a recent graduate of the Los Angeles Police Academy.

✳

Just as Brian Wilson could sometimes be unintentionally disrespectful, as during the intense "Help Me, Rhonda" session, he could also be intentionally generous and kind to his musical charges. And it often came when it was least expected.

Billy Strange, one of Wilson's favorite guitarists and the composer of "Limbo Rock," got a call one Sunday afternoon from the maestro himself, who had somehow tracked him down at his ex-wife's house in the Hollywood Hills.

"Billy, it's Brian Wilson. Sorry for the intrusion, but you gotta come down to Western Three right now. I need you to listen to this song I'm cutting to see if there is something you can do on it."

"Brian, I'd love to," Strange replied. "But it's Sunday and I've got my son this weekend. Besides, I don't have a guitar with me."

A divorced father, Strange loved spending time with his son. His own dad—a little-known cowboy singer named George Strange—never was around all that much and Billy sure wasn't going to end up being that kind of parent. Plus, he only had weekend visiting privileges. His ex-wife had made sure of that.

"That's okay. Don't worry about it," Wilson said brightly. "Bring your son with you. See you in a few."

What the heck, Strange thought as he hung up the phone. Maybe Billy Jr. would actually get a kick out of visiting one of the places where his old man earned his living. So, with the winds of optimism firmly at their backs, father and son jumped into Billy Sr.'s car and headed down the hill for the corner of Sunset Boulevard and Gordon Street, filled with a shared sense of adventure.

By this time, the thirty-five-year-old Strange had finally settled into his role as one of the best studio sidemen in the business. Someone not only able to play the hell out of any stringed instrument placed in front of him but also possessed of the ability to sight-read "fly shit"—industry vernacular for tiny, complex passages of written musical notation. Strange excelled, too, at crafting arrangements (his work on "These Boots Are Made for Walkin'" by Nancy Sinatra helped push that song all the way to number one), and he was now producing as well. All valuable skills in the increasingly competitive pop music scene of the mid-Sixties.

As Billy Strange and his nine-year-old boy arrived at the studio and entered Western 3's cozy control room, Wilson greeted them both warmly and then got right down to business.

"Here, listen to this section, Billy. What I need is an electric twelve-string guitar solo right here."

"Brian, I don't even own an electric twelve-string guitar."

"Well, let's get one then."

The next thing Billy Strange knew, the young producer was on the phone with Glenn Wallichs, the co-founder of Capitol Records (with famed songwriter Johnny Mercer) and also the owner of Wallichs Music City, Hollywood's best-known purveyor of musical instruments. Within minutes, two deliverymen showed up at the studio's back door carrying a brand-new

Fender electric twelve-string guitar and a Fender Twin Reverb amplifier—
both from a shop that was closed on Sundays.

An impressed Strange sat down, cradling the gleaming new guitar in his
hands, and began tuning up, carefully adjusting the amp's tone controls in
precise increments along the way. Satisfied that he'd achieved just the right
sound, he then made one quick pass at playing the short eight-bar section
Brian wanted to place right in the middle of what proved to be the future
hit "Sloop John B."

"That's it!" Wilson yelped with glee. "You nailed it, Billy."

And so, just as quickly as it had begun, the world's shortest recording
session had now ended. Almost.

As Strange and his son stood to leave, the Beach Boys' leader pulled out
a wad of hundred-dollar bills and peeled off several of them, stashing them
in Billy's front shirt pocket.

"Thanks, man, for the great riff and for coming down today. And don't
forget your guitar and amp."

Billy Strange stood bug-eyed. Brian Wilson—a world-famous producer
under tremendous pressure to finish a new album on time and within
budget—had just given him five hundred dollars in cash and a brand-new,
expensive set of equipment worth well in excess of two thousand dollars.
All for a few minutes of work.

This is some rate of pay, a grateful Strange thought to himself as he
thanked Wilson for the unexpected largesse.

But, then, that was Brian Wilson—when you least expected it, he was
generous to a fault. But, sadly, it was precisely this range of behavior—
mostly good, other times questionable—that would soon conspire to spell
the demise of his long-standing musical partnership with Strange and all the
rest of the Wrecking Crew.

✳

In December of 1965, the playing field within the realm of contemporary
music suddenly experienced a seismic shift in terms of creativity and vision, tilting the advantage decidedly toward the British Isles. Because during that month and year the Beatles released their groundbreaking *Rubber*

Soul album. Replete with a variety of cleverly crafted odes to love that took the notion of the popular song to a new level of lyrical sophistication and perspective, the LP was a smash, going straight to the top of the charts.

No ordinary album in terms of content, *Rubber Soul* evidenced a maturity and conceptual cohesiveness that forever altered how vinyl albums were to be utilized. Since the Beatles first released "I Want to Hold Your Hand" in January of '64, American musicians had mostly been able to hold their own in the face of the so-called British Invasion in what was essentially a song-by-song Top 40 battle of 45 rpm records. Long-play 33⅓ rpm albums had yet to be considered as anything more than vehicles for a hit single or two, plus the addition of several "filler" tracks to pad things out ("two hits and ten pieces of junk," as Phil Spector liked to say). But the arrival of *Rubber Soul* changed all that. The days of "yeah, yeah, yeah" were clearly oh, oh, over.

With each song seemingly more brilliant than the one before it, *Rubber Soul* also offered an exquisite and unprecedented variety of instrumental surprises, such as the fuzzed-out bass line on "Think for Yourself" and the first use of a sitar on a major pop recording ("Norwegian Wood"). The Byrds' David Crosby (whose band the Beatles greatly admired) had enthusiastically introduced the complicated stringed instrument to a fascinated George Harrison, who subsequently worked night and day to try to master its intricacies. Ironically, just months earlier Crosby had been unceremoniously replaced on the much-simpler-to-play rhythm guitar by Wrecking Crew member Jerry Cole during the recording of the Byrds' "Mr. Tambourine Man."

As with the Byrds, the Beatles also maintained a friendly rivalry with the Beach Boys, and the two bands kept close tabs on each other's chart successes. Label mates in the United States on Capitol Records, they would also occasionally visit each other when on tour. And Mike Love, the Beach Boys' lead singer, would even one day join the Beatles in visiting the Maharishi Mahesh Yogi in Rishikesh, India—a trip that helped inspire much of what would eventually become the Beatles' *White Album*.

But for now, their cordial game of one-upsmanship had just one name: *Rubber Soul*.

With almost universally glowing reviews and substantial sales success on both sides of the Atlantic, this latest record by the Fab Four also naturally caught the ear of ambitious musicians everywhere, causing many—like Brian Wilson—to scramble in reevaluation of their own efforts. He wondered how the Beach Boys would even be able to compete.

It turned out the answer came in the form of a little album with the cute-sounding name of *Pet Sounds*.

Having recently completed the hastily conceived *Beach Boys Party!* album in late '65—an in-studio effort passed off as a "live" party recording in order to fulfill contractual obligations with Capitol—Wilson set out in earnest during January of the new year to begin work on what he hoped would become his magnum opus, something even the über-talented Beatles couldn't top.

Assembled with the other Wrecking Crew members this time around in Western's much larger Studio 2, Hal Blaine could immediately sense that something was different on this project. There was a seriousness of purpose in the air, almost as if all the previous Beach Boys dates on which he'd worked were merely preambles to something bigger and better to come. And he was right.

"Brian is sure focused today," remarked guitarist Jerry Cole to both Blaine and stand-up bass player Lyle Ritz between takes during an early *Pet Sounds* session for what would soon become "Wouldn't It Be Nice," one of the band's biggest all-time hits.

Ritz, a small, mild-mannered, balding man blessed with a pitch-perfect ear and impeccable technique, nodded his head in agreement. But he had also noticed something else that day. As he played the song's bass line in the key of D, the rest of the band seemed to be in another key altogether. Something's not right here, he thought.

"Hey, what key are you guys in?"

"Key of A—it's right there on the sheet music," said Cole, pointing, while working to replace a broken string on his Fender Telecaster.

"Well, my sheet music is in D," replied Ritz. "Go figure."

As the bass player got up and walked around the room, glancing curiously at everyone else's music stands, he came to the startling realization that he was the only one in the studio playing in a different key. The only one, it appeared, who was *supposed* to be in a different key. That can't be done, thought Ritz.

But it could. And it was. For Wilson had outdone himself this time by writing a countermelody for the bass line that fit neatly within the song— all based on a completely different harmonic center or tonic. Something neither Ritz nor the Wrecking Crew had ever experienced during a rock-and-roll gig. That was something a jazzer might do. Maybe. But, then again, these were the *Pet Sounds* sessions and all creative bets were off. There would be nothing prosaic about this album.

Son of a gun, Ritz said to himself, smiling. Son of a gun if he didn't pull it off.

✳

For three grueling months, Glen Campbell, Carol Kaye, Hal Blaine, and the other musicians toiled on *Pet Sounds,* sometimes working in the studio from seven at night until early the next morning—often on just one song. And on more than one occasion, Blaine found the need to lie down on the floor in the middle of the night next to his drums, hoping to catch a little sleep before the next session began only a few hours later. Though the extra studio time was certainly a financial boon (overtime could add up fast), the extended absences from home too often took a toll on the Wrecking Crew's personal lives. Birthdays and anniversaries were forgotten, school plays were missed, and in several instances marriages sadly ended.

In creating *Pet Sounds,* Wilson wanted the music to be perfect and the boys (and one girl) in the band were right there with him. He was their leader, the guru, the youthful genius whose artistic inclinations were golden. They were a team now and he was the undisputed captain. So while the real Beach Boys continued to travel America and the rest of the world on what seemed to be a never-ending tour, Brian and the Wrecking Crew stayed home and made studio magic.

With them smoothly playing as a seamless unit after so many Beach Boys sessions together, it now seemed to Blaine as though they could almost read Wilson's mind. The producer also sought innovation at every turn. If this album was to be his crowning achievement, then *any* idea was fair game. A distinctive sound was simply a must. During one session, when the percussion on "God Only Knows" seemed to be lacking an indefinable "something," Blaine suggested that maybe he should try playing his drumsticks on some taped-together plastic orange juice bottles instead. Wilson loved the result.

Another time, Wilson felt that the bass pedals underneath the Hammond B-3 organ just weren't providing the right sound. So he instructed the organ player, Larry Knechtel, to lie on the floor and instead play them with his hands during the song. An unorthodox move to say the least. But neither Knechtel nor Blaine nor any other member of the Wrecking Crew minded. Whatever worked was okay with them.

Released in early April of '66, *Pet Sounds* was an immediate home run with critics and the band's music biz compatriots alike. The *Los Angeles Times* raved about it. The Rolling Stones loved it. Paul McCartney—Wilson's main competitor—practically worshiped it, considering *Pet Sounds* to be the greatest pop album of all time.

But a funny thing happened once this future classic made its way to the nation's record stores: it landed with a resounding thud. A confounded public just didn't know what to make of all the melancholy and introspection. Was this really the Beach Boys? The same fun-loving band that used to sing about waxing down their surfboards and liking California girls the best?

Despite brilliant playing by the Wrecking Crew and equally brilliant songwriting that was in many ways ahead of its time—or perhaps exactly because of it—sales were lukewarm from the start and the vaunted album failed to even achieve Gold status. Certainly a first for the Beach Boys and simply an unthinkable proposition only six short months before.

Brian Wilson was crushed. Despite the critical acclaim surrounding *Pet Sounds,* he couldn't get over the public's failure to embrace his most important and personal musical creation.

"I've never seen him like this," Knechtel said to Blaine one evening a few weeks later during a hastily arranged session for some overdub work on the soon-to-be-released stand-alone single "Good Vibrations."

"Neither have I," admitted the drummer.

Though he tried to put on a brave face, Wilson's ever-fragile spirit had been irretrievably broken. Though more sessions with the Wrecking Crew would occur later in the year and into the next in what would be a half-hearted attempt to create a new album—most notably the time he had them all don little red fire hats while playing the instruments on the "Fire" portion of a musical suite he called *The Elements*—the damage had been done. Wilson's own fire was essentially out.

✳

As Hal Blaine pressed the buzzer at the gate in front of Brian Wilson's massive pale yellow Mission-style mansion along Bel Air's tony Bellagio Road, he knew something just wasn't right. He had been recording there on and off for several months—it was now the fall of 1967—and rumors were starting to swirl about Wilson's possible mental illness and drug use. But a call to do another recording date at Brian Wilson's home at least seemed like a positive sign. Maybe the kid was on the road to turning things around.

After entering through the front door and being escorted down a long hallway, Blaine found himself, as usual, in a former den with a very tall ceiling that had been converted into a makeshift recording studio. The fireplace opening had been covered with plywood and his drums were already set up in the corner, courtesy of his trusted drum tech and friend, Rick Faucher. Several mic stands were in position and a grand piano sat front and center.

For some reason, the control booth itself—the heartbeat of any studio—had been placed in a strangely detached location far above the main floor on what looked to be a balcony on the home's second level. The eerily foreboding structure featured an ominous series of small, slit-like windows that overlooked everything below, like some sort of fortified citadel straight out of medieval wars. Hardly the best environment for creating music, Blaine thought.

Several other Wrecking Crew regulars were there, too—guys like Jerry Cole, Larry Knechtel, Ray Pohlman, and others. Everyone had come prepared, as always, hoping to cut something special, just like in the old days. But despite their expectations, the three-hour date turned out to be nothing more than the usual oddball recording session up at Brian's house, where nothing ever seemed to come to fruition. And just like on so many previous visits, the musicians on hand never even personally interacted with Wilson. They took their instructions straight from the engineer over the talk-back mic.

On the way out that day, a few of the Wrecking Crew players suddenly caught a glimpse of—*could it be?*—Brian Wilson. Or at least somebody who vaguely looked like him. Gone was the affable, trim, energetic soul who had so skillfully guided their musical efforts at Gold Star and Western Recorders. In his place was an overweight man with unwashed, stringy hair, wearing an old bathrobe and slippers. As he silently passed along in the shadows, his gaze, if you could call it that, seemed to look right through them. The famed producer and recording star clearly had retreated within himself to a private world—a world where the Wrecking Crew were not invited.

The group of musicians stopped in surprise.

"Hi, Brian, how are you doing?" one of them said.

Wilson made no response.

"Hey, Brian, we've missed you, man," offered another.

Still no response.

As they watched the onetime leader of America's most popular band shuffle his way down the hall into the half darkness, an ineffable sadness filled the air. Not just at the heartbreaking sight before them but also at the realization that the time they had spent as part of something so rare, so world changing, was finally, officially over. Forever.

And so it came to pass that after almost five years of Brian Wilson and the Wrecking Crew together in the studio night and day as a virtual musical family in creation of an almost unprecedented string of twenty-two Top 40 hits, he didn't even seem to know who the members of the Wrecking Crew were anymore.

12

Let's Live for Today

Never have so many played so little for so much.
—BARNEY KESSEL

In late 1965, two young music-loving producers, Bob Rafelson and Bert Schneider, had a brainstorm. What if they took the basic concept of the Beatles' movie *A Hard Day's Night*—the fictional story of four zany, cute-looking twentysomething male musicians running amuck in a comically skewed world—and turned it into a weekly TV series specifically targeting teenage girls? With tapping into the burgeoning youth market a known priority for ABC, CBS, and NBC and with animal-oriented band names currently in vogue, the enterprising duo immediately began making a series of pitches around Hollywood for a program they wanted to call *The Monkees*.

After finagling a one-episode pilot deal with Columbia Pictures' TV subsidiary, Screen Gems—a major supplier of shows to all three networks—Rafelson and Schneider, now going by the corporate name of Raybert Productions, set about the task of coming up with four suitable musicians, or at least a reasonable facsimile thereof. Though they first considered using a novice band they had befriended called the Lovin' Spoonful ("Do You Believe in Magic," "Daydream," and "Summer in the City" would be among their eventual hits), the producers ultimately chose to go the casting-call route in order to find their perfect set of joyful anarchists.

Accordingly, in early 1966 Raybert put a small, pithy advertisement in *Daily Variety* and in *The Hollywood Reporter* that read: "Madness!! Auditions: Folk & Roll Musicians-Singers for acting roles in a new TV series. Running parts for 4 insane boys, age 17–21. Want spirited Ben Frank's-types. Have courage to work. Must come down for interview."

With swarms of young male hopefuls easily several hundred strong descending upon their offices, the producers ended up with plenty of warm bodies from which to choose, including future well-known musicians Stephen Stills, Van Dyke Parks, and Gary Lewis. After hour upon hour of freewheeling auditions stretching over an exhausting two-month period, Rafelson and Schneider finally settled on their ideal fabricated foursome: Micky Dolenz, a former child actor and natural mimic, best known for playing the lead role in the Fifties TV series *Circus Boy*; Davy Jones, a diminutive British-born song-and-dance veteran whose most recent work had him on the Broadway stage in *Oliver!* as the Artful Dodger; Michael Nesmith, a laconic Texas-born guitarist and singer with minimal performing experience; and Peter Tork, a sometime-musician now washing dishes for a living in a Santa Monica restaurant.

Given that *The Monkees* was a show about a band, the first order of business, along with filming the pilot, was to record some music. Choosing to employ the services of a number of established songwriters, with Neil Diamond, David Gates, and Carole King among them, music publisher and Screen Gems music division president Don Kirshner—who had assumed the role of music supervisor on the show as well—also saw the need to bring in studio musicians to help cut the made-for-TV group's records. In his view, the four actors were in no way ready to assume the duties of actually playing their own instruments.

Once the decision was made to go with the in-house Screen Gems songwriting team of Tommy Boyce and Bobby Hart as the program's primary music producers, for a while everything went along smoothly. The pilot sold to NBC, who then made a commitment for a full season to begin in the fall of 1966. Recording also began on what would become over two albums' worth of initial material, with Dolenz and Jones supplying most of the lead vocals.

After a huge promotional push from Colgems, the band's newly created record label (a partnership between Screen Gems and RCA), and with the instant exposure provided by their recently launched Monday night show, the Monkees' first 45, "Last Train to Clarksville," shot to number one on the charts in October of 1966. Their first LP, *The Monkees,* did the same, with their mostly adolescent (and younger) fans blissfully unaware that the musicians playing on the vinyl discs really weren't their heroes at all. Instead, the instrumentation consisted of a mixture of the Wrecking Crew (often including Glen Campbell, Carol Kaye, and Hal Blaine) and the Candy Store Prophets (Boyce and Hart's personal band).

From children's lunch boxes to teen magazines to miniature toy Monkeemobiles, the phenomenon known as Monkeemania was suddenly at full throttle. Yet despite the quartet's virtually instantaneous rise to fame and fortune—with a level of adulation matched in intensity only by the fans of the Beatles themselves—the behind-the-scenes action was already beginning to head sideways. Just a few months into their first season on the air, Mike Nesmith, generally the quietest of the four, had become exceedingly vocal about his unhappiness. He wanted the Monkees to be allowed to play and sing as a band on their own records, particularly on the songs he continued to write. Nesmith had little interest in continuing as part of what he considered to be a colossal charade. The public was being duped and he wanted no part of it.

Arriving for a meeting one afternoon in January of 1967 at Don Kirshner's bungalow at the Beverly Hills Hotel, the Monkees gamely participated in a made-for-the-press ceremony where they were each given a gold record and a check for $250,000, their share of the record royalties that had accumulated so far. After posing for endless photos and good-naturedly mugging their way through the rest of the event, the four then stayed behind with Kirshner and a few Screen Gems staffers to go over some business.

As Kirshner, who was always looking ahead in terms of generating more revenue, presented the boys with several new songs that were being considered for their next single release (including "Sugar, Sugar," the future number-one hit by the Archies), he made the fatal mistake of saying, "The tracks have already been cut. We just need to add your voices."

That was all Mike Nesmith needed to hear. It was finally time to make a stand. He was sick to death of singing on other people's songs played by still other musicians while Screen Gems happily slapped the band's name on the little red and white Colgems record labels.

"We're not recording for you *anymore*," Nesmith exploded, staring down a stunned Kirshner. "We want to do our own thing."

A tense silence instantly filled the room. The line had been drawn.

Wide-eyed, the other three Monkees could do nothing but watch the showdown now unfolding between a determined Nesmith and their equally intransigent music bosses. Screen Gems, with Kirshner at the helm, was making a bundle off the Monkees, and there was no way they were about to jeopardize any of it just to assuage some guitar player.

Feeling the need to set an obviously misguided employee straight, Kirshner's fellow executive (and lawyer) Herb Moelis stepped into the fray.

"Don Kirshner, as the music supervisor on *The Monkees,* has every right to pick whatever songs he wants for release," Moelis reminded.

Nesmith, however, would have none of it. To him, the whole thing had become insipid.

"We could record 'Happy Birthday' with a beat and it would be a million-seller," he replied in disgust. "If something doesn't change, I'm out of here."

Moelis then reached into his briefcase and pulled out a sheaf of papers.

"You had better read your contract, Mr. Nesmith," he said sharply, wagging a copy of the document. "We have a legally binding agreement with you."

As the two alpha males warily eyed each other during what had now become a standoff, a frustrated Nesmith suddenly lost his temper. Whirling around, and with all his might, the guitarist slammed his right fist through the hotel room's wall, sending out a shower of plaster. Turning back toward Moelis, Nesmith then made sure his position was perfectly understood.

"That could have been your face, motherfucker."

✳

Around the time of the Monkees' incandescent debut, another pop act that routinely relied on the Wrecking Crew's services also found itself squarely in the spotlight. Such was the worldwide impact of "I Got You Babe" back in 1965 that Sonny & Cher had been able to coast on its success for the better part of a year. Several songs they had recorded before anyone knew who they were, such as "Just You" and "Baby Don't Go," had also swiftly skated onto the higher reaches of the national charts. The funky-dressing couple with the almost atonal singing style had become, by mid-1966, one of the hottest acts in show business.

But Sonny Bono was nothing if not honest with himself. The latest records he had been putting out were doing okay, too, but *just* okay. They were creeping their way into the teens and twenties, a moderate success by most music industry standards. But singles like "What Now My Love" and "Little Man" were far from turning anyone's heads. And with this, Bono could feel the duo's momentum beginning to slide. The sweetly sentimental love songs that he and Cher favored could no longer adequately compete in an increasingly hip marketplace. Music was changing once again. Folk rock, with its often-overt social commentary, had become the new darling of Top 40 radio. Songs like "The Sound of Silence," "Like a Rolling Stone," and "Turn! Turn! Turn!" were now setting the musical tone. Alienation was in.

Riding high though he and Cher might have appeared to the outside world as the months passed in 1966, behind closed doors Bono knew they needed to develop a different sound fast if they were going to keep their recording careers alive. They needed a hit song that would make them relevant again. Something that grooved, something that *mattered*.

Once again, Sonny Bono found himself sitting alone in a lousy mood late one fall evening in front of his battered piano. While messing around for several hours, he unexpectedly hit upon a melody idea that he especially liked. Adding some autobiographical lyrics about his belief in the need to persevere no matter how life seemed to change, Bono sensed that he might just have a winner on his hands.

Gathering at Gold Star with the Wrecking Crew several days later, Bono got to work on trying to shape his song into a possible hit. On hand were many of his favorites, including Michel Rubini on piano, Frankie

Capp on drums, and Carol Kaye, this time on acoustic guitar. Another familiar face was that of Barney Kessel, and the old pro just couldn't resist giving Sonny Bono the business one more time.

As the musicians ran through the song, called "The Beat Goes On," for over two and a half hours, they began to wear down. Not just from the repeated playing but also from the unprecedented monotony of it all. Bono had written the whole thing in just one chord (F), and the musicians were about to fall out of their chairs from boredom.

Finally, the Kerouac-cool, bebop-schooled Kessel could take no more. His world was about anything *but* strumming the same chord over and over. He was a flat-out jazz guitar legend. Rising to his feet, with instrument in hand, the normally silent, poker-faced guitarist announced to one and all, "You know, guys, this song has got a *great* change."

As the musicians all chuckled, Kessel then turned toward the control booth and grandly proclaimed in his finest stentorian voice, "Never have so many played so little for so much." With that, he sat down. Everybody in the place—even Bono—dissolved in laughter.

But the all-important session also had a very serious problem. With no chord changes and a relatively ordinary melody line, the song just wasn't happening; it didn't swing. Sonny Bono's last-gasp hope for a hit record was in danger of never making it onto vinyl. He needed help, and he needed it now.

＊

In 1963, Betty Friedan, a freelance magazine writer and suburban New York housewife, dismayed by the prevalence of what she called "the problem that has no name," published a book called *The Feminine Mystique*. In her expository essay, Friedan analyzed the trapped, imprisoned feelings that she believed many women (including herself) secretly held regarding their roles as full-time homemakers. Friedan vehemently argued that women were as capable as men to do any kind of work or to follow any kind of career path and that they would be well served to recalibrate their thinking accordingly.

Some considered it a call to arms; others found it to be an outrage. Either way, Friedan's groundbreaking treatise not only ignited a nationwide firestorm of controversy and debate; it also became an instant bestseller, in the process helping to launch what came to be known as the "second stage" of the Women's Movement.

At the same moment in time, deep inside the rock-and-roll recording studio world of Los Angeles existed an important, pioneering exception to the female status quo that Friedan wrote so passionately about. And that exception was Carol Kaye.

With Kaye self-reliant from an early age, it never entered her mind that she couldn't perform either in the same profession or at the same level as men. She had played alongside many women in her earlier jazz days, when greats like the organist Ethel Smith, the pianist Marian McPartland, and the alto saxophonist Vi Redd were at the height of their careers. So the notion of being a woman who happened to play guitar seemed as normal to her as any other line of work. And when rock and roll came along in the late Fifties, Kaye naturally made the transition, where other women, for reasons of their own, decided to leave the business or stick purely with jazz. There was no particularly evident gender bias in the studios, either. If you could play, the producers would pay.

Over the years, Kaye had more than held her own while moving up the studio ladder, too, and she was not at all shy about defending her turf. Whenever some wise-guy male musician would comment, "Hey, that's pretty good for a woman," she would immediately counter his backhanded compliment with, "Well, that's pretty good for a man, too." That was also a big part of why Sonny Bono liked having her on his sessions: she was quick and she was creative.

As Kaye carefully listened that day in the studio as she and her fellow musicians ran through "The Beat Goes On" several times in order to try to make sense out of it, she knew that she was going to have to come up with something inventive. In her opinion, the droning, one-chord tune was a real dog; it just lay there. Playing around with several bass lines on her acoustic guitar, she then came upon a particular pattern that had some real hop to it. *Dum-dum-dum-da-dum-dum-da-dum-dum.*

Bono immediately stopped the session.

"That's *it*, Carol," he whooped. "What's that line you're playing?"

Maybe he couldn't really play an instrument himself, least of all the bass, but Bono instinctively knew a signature lick when he heard one. And Kaye had just come up with an all-timer. As she dutifully played her creation once more for the producer, Bono had Bob West, the electric bass player on the date, learn it on the spot. Kaye and West then proceeded to play the simple yet transformative line in unison on the final recording, turning a previously lifeless production into a surefire hit.

Entering the charts in January of 1967, "The Beat Goes On" made it all the way to number six, giving Sonny & Cher their biggest Top 40 showing in almost two years. Stepping in as the song's de facto arranger, the independent-thinking Carol Kaye had just saved Bono's composition, and likely Sonny & Cher's tepid recording career, from an almost certain demise.

But the beat also went on for scores of others trying to gain a measure of their own fame and fortune in the high-flying, competitive Top 40 market-place of the mid-Sixties. There was always another Sonny Bono or Jan and Dean or Roger McGuinn waiting in the wings someplace, anonymously dreaming the same fevered dream. The "kids" music that label execs like Mitch Miller at Columbia had once derisively dismissed as a passing fad had now become firmly entrenched as the biggest-selling genre of them all. Rock and roll had gone mainstream. Which gave the Wrecking Crew players more session work than they knew what to do with. And it provided an inevitable destination for every kind of struggling garage band, vocal group, and wandering minstrel. Even if they didn't always know it yet.

✳

Sitting at a table in a tiny outdoor café overlooking the Mediterranean Sea on the sun-bleached island of Crete, tall, lanky, twenty-one-year-old Chuck Ertmoed could visualize his future as clearly as he could see the local fisher-men returning with their catches on the sparkling blue waters of the harbor below.

As part of a folk-singing group called the New Californians, out on a two-year-plus, shoestring-style world tour, the young vocalist and guitarist had recently arrived in Greece for a series of small concerts. He now found himself enjoying dinner late one afternoon with a married couple from Oregon after randomly having met them during a bit of sightseeing in Crete's capital city of Heraklion. As their impromptu alfresco get-together merrily rolled along, with one glass of ouzo becoming two and two glasses soon enough becoming several bottles, the well-oiled conversation between the three tablemates eventually made its way around to the subject of dreams.

"You know, I can see it all in my mind's eye," Ertmoed confided, taking a last bite of his *karidopita,* a rich walnut cake flavored with cognac. "I'm going to go back home and become successful in music. I can feel it."

Whether it was the shared liquid fortification or the powerfulness of his conviction, the musician's newfound friends instantly became fellow believers in his career prospects. They even went so far as to pick possible stage names for him to use, writing them on individual scraps of paper. One thing everyone agreed upon for sure was that the surname of Ertmoed would have to go; it sounded too much like somebody in the throes of up-chucking.

After a number of hours together under what had become a coal-black sky illuminated by a galaxy of glimmering Greek-named constellations, the woozy threesome finally decided to call it an evening. "Maybe we'll run into each other again sometime back in the States," the woman said brightly.

Grabbing his ever-present rucksack, Ertmoed warmly hugged them both good-bye, gave a quick wave over his shoulder, and then disappeared down a dark cobblestone street to the old-world-style inn where he and his group mates were staying. With a big show scheduled for the next day, it was time to get some sleep.

As he gratefully crawled into bed inside his small room, just like every night, Chuck Ertmoed mentally tucked away his career aspirations for safekeeping, content in the knowledge that he was now one day closer to realizing his musical destiny, whatever it may be.

✳

As the local band known as the 13th Floor entered the offices of Dunhill Records in early 1967, it was with a great sense of anticipation and excitement. The quartet's managers had scored them a hard-to-get record deal, and they were there that day to sign the contracts. Eagerly stepping forward with pens in hand, Rick Coonce, Warren Entner, and Rob Grill immediately signed their names on the line, no questions asked. The fourth member of the group, however, hesitated. Wordlessly he began fishing around for something in one of his pockets, finally pulling out a crumpled slip of paper. After carefully smoothing it out on the table and reading its contents, the guitarist then proceeded to add his signature to all the rest.

"Creed Bratton?" one of his bandmates asked, looking over his shoulder. "Who is *that*?"

"That," Chuck Ertmoed said proudly, "is my new name."

Having returned to the United States from his vagabond days abroad, Ertmoed had finally settled down to form a rock-and-roll band with three like-minded musicians. Based in Los Angeles, they played popular nightspots like the Middle Earth in the Valley and the Fog Cutter on the Sunset Strip and soon began building a following. With one of their songs, "Beatin' Round the Bush," being good enough to get them a recording session for Dunhill over at Eldorado Studios on the corner of Hollywood and Vine (a smaller facility sometimes used when Western 3 was unavailable), the next thing they knew the foursome had a contract. And their timing couldn't have been better.

With a studio-concocted hit song on their hands called "Where Were You When I Needed You"—featuring Larry Knechtel (keyboards) and Joe Osborn (bass) from the Wrecking Crew, plus multi-talented engineer Bones Howe moonlighting on drums—Dunhill producers Steve Barri and Phil Sloan (who also played guitar and sang on it) were suddenly in a fix. In order to capitalize on the single's unexpected Top 30 success, they needed to put an actual band together as soon as possible. Tour offers were starting to come in and there was money to be made. For a while they thought they had the perfect solution in the Bedouins, a San Francisco blues rock outfit. But that group proved to have other ideas, mainly regarding the desire to record their own material, which was decidedly *not* part of Dunhill's plans. After four months, the Bedouins migrated back to the Bay Area, leaving Barri and Sloan band-less once again.

Listening to the 13th Floor record that day in the studio, Barri and

Sloan realized that they had finally found their band. Staring them in the face were four good-looking local kids who could sing and had a definite pop vibe to their music. They also seemed to take direction well, an important selling point. Upon working out the business details with the 13th Floor's manager, Sloan and Barri then made sure everyone involved understood one more, nonnegotiable deal point. Coonce, Entner, Grill, and Bratton would *all* have to use a different name from now on.

They would be the Grass Roots.

✳

After all the drama of Mike Nesmith's heavy-duty hotel room encounter with Don Kirshner and his corporate counsel, the guitarist's message apparently had hit its mark. A sympathetic Bob Rafelson and Bert Schneider, who were also embroiled in their own issues with Kirshner, went to the head of Columbia Pictures and had the Screen Gems executive fired. Of course, it didn't hurt that Schneider's father *was* the head of Columbia Pictures. Regardless, the net result gave the Monkees their creative freedom, and under the leadership of Nesmith they intended to make the most of it. Beginning with album number three, to be called *Headquarters,* they were determined to play all their own instruments and finally become a real band for all to see and hear.

Spending several weeks locked away in RCA's Studio C during March of 1967, the Monkees feverishly worked to cut what would become fourteen songs. Dolenz, who had only recently learned to play the drums, held down the beat as best he could. Nesmith and Tork handled all the guitar and keyboard work. And Jones played percussion, with their producer, Chip Douglas, sitting in on bass. Their collective skills weren't nearly in the same league as that of the Wrecking Crew, but they were still the Monkees and this was their great moment of unification and redemption.

In spite of their best efforts, however, *Headquarters* fell flat. Though it did hit number one on the album charts for exactly one week (to then be knocked off by *Sgt. Pepper's Lonely Hearts Club Band*), the LP failed to generate any hit singles, a devastating development. In 1967, the sales of relatively inexpensive 45s were still the lifeblood of most bands, especially for those making their living on the pop end of the scale like the Monkees. With their predominantly junior high–aged demographic, the continued inflow of their fans' allowance money was vital.

Dispirited by radio's indifference to the music they had worked so hard to create on *Headquarters*, the Monkees essentially devolved into four separate music-making entities for the rest of their recording career as a band. They each used the Wrecking Crew (and other musicians) to play on their own sessions on the group's final six studio albums. The Prefab Four had made their point; it was now time to get back to making some hits.

At the same time that the Monkees were learning the harsh realities of the record business, the Grass Roots were beginning their musical journey filled with optimism. With Sloan and Barri providing the tunes and the production expertise, along with instrumentation by the Wrecking Crew, the quartet immediately found success on the airwaves. Their first single, "Let's Live for Today," made it all the way to the Top 10 during the summer of 1967, with its follow-up, "Things We Should Have Said," hitting the Top 30 not long after. Suddenly the Grass Roots were getting hot.

But just as with Mike Nesmith before him, the almost instantaneous success felt less than satisfying to Creed Bratton. More than anything, he wanted to be an artist, to be allowed to grow and flourish by writing and playing on *all* the records, along with the rest of his band. But Barri and Sloan held a tight grip on the reins, only allowing the Grass Roots to contribute their instrumental skills on the occasional album track, certainly *never* on the songs the two producers knew would be released as singles. Those were reserved strictly for the Wrecking Crew.

By the time of the Grass Roots' next big hit, the Top 5 "Midnight Confessions" (during which Carol Kaye played yet another memorable opening bass lick), Bratton, for better or worse, had begun to openly express his artistic frustrations. He didn't want the Grass Roots to become Dunhill's version of the Monkees. Riding one day in the back of a limousine in New York City with his bandmates, the lead guitarist could no longer keep his fragile emotions in check.

"Look, guys, I can see it," the high-strung Bratton said, breaking into tears. "If we don't come up with our own songs and play our own instruments in the studio, we're not going to get any respect. We'll fall by the wayside."

Despite the impassioned plea, his fellow group members remained unmoved. They had no interest in making any waves. To them, the money, women, and fame far outweighed the fact that most of their songs were provided by others and that the Wrecking Crew usually played the instruments. They *did* get to sing on all the records, didn't they? And on tour, there was nobody onstage but them.

"Let it go, Creed," they said. "Things are fine."

But Bratton couldn't let it go. It was a matter of principle. As the months passed, the guitarist became ever more petulant, whining and complaining incessantly, driving the rest of the band crazy. He also began to act out in wildly inappropriate ways, even by music business standards.

One afternoon on tour in San Francisco, Bratton and Rick Coonce, the band's twenty-two-year-old drummer, decided to wander over to Golden Gate Park to check out the action. Located next to the much-publicized counterculture neighborhood of Haight-Ashbury, the sprawling public recreation area offered every kind of adventure imaginable, legal and otherwise. The pair soon found themselves happily engrossed in playing African hand drums along with a bunch of free-spirited locals. During their heated jam, a small hippie-looking girl in tie-dyed clothing bopped her way over to Bratton, slid a tab of acid into his hand, and said, "For you, brother."

Never one to turn down a new life experience, on the way back to their show at the Fillmore West on South Van Ness Avenue Bratton ingested the tiny piece of paper containing the LSD. Giving it no further thought, he then focused himself on the evening's gig. He loved playing live; it was the one place where he felt that he could truly express himself. There was precious little chance for that in the recording studio.

Shortly thereafter, with all four members now in position on the darkened stage, ready to play their growing string of hits, the promoter Bill Graham announced over the house sound system, *"Ladies and gentlemen, here they are, the Grass Roots!"* And at that exact moment, just as they were to launch into the first number, Creed Bratton's hands began to glow. Or, more accurately, the lead guitarist *thought* they were glowing.

Mesmerized by the strange phenomenon, Bratton then strummed a chord and watched as the chord itself came flying out of the monitor next to him. Only now it was somehow written on sheet music, complete with the individual notes. Then, like out of a cartoon, the note heads and stems all slid off the paper and tumbled to the floor, landing in a pile. As Bratton walked over to pick them up, thinking that he would somehow need the jumble in order to continue playing his guitar, he could hear his bandmates in the background all yelling in a strangely distorted, slow-motion kind of way, *"Plaaaay, Creeeed, plaaaay!"*

By this time, Graham, the famously dictatorial impresario, was going berserk just offstage. "Play, goddammit," he shouted angrily, his neck veins bulging. Trying to comply, Bratton picked up his guitar, but he could no longer figure out how it worked. Turning toward the audience, he then did the only other thing he could think to do in such a situation: he undid his belt and dropped his pants, giving the audience a clear view of all he had to offer. Bratton then unabashedly waved at everyone while initiating a rap on the true meaning of life. With the rest of the Grass Roots quickly mobilizing to hustle him out of sight, Bill Graham canceled the concert.

Not long after Bratton's drug-fueled, Johnson-baring onstage incident, the other three band members, along with their manager, held a meeting with him back in Los Angeles. And their message was neither unexpected nor lengthy.

"Creed, we'd like you to leave the group," they said bluntly, offering an immediate buyout of his interest in the Grass Roots.

"Okay," Bratton replied with a sigh. "Whatever you guys want."

There would be no fighting, no protracted haggling. There were no hard feelings, either. Yes, the guitarist had made some errors in judgment. And for that he was sorry. But mostly Bratton was simply burned out from the constant stress of wanting so badly what the rest of the band did not. They obviously did not place the same value on artistic freedom that he did. But that was okay; to each his own.

With the vision that he had seen so clearly that evening in Greece now coming around full circle, Bratton decided that he would return to his own unique musical roots, to become a globe-trotting balladeer once more. The

Grass Roots were more than welcome to continue with *their* vision, singing on material secretly played by the Wrecking Crew. And so the band did. They quickly added a new member and then enjoyed a run of eight more Top 40 hits over the next two and a half years, all with the public none the wiser. Just the way Dunhill wanted it.

13

Up, Up and Away

Sounds more like an album cut than a single to me.
—BILLY DAVIS, JR.

When shy, bespectacled songwriting prodigy Jimmy Webb first made his way out west with his family to lush, palm tree–lined Southern California from the arid, hardscrabble lands of his youth along the edge of the Great Plains, he simply couldn't believe what his eyes, ears, and nose were suddenly telling his brain. It was paradise times ten for the seventeen-year-old music hopeful.

From where he had grown up as the son of a strict Baptist minister in various Oklahoma and West Texas prairie towns, the frequent dust, desolation, and despair were stark reminders of all that might have been. In his new home of San Bernardino, the air on a typically translucent Inland Empire evening could be simply intoxicating, almost like perfume, with night-blossoming jasmine everywhere. And with songs such as "Don't Worry Baby" by the Beach Boys seemingly wafting in the breeze from house to house through open windows, the whole experience was, for Webb, like being in some kind of warm, languid, impossibly optimistic dream.

In 1964, American innocence was embodied in the Beach Boys. With

John F. Kennedy's assassination still resonant and the Vietnam War growing in intensity, songs about cars, girls, and surfing provided a welcome escape to simpler, happier times. And it was for that very reason—the overwhelming desire to also create music for a living—that Jimmy Webb was where he wanted to be, *needed* to be: a mere two-hour drive from Hollywood.

During those magical moments, when all seemed so right with the world, as Webb allowed his mind to drift along with the soothing sounds of one of the biggest bands in the world he was, instead, unknowingly listening to something even he could never have imagined: a highly paid group of hired musicians sitting in for the Beach Boys who would soon help *him*—a skinny kid from the sticks with absolutely no music industry connections—generate an astounding eight Grammy Awards all in one night.

✳

In the late summer of 1965, in a poor inner-city neighborhood of Los Angeles known as Watts—only twenty geographic miles yet worlds away from the insular music industry enclaves of Hollywood and Beverly Hills—a California Highway Patrol motorcycle officer out on routine duty arrested a driver for possible drunk driving. Though it was seemingly an ordinary traffic stop, on this occasion the officer was white, the motorist was black, and it was a steamy August afternoon at a time when racial tensions across America were already reaching a boiling point, especially in this predominantly African-American area.

With one thing quickly leading to another, as various locals gathered in rising anger, the worst-case scenario became a frightening reality for all: an ugly full-scale riot broke out. The residents of Watts had simply had enough. Fires, looting, and gunfire burst forth onto mile after mile of neighboring streets, shutting down a large portion of the city.

After nearly a week of violence, thirty-four people lay dead. And over a thousand more were injured, many severely. Hundreds of buildings were damaged or destroyed. Thriving business districts, their stores mostly white owned, were burned to the ground. Eventually, the National Guard cordoned off a vast region of South Los Angeles, further underscoring the social, economic, and geographic divide among the races. Many wondered whether the biggest city in California—or, for that matter, whether the country itself—would ever be the same.

Following all the tumult, with black/white relations in Los Angeles at their most divisive, a sweet-singing African-American vocal group with big aspirations and an infectious optimism seemed to somehow magically spring forth from all the devastation in Watts. They called themselves the Versatiles, and their sound and image were smooth, refreshing, and non-controversial—a welcome, if unwitting, antidote for a city at war with itself. But what this quintet *really* wanted was a record deal.

During the early-to-mid-Sixties, few major black pop music acts came out of Los Angeles. Whether for reasons of proximity, musical style, or simple opportunity, the Hollywood-based record labels mostly seemed uninterested. There were exceptions, of course, such as Sam Cooke, the Platters, and the Phil Spector–produced Ronettes, but the studios were, in the main, the provinces of white singers. Most popular black recording artists at the time worked elsewhere, such as Detroit, New York, and Memphis.

Those cities, along with Nashville, also each had their own versions of the Wrecking Crew. In the Motor City, a disparate group of local musicians hired by Motown Records founder Berry Gordy collectively came to be known as the Funk Brothers. Unbeknownst to the public, just as with their LA counterparts, these Detroit-based freelancers (who became the in-house Motown "band"—a clever, if questionable, way for the label to sidestep the local musician's union) played virtually all the instruments on the lion's share of a massive number of recordings. From Smokey Robinson's "Shop Around" to the Supremes' "Stop! In the Name of Love" to the Temptations' "Ball of Confusion," the mostly African-American Funk Brothers provided the backing on countless soul hits, with standouts like James Jamerson and Bob Babbitt on bass; Johnny Griffith, Earl Van Dyke, and Joe Hunter on keyboards; Eddie Willis, Joe Messina, and Robert White on guitar; William "Benny" Benjamin, Richard "Pistol" Allen, and Uriel Jones on drums; and Jack Ashford and Eddie "Bongo" Brown on percussion.

By the mid-Sixties, with the locus of pop music having permanently shifted from the busy streets of Manhattan to sunny Los Angeles (which had become the undisputed recording Mecca for making it big on mainstream

Top 40 radio), New York still managed to garner—at least for a while—its fair share of important sessions, too. Well-known artists like Roberta Flack, the Four Seasons, Tom Jones, Fats Domino, the Rascals, Jackie Wilson, and Dionne Warwick all cut the bulk of their work there. The most prominent players on these sessions regularly included AFM Local 82 members like Chuck Rainey and Anthony Jackson on bass; Paul Griffin, Artie Butler, and Richard Tee on keyboards; Al Caiola, Eric Gale, Vinnie Bell, and Carl Lynch on guitar; Grady Tate, Gary Chester, Bernard "Pretty" Purdie, Jimmy Johnson, and Donald McDonald on drums; and Ralph MacDonald and Specs Powell on percussion.

With Memphis home to famed label and studio combos like Stax/Volt, Hi!/Royal, American Sound Recordings, and Sun Records, artists such as Elvis Presley, Wilson Pickett, Otis Redding, Al Green, Booker T. & the MGs, Isaac Hayes, and the Staple Singers made this riverside port—often referred to as "Soulsville, USA"—their recording home. That city's first-call session players through AFM Local 71 included Mike Leach, Jerry Scheff, Leroy Hodges, Duke Bardwell, Emory Gordy, Jr., and Donald "Duck" Dunn on bass; Bobby Woods, Charles Hodges, Booker T. Jones, Dan Penn, and Glen D. Hardin on keyboards; Steve Cropper, Teenie Hodges, John Wilkinson, Tommy Cogbill, and James Burton (who also often sat in with the Wrecking Crew in LA) on guitar; Gene Crispian, Ronnie Tutt, Howard Grimes, and Al Jackson on drums; and the renowned Memphis Horns—Andrew Love and Wayne Jackson.

Made famous in song by the Lovin' Spoonful, Nashville also had its so-called cats—better known in country music circles as the A-Team. These studio pros and AFM Local 257 members played with everyone from Roy Orbison to Tammy Wynette to Patsy Cline—even with Bob Dylan on his *Nashville Skyline* album. The A-Team's ranks included, among others, Bob Moore on bass; Hargus "Pig" Robbins and Floyd Cramer on keyboards; Ray Edenton, Hank "Sugarfoot" Garland, Harold Bradley, Fred Carter, Jr., and Grady Martin on guitar; Buddy Harman on drums; Pete Drake on pedal steel; Charlie McCoy on harmonica; Boots Randolph on sax; Tommy Jackson on fiddle; and the Jordanaires on backing vocals.

But back in Los Angeles, some much-needed good fortune and the presence of the Wrecking Crew were about to come the Versatiles' way. With a vibrant vocal style and a fresh-scrubbed, charismatic presence that uniquely appealed to both black *and* white audiences, the group's five members (three men, two women) were an act that fit the times perfectly. An ensemble just *waiting* to happen.

With the buzz surrounding their live gigs coming to the attention of Marc Gordon, an up-and-coming young artist manager who had recently left his job as the West Coast head of Motown Records, he decided to check things out. Catching the Versatiles' show one evening, he liked what he saw. In fact, he more than liked it. The group had the rare potential to transcend racial lines, to become breakout national stars. They just needed some good songs to sing, a few connections. And Gordon had just the guy in mind who could make it happen: Johnny Rivers.

Rivers, a small, intense, dark-haired man sporting an ever-so-fashionable goatee and soul patch (sans moustache), had become the hottest singer on the Sunset Strip just two years before by virtue of his storied live performances at Gazzarri's and the Whisky A Go-Go. Several Top 10 singles later, including "Memphis," "Mountain of Love," and "Seventh Son," Rivers had become a nationwide star.

Outside of his burgeoning singing career, Johnny Rivers also had his hands in a variety of other music-related pursuits. One of those endeavors included founding and owning a new record label called Soul City, where he planned to release not only all of his own recordings but those of other young musicians as well. Rivers knew firsthand that the really big money in the music business lay on the side of the labels and publishers. They had the cash and they had the control. It was all about power, baby. And with the newly formed Johnny Rivers Music as his publishing arm, the shrewd and ambitious young Louisiana transplant felt ready to join their ranks. Now all he needed was a talented first act to produce.

Within minutes of meeting with the Versatiles and their new manager, Johnny Rivers knew he had struck gold. The demo they played for him evidenced a vocal blend that was magnificent, soaring. Nothing like he had heard before. And the two women, well, they were simply gorgeous, a nice bonus for album covers. He signed the five singers on the spot.

Just two things were missing, Rivers thought, as the elated group practically danced their way out of his offices: a better name and a good first song to cut.

Marc Gordon, ever the opportunistic operator, figured that he would handle the song acquisition part of the equation. After all, if he could find the Versatiles a solid hit to sing, his 10 percent commission would get really meaningful really fast. And he had an idea. When he mentioned to Rivers one day that he knew an unusually gifted young kid who had a knack for writing songs with killer lyrics and irresistible melodies, they decided to drop in on an unsuspecting Jimmy Webb.

"Jimmy, this is Johnny Rivers," Gordon said. "He's got a new record label and publishing company. How would you like to work for him?"

Webb didn't have to be asked twice.

Negotiating a quick and cheap buyout of the blooming songwriter's low-paying contract from the tiny mom-and-pop recording studio on Melrose where he'd been working, Rivers landed the skilled tunesmith he so desperately needed. More so, Rivers now owned the publishing rights to Jimmy Webb's growing catalog of songs. A cache of material that would soon help propel the Versatiles—newly renamed the 5th Dimension—to worldwide acclaim.

✳

At a little before seven on a beautiful Tuesday evening in mid-July of 1966—the summer after the Watts Riots and a year before the Summer of Love—a handful of the Wrecking Crew's best began to assemble inside Western 3 for what was expected to be a typical three-hour Johnny Rivers recording session: Hal Blaine behind the drum kit, ready to tell some of his endless supply of hilarious Borscht Belt–like stories and jokes ("What do you call a guy who hangs around with musicians? A drummer!"); Joe Osborn with his timeworn Fender Jazz Bass propped across his lap; Tommy Tedesco placidly parked in a folding chair next to an army of guitars pulled from the trunk of his car; and Larry Knechtel, half-hidden behind a grand piano, watching, waiting.

As they all settled into position, a terrified nineteen-year-old kid timidly pushed his way through a set of heavy, soundproof wooden studio doors in order to join them.

"Hey, good to see you, man," came a quick hello from Johnny Rivers himself.

Now looking to update his sound, Rivers wanted to become a little more contemporary, deeper. His new album would be called *Changes*, and he had already zeroed in on the person who could help him get there.

"Everybody, this is Jimmy Webb, the songwriter I've been telling you about."

Squinting through a pair of thick black-framed eyeglasses underneath the glare of the studio's fluorescent lighting, Webb self-consciously gave a quick half wave. The musicians simply nodded in return.

"Jimmy, have a seat over at the piano and we'll do a quick run-through of your new song before we roll tape."

A palpable coolness immediately fell over the room.

Western 3 only *had* one piano. And Larry Knechtel, one of the most esteemed keyboard men in the business, was currently sitting behind it, looking considerably less than pleased about the prospect of having to vacate his seat, especially for some goofy-looking kid he had never heard of.

"Mind if I give it a go for a minute?" Webb nervously asked a stone-faced Knechtel, who silently rose and stepped to the side.

As Webb assumed his position behind the large Steinway grand, he could feel the stares of the other session players cutting right through him. Who does this guy think he is, taking the place of the great Larry Knechtel?

This is crazy, Webb thought. They know it and I know it. Larry can absolutely play me under the table. They all can. But if that's the way Johnny wants it...

That was indeed the way Johnny wanted it. He was convinced that Webb, being the song's writer, had just the right feel for how to play it.

But before Webb could give the situation any further thought—or dash back out of the room—the producer Lou Adler called out from the control booth through the talk-back speaker, "Okay, guys, take one."

Too late now, the show was on.

Hal Blaine counted off "one-two-three-four" and the musicians simultaneously launched into playing the notes written on the charts sitting before them. Notes that a devastated Jimmy Webb had painstakingly—and painfully—crafted through a haze of tears and self-recrimination in the wake of his recent breakup with his beloved girlfriend, Susan. A heartfelt tune he had written called "By the Time I Get to Phoenix."

While Webb worked his way through the chords and lead lines he had practiced so many times before, the rest of the musicians began to take notice as they kept pace. Not bad, they thought. Not only did the kid seem to have some decent piano chops, but also the song itself had a melodic sophistication and lyrical poignancy that set it apart from much of what often passed through the studios. Even Larry Knechtel began to warm to the idea, watching over Jimmy's shoulder as he played, offering occasional alternate chording suggestions. Maybe Johnny was right—maybe this teenager really did have the goods.

"Ah, that was great, just great," enthused Rivers with a big smile as he and the musicians rolled to a stop.

By the time the session ended that evening, Jimmy Webb was both exhausted and exhilarated. Tired to the bone from the anxiety borne of sitting in with the exalted Wrecking Crew. But also excited to finally have one of his songs—a *good* song, he thought—recorded by one of the biggest singers in the business. That's what songwriters live for. Sure, the Supremes had recorded his "My Christmas Tree" the year before for their holiday album, but that song was sort of a throwaway, certainly not his best work. This session, though, was the *real* deal. And for better or worse, it was now in the can.

"Okay, we got it, guys. Come and listen to the playback," Adler announced.

And just when Webb thought his day couldn't get any more overwhelming, he was in for a further surprise. Standing up from the piano to stretch his arms and legs, Webb took a casual glance toward the control booth window, where he noticed what appeared to be a familiar face. A guy standing against the back wall with very short dirty blond hair who looked kind of like Steve McQueen, the movie star.

Nah, it couldn't be, Webb thought. But it was.

Squeezing his way into the already-crowded booth along with Hal and the other guys to listen to the completed version of his song, Jimmy Webb was amazed to see the famous actor in the flesh. Probably a friend of Johnny's from all the wild celebrity-filled shows down at the Whisky, he guessed.

As he inched past the stolid McQueen, star of such major motion pictures as *The Great Escape* and *The Sand Pebbles*, Webb couldn't help but notice the bluest eyes he had ever seen. Blue eyes that seemed to silently take in everything, just like in the movies.

Man, this is something, Webb mused, feeling like he was going to burst from all his good fortune. I've just played a session on my own song with the best studio musicians in the world, and now I'm standing next to Steve McQueen of all people. What could be any greater than this? For the teenage Jimmy Webb and the men in the Wrecking Crew, however, the best was by far yet to come.

✳

By the spring of 1967, with the Vietnam War, campus unrest, and racial strife increasingly preoccupying American youth, Top 40 radio playlists also began to take a more serious turn. Innocent fare like "Everybody Loves a Clown" by Gary Lewis and the Playboys and "Cherish" by the Association gradually ceded airtime to more provocative social anthems like "Respect" by Aretha Franklin and "All You Need Is Love" by the Beatles. Songs increasingly needed to have a message, some *meaning*—a commercial reality not lost on either Johnny Rivers or the 5th Dimension.

One day, in the absence of Rivers (who was overseas attending a music festival), Jimmy Webb stopped by Sound Recorders at the corner of Yucca and Argyle in Hollywood with an idea. The 5th Dimension were coming to the studio to rehearse and he wanted to try out a buoyant little number for them he had just written called "Up, Up and Away." Inspired by the exhilaration he had experienced during a hot-air balloon ride back home in

San Bernardino, Webb felt certain his creation would be a success. But with happy, hopeful lyrics and a bouncy, hook-laden melody, it seemed better suited for *The Lawrence Welk Show* than for a soul group launching a career. The 5th Dimension wanted relevance, to catch the ear of a changing pop marketplace. A song about a balloon wasn't exactly what they had in mind.

"Sounds more like an album cut than a single to me," observed Billy Davis, diplomatically, as Webb demoed the song on piano. Davis, the group's lead male singer, always leaned more toward R & B anyway.

"It's just too pretty, Jimmy."

But Webb would not—could not—be deterred. Time to bring in the heavy guns. A call went out to Hal Blaine, Joe Osborn, Tommy Tedesco, and Larry Knechtel from the Wrecking Crew to come over and cut the basic instrumental tracks. With Webb encouraging them to "let it fly," Tedesco, in particular, came with his "A" game, adding a series of improvised, flamenco-flavored flourishes on the acoustic gut-string guitar that really helped knock the song out of the park.

Webb then one-upped himself, scoring a complex, lilting vocal arrangement that actually *sounded* like a beautiful balloon in flight. By the time they recorded the last of the vocals, the 5th Dimension stood in awe. After listening to the final playback, now complete with a full string section, they knew Webb was right all along. "Up, Up and Away" was definitely like nothing else on the radio, but in a good way. A very good way.

Having played on literally thousands of recording sessions to this point, the Wrecking Crew also knew a surefire hit when they heard one. You couldn't always tell, but every once in a while, when all the pieces came together, a song could take on a life of its own. "Be My Baby" was like that. "Good Vibrations," too.

"It's got 'hit' written all over it," Blaine said. "A real winner."

"Up, Up and Away" did indeed become a hit, worldwide. In addition to being rush-released as a single, it also became the title of the group's first album. Both quickly went gold, in the process rocketing the 5th Dimension to international fame. Webb, too, became *the* hot songwriter with whom every Hollywood music producer suddenly wanted to get cozy.

But despite the heady success of "Up, Up and Away"—something most songwriters and musicians could only dream about—the astoundingly fruitful collaboration between Jimmy Webb and the Wrecking Crew had barely even begun.

*

In the fall of 1967, at the same time the 5th Dimension began their climb to stardom, Wrecking Crew guitarist Glen Campbell was in the process of taking some serious steps of his own. In a last-ditch attempt to jump-start his flagging solo career as a singer, Campbell's label, Capitol Records, assigned fellow Wrecking Crew member (and ace pianist) Al DeLory to produce Glen's next—and maybe last—recording. "See what you can do with him," came the word from on high.

Campbell's previous personal recording efforts had done poorly. Try as he might, he'd never been higher than number forty-six on the pop singles charts. He'd had a couple of flirtations with the country charts that did a little better. But after five frustrating years, Capitol was running out of patience. With several promising new artists on their roster like Bobbie Gentry, the Stone Poneys (featuring a young Linda Ronstadt), and a psychedelic rock group out of San Jose called People! label execs had other, better ways to spend their time and money.

Just when Glen Campbell needed it most, however, serendipity—or perhaps divine intervention—appeared from an unlikely source. Coming into Western 3 one day for another session as a sideman with the Wrecking Crew, Glen happened to notice a record album lying on a table. It was by Johnny Rivers and contained a track that caught his eye called "By the Time I Get to Phoenix." Now that's an interesting title, Campbell thought. Is it about the city or that bird that rose from all the ashes?

Out of curiosity, having gigged around the Phoenix area many times over the years, Glen decided to give the song a quick spin on the studio's turntable. What could it hurt? Didn't they used to say back home that a stone unturned is opportunity lost? Or something like that.

Within seconds of listening, the one-day Rhinestone Cowboy experienced a life-altering epiphany. A feeling he'd never had before. He knew—

instinctively *knew*—that this semi-obscure album track was going to be not only his next single but also his first bona fide pop hit.

Rushing to meet with DeLory in Capitol's Studio B the next day, Campbell couldn't wait to share his discovery.

"I've found our song, Al."

With the help of fellow Wrecking Crew mates Hal Blaine, Carol Kaye, Al Casey, and Mike Deasy, "By the Time I Get to Phoenix" did in fact become Campbell's first pop success. Released in November, it nosed into the Top 40 at a respectable number twenty-six (with a number-two showing on the country charts), reinvigorating Campbell's shaky solo career in the nick of time. It also set the stage for an event so far-fetched, so surreal, that those involved could scarcely believe their good fortune.

✳

Back in 1961, as the soaring production costs for the infamous box-office dud *Cleopatra* finally pushed the 20th Century Fox Film Corporation in West LA to the verge of bankruptcy, the powers-that-be made a momentous decision. They decided to do the unthinkable and sell off a good share of the studio's historic back lot, the filming location of such classics as *The Ox-Bow Incident, Gentlemen Prefer Blondes,* and *Carousel.* Striking a deal with developers, Fox parted with 180 prime acres of land, which became a futuristic "city within a city" called Century City.

Easily the most prominent addition to this new office, retail, and residential development occurred in 1966 with the construction of the nineteen-story, crescent-shaped Century Plaza Hotel. The five-star hostelry immediately became the luxurious home to a variety of awards shows and also a popular social destination among politicians and celebrities. The *Apollo 11* astronauts were enthusiastically welcomed back there from the moon at a big ballroom ceremony by President Richard Nixon. Old Hollywood stars like Cary Grant, Bob Hope, and Debbie Reynolds often dined in the swanky Lobby Court restaurant. And perhaps most infamously, in 1967, President Lyndon Johnson spoke at a Democratic fundraiser at the hotel while ten thousand raging Vietnam War demonstrators clashed in a bloody melee out front with thirteen hundred club-swinging riot police.

But on February 29, 1968, all was glory and good cheer. It was the tenth annual Grammy Awards ceremony, grandly taking its first bow on center stage at the opulent hotel. Always a much-anticipated event among music business insiders, the show had also in recent years become a highly rated TV special, too. Though not broadcast live, the NBC-TV show, called *The Best on Record,* served to spotlight the most important performers and categories. And with home viewership levels providing a direct stimulus to record sales in retail stores across America (and, for that matter, around the world), the Grammy Awards had essentially evolved into a lucrative promotional vehicle for everyone involved.

As Hal Blaine walked through the Century Plaza's front doors that evening, he couldn't have felt more proud. He'd come such a long way from his early days playing drums around town for the Diamonds, Jan & Arnie, and other fledgling LA rock and rollers. Now here he was at the Grammys. Blaine (just like the rest of the Wrecking Crew) had played on a covey of songs in '67 that were nominated in a variety of categories, so chances were good that his efforts might win at least something. Of course, as a hired drummer he wouldn't actually qualify to take home a statuette of his own. But still, just to be in the company of so many great talents all in one room, with the whole world looking on, was an unbelievable thrill all by itself.

Once the ceremonies got under way it quickly became clear that this was no ordinary Grammy show. Something was in the air, the smell of an upset. Powerhouse performances on nominated albums like *Sgt. Pepper's Lonely Hearts Club Band* by the Beatles and songs like "A Whiter Shade of Pale" by Procol Harum were getting overlooked.

Stunning the crowd, three songs, two by solo artists and one by a group—"By the Time I Get to Phoenix," "Ode to Billie Joe," and "Up, Up and Away" by Glen Campbell, Bobbie Gentry, and the 5th Dimension, respectively—virtually swept the pop categories.

Further, in an improbable coup, the 5th Dimension's version of "Up, Up and Away" didn't just win; it *dominated* by earning awards for record of the year, song of the year, best performance by a vocal group, best contemporary single, and best contemporary group performance. Another recording of the tune, by the Johnny Mann Singers, also got the nod as best performance by a chorus.

But the ripple effects of young Jimmy Webb's magic pen didn't stop there.

As the rest of the Grammys were announced, "By the Time I Get to Phoenix" won Glen Campbell the awards for best male vocal performance and best contemporary male solo vocal performance. Campbell also walked off with awards for the best country and western recording and best country and western male solo vocal performance for another song he had cut almost a year before called "Gentle on My Mind" (also featuring the Wrecking Crew on the instrumentation). Quite a showing for a guy who came within one more failed 45 of getting dropped by his label.

In a memorable aw-shucks-style acceptance speech, the prolific Campbell bashfully thanked "all the people I've backed up on guitar over the years for their votes," providing the knowing audience with its biggest laugh of the evening.

Jimmy Webb, for his part, ran up to the stage so many times during the show that he thought he was in a dream. And in an act of generosity and gratitude not always on display in an industry known for its me-first myopia, Webb singled out a beaming Hal Blaine from the podium, asking the audience to give the well-respected drummer a round of applause for all his contributions.

At final tally, the Wrecking Crew's instrumental prowess supplied the musical foundation for no fewer than nine Grammy Awards that February evening. And if people hadn't heard of Jimmy Webb before the show, they sure as heck had afterward. Writing two songs that generate eight Grammys in one night can do that. The kid who used to unknowingly listen to the Wrecking Crew on his transistor radio late into the night back home in San Bernardino had done all right.

Classical Gas

I've been working on this ... idea for orchestrated rock and roll.
—MIKE POST

By 1967, network television, like the pop music charts, had begun to change. Slowly at first, perhaps, but a metamorphosis nonetheless. The social and cultural voices of a big segment of young America—the so-called New Left—were simply getting too loud to ignore.

Programming executives at the Big Three (ABC, CBS, and NBC) knew that continuing to offer up a steady diet of silly sitcoms about flying nuns, maladjusted hillbillies, and dim-witted secret agents could only last so long. With the country at war, rioting in the streets, and changing views on sex and drugs, those in their teens and twenties now wanted more. They hungered for television that would finally reflect *their* realities. And just as in radio, advertisers—the lifeblood of all three TV networks—wanted to reach as many young people as possible. Those under thirty, so the theory went, were the ones most easily swayed into buying more stuff.

Among the new TV entries that year was an innocent-sounding variety show called *The Smothers Brothers Comedy Hour.* Starring the folk-singing comedy team of Tommy and Dickie Smothers—famous for their immortal sibling rivalry routine, "Mom Always Liked You Best"—the series premiered on CBS in February of 1967 (as a mid-season replacement) to instant ratings success and widespread acclaim. For its part, the network loved having a new Top 20 program that appealed to a more youthful demographic, one that could perhaps give the number one–rated *Bonanza* some real competition on Sunday nights for a change. CBS execs did not, however, love all the controversy that came with it.

Irreverent from the start, *The Smothers Brothers Comedy Hour* pointedly poked fun at just about every American institution possible, from church to government to motherhood. It was nothing like *The Red Skelton Show* or *The Andy Williams Show*, but that was all very much by design. That was the old way of doing things. Sly wit, with a decidedly left-leaning political bent, all couched within a highly entertaining, fast-paced presentation, was the new order of the day, giving the program a unique, almost subversive appeal, especially among the young.

Pete Seeger, a musician and ardent civil rights activist long blacklisted on network television, appeared during one taping, for example, singing a protest song called "Waist Deep in the Big Muddy," sparking an immediate uproar among the censors. The lyrics, it seemed clear, presented a not-so-subtle allegory for President Johnson's continued failure to end the war in Vietnam. A hot-button issue if there ever was one in an increasingly polarized country.

Further pushing the boundaries of the era's broadcasting standards, the series also featured a regular segment called "Share a Little Tea with Goldie," during which resident hippie Goldie O'Keefe (played by actress Leigh French) parodied afternoon advice shows for housewives, offering "helpful" household hints laced with double entendres about sex and drugs. At the time, the word "tea"—for those in the know—was counterculture code for marijuana. CBS never did catch on to that one.

All tame stuff by today's standards, but a very big no-no in the mid-Sixties. Anti-war rhetoric and drug references, no matter how veiled, were a quick way to stir up the public and cause corporate advertisers to blanch. In other words, it made the Establishment react. Which, of course, was just what the Smothers Brothers had in mind.

Besides Tommy Smothers (the act's driving force), one of the other main architects of this mixed bag of groundbreaking comedic anarchy was a mild-mannered folk musician and satirist named Mason Williams. Something of an eccentric balladeer, the Oklahoma-raised Williams, in addition to possessing an offbeat, well-honed sense of humor, was also an accomplished songwriter and classically influenced guitarist. The Kingston Trio, Glenn Yarbrough, and other prominent folk artists covered several of Williams's compositions in the early Sixties.

Traveling in the same LA folkie circles, the Smothers Brothers soon became aware of Williams's quirky comedy songs. Knocked out by what they heard, they decided to record several of his compositions for their *Tour de Farce* album, on which Williams also backed them up on twelve-string guitar and five-string banjo. The relationship flourished, with the brothers subsequently taking him on tour to play various instruments onstage behind their routines. And, as an added bonus, by virtue of watching the duo painstakingly work out their material in the dressing room before each night's show ("Slow down here, Dick—don't step on my line"), Williams quickly absorbed the delicate art of crafting first-rate comedy dialogue. Valuable lessons he would soon carry forward as the new head writer for *The Smothers Brothers Comedy Hour,* where, among other things, Williams would eventually give future "Wild and Crazy Guy" Steve Martin his first entertainment industry job as a member of the writing staff.

As the red-hot show began its second season in the fall of 1967, an executive at Warner/Reprise Records—delighted to have had several of his label's newest acts make breakthrough appearances on the weekly telecast (the First Edition, the Electric Prunes, and the Association among them)—asked Tommy if there was anything he could do for *him.* "Yes," Smothers replied, "I think Mason would like to make a record."

And with that, Mason Williams—a little-known folk musician who couldn't seem to write any song lyrics that didn't come out just plain funny—suddenly had a very serious recording contract on his hands with one of the most important record labels in the world. Now he just needed to find some people to help him finally make an album that would sell.

*

Having been around the music business for some time, Mason Williams knew he needed to come up with something special this time around. The new deal with Reprise was a real cherry, something to make the most of. Major labels liked hits; expected them, even. And Williams wanted one, too. His earlier folk albums, while well crafted, had found only niche markets and little or no radio airplay. Though he had at least a hundred songs—maybe closer to two hundred—sitting around in various stages of completion, none seemed quite right to help him make the transition from relative obscurity to the Top 40.

Noodling around one day on his favorite old acoustic guitar, a vintage Stella he had once purchased from a friend for the princely sum of thirteen dollars, Williams stumbled across a lick that particularly jumped out at him. Building on it, he began to expand an intricate, classical-style finger-picking progression into the semblance of what he thought just might make a catchy song. At least, he figured, it might help him stand out during parties when people passed around the guitar. Girls liked that.

Living at the time with Tommy Smothers in an apartment on Kings Road in West Hollywood (both men were recently divorced), Williams continued to practice the embryonic tune over and over at home while Smothers offered feedback along the way. As it took shape, it became clear that the piece of music had unusual potential. "You've got to record that," Tommy said.

With the mid-November recording date for Mason Williams's new album drawing near, Ken Kragen, the Smothers Brothers' co-manager (who, with partner Ken Fritz, also managed Williams), put in a call to a hot young producer he had recently worked with named Mike Post. Originally, by trade, a Wrecking Crew third-stringer on guitar, the twenty-four-year-old Post had a natural ear for song structure, with a special knack for creating just the right production values and arrangements. Most recently he had produced the Kragen/Fritz-managed First Edition's debut album (featuring a young Kenny Rogers), whose intensely psychedelic "Just Dropped In (to See What Condition My Condition Was In)"—featuring Hal Blaine and Earl Palmer on double drums—would soon become the surprise hit of 1968. And Post came complete with the imprimatur of none other than

Frank Sinatra's mega-hit-making producer Jimmy Bowen, who was Post's boss at Amos Productions. That endorsement alone carried its weight in gold. If the kid's good enough for the guy who put the Chairman of the Board back on the top of the charts, well then...

After exchanging a few quick pleasantries, Ken Kragen got down to business.

"We love what you did for us with the First Edition," he told Post. "Now, one of our other acts, Mason Williams, also just signed a record deal with Warner/Reprise. And the guy is a *genius*. Would you be interested in producing him?"

Minutes later Kragen had his man.

A couple of weeks down the line, as Mason Williams and Mike Post sat across from each other over at United Recorders, the newly hired, supremely confident young producer had but one question on his mind.

Williams had just run through the instrumental song he'd been working on—now called "Classical Gasoline"—and Post liked it. He also thought he knew a way to really bring it to life. Maybe even make a hit out of it. But first he wanted to assess the guitarist's vision for the tune. Being a fellow musician, Post knew all too well about the need to tread lightly when it came to someone else's artistic handiwork.

"So, Mason, how do you see this song going?" Post gently inquired.

"Piano, bass, drums, and guitar, I guess."

"Well," Post continued, "I've been working on this thing, this idea for orchestrated rock and roll. I think it might really work on your song."

Williams seemed skeptical but game.

"Uh, okay, if you think so. We could try it."

Soon, however, any hesitancy Mason Williams may have felt about someone tinkering with his prized guitar composition had changed into nothing short of unbridled admiration. Mike Post, the young producer he'd never even heard of a few weeks before, simply took hold of the now retitled "Classical Gas" and lit the whole damn thing on fire.

Realizing that the song needed a middle section or "bridge" in order to provide the listener with a respite from the repetitive (and signature) melody, Post drew inspiration from his love for the work of the late German composer Richard Wagner, something he grew up listening to on the family record player. Taking the notion one step further, he decided to write the score for a rare instrument Wagner had invented back in the 1800s known as a tuben horn, something like a cross between a tuba and a trumpet. Its unique timbre came closest to resembling that of a French horn. Certainly not a sound found on contemporary pop radio in the 1960s. But to Post, that was exactly the point. It was *different.*

On November 14, 1967—the same day that the Monkees released their fourth album (*Pisces, Aquarius, Capricorn & Jones Ltd.*) and *The New York Times'* Howard Taubman wrote a presciently positive review of a little-known Off-Broadway play called *Hair*—key Wrecking Crew members, including Jim Gordon (drums), Mike Deasy (guitar), Larry Knechtel (piano), Al Casey (guitar), and Gary Coleman (percussion), took their places in United's oversized Studio A, along with a couple of dozen string and horn players.

After a quick read-through of the charts written by Post and his co-arranger Al Capps (who had previously arranged "Woman, Woman" for the Union Gap), the musicians, to a man, could tell that this was not going to be the usual three-chord rock-and-roll date. No sir, not with those sophisticated passages it wasn't. Coleman, for one, heard several of the guys commenting on how the arrangement was "more involved" than usual. The ubiquitous Larry Knechtel, one of two pianists hired for the date, could feel the electricity in the air.

As the engineer called from the booth, "Roll tape, take one," Williams counted off "one-two-three-four," and began alternately strumming and finger-picking the song's delicate and doleful—almost unassuming—intro on his Cordova classical guitar (a recent gift from Tommy Smothers). The beautifully stylized piece sounded a bit like the work of famed Gypsy guitarist Django Reinhardt, with perhaps even a dash of the great Andrés Segovia thrown in for good measure. But it all came packaged within Williams's distinctive playing pattern and provided no hint whatsoever as to the power and majesty about to follow. With his trademark sense of humor intact, the poker-faced comedy writer clearly liked to play his sonic cards close to the vest.

But the second the drums, bass, piano, and other guitars—the Wrecking

Crew rhythm section—joined in a sense of urgency leaped forward. The ruse was now up; this song was going places.

A few bars further came the strings, bold and striking—building, building. Just as Post had envisioned. Back and forth they cajoled and seduced, begging the listener with all their sweetness and might to travel along toward an inevitable, crashing crescendo. The ultimate payoff came swiftly in a monumental moment of pure aural euphoria, with the song's soaring signature riff repeating over and over: *dee-dee-dee* dee dee dee.

And that wasn't nearly the end of it. When the battery of tuben horns finally burst forth during the bridge, it was lights-out, like the second coming of the Boston Pops Orchestra from the Charles River Esplanade on the Fourth of July. The song simply exploded, but in a different, wholly unexpected direction, abruptly changing keys from A-minor up to E-flat in the process, something Post referred to as "storm-trooper modulation."

As the sweat-soaked production eventually began to wind its way down with an equally delicate acoustic guitar outro, Mike Post knew he had a hit on his hands. Top 40, here we come. The horn and string arrangements he had co-written and produced had taken a pretty guitar piece and turned it into an absolute monster, an epic. And it didn't hurt, either, that the inspired, in-the-pocket drumming performance by his childhood pal Jim Gordon had maybe been Gordon's best work yet. In fact, all the musicians present—from the Wrecking Crew regulars on down to the violinists, cellists, and tuben-horn guys—had played a major part in creating a masterpiece.

Making his way out of the control booth, an obviously pleased Post headed straight for Williams. Time to get some feedback from the composer himself.

"What'd you think, Mason?"

In the understatement of the day, the low-key Williams turned to Post and said what everybody else in the room was already thinking.

"Jeez, man, that was *something*."

* * * * *

After hearing the exciting news about Mason Williams's big studio triumph on "Classical Gas," Tommy Smothers very much wanted to check out the new record for himself. He felt a strong sense of pride in the song *and* in his close friend, having been there every step of the way—from cradle to lathe, so to speak.

Stopping by United's Studio A, where Post and his engineers were busy working on the final mastering and acetate cutting, Smothers poked his head in the door. He had been around enough during the preproduction phase that everybody was used to seeing the now-famous TV star in their midst.

"Hey, guys, mind if I give the playback a listen?"

Post, understandably proud of his musical achievement, was happy to oblige. He promptly asked his engineer to cue up "Classical Gas" on the reel-to-reel tape deck. This would be the first actual test of its appeal on an outside set of ears, piquing everyone's curiosity.

But as the recording began to play through the control booth's state-of-the art monitors—particularly as it moved into the bridge section, Mike Post's shining moment—it gradually became clear that something was amiss: Smothers didn't seem to be digging the tune at all.

When the roughly three-minute playback finished, the room fell quiet, thick with anticipation. What had gone wrong?

Smothers finally broke the silence. "That's the most overarranged piece of shit I've ever heard in my life," he declared. "Mason's song has been obliterated."

For a self-admitted "cocky little guitar player" like Mike Post, who, when scared, came on the strongest, those were fighting words. Pure and simple. Nobody was going to walk into the middle of one of his productions and talk to him that way. Nobody.

Young, ego-driven, and not afraid to speak his mind—especially about something that he believed in so strongly—Post immediately wheeled on a surprised Smothers and said, "Get the fuck out of my studio."

And Smothers did.

But, within twenty-four hours, something miraculous happened: Tommy Smothers completely changed his mind. And was big enough to admit it. After talking things over with Williams, Smothers had decided that the over-the-top production really was the right way to go. It had just been an initial shock to the system, that's all. He told Post as much, with both men quickly putting the brief flare-up behind them. The important thing now, they all agreed, was to get the song some much-needed exposure.

With the Smothers Brothers graciously allowing Mason Williams to perform "Classical Gas" several times on *The Smothers Brothers Comedy Hour* over the next few months, it finally began to catch on with the public. Just as season two of the increasingly controversial show came to a close in June of '68, the record finally slid into the upper reaches of the Hot 100. Seven weeks later, "Classical Gas" had blown by virtually all comers on its way to number two, held off from the top spot only by the Doors' "Hello, I Love You."

But the momentum didn't stop there. "Classical Gas" would soon go on to win three Grammy Awards, two for Williams and one for Post. And, because of the massive amount of airplay the song continuously received, even after falling off the charts, it would eventually become nothing less than the most played instrumental in the *history* of American radio. Not bad for a homegrown acoustic guitar riff initially written in humble hopes of attracting some female attention at parties—but recorded with a little help, of course, from the Wrecking Crew.

15

Wichita Lineman

It's not finished yet. There's no middle part.
—JIMMY WEBB

At a little before 9:30 A.M. on a mid-August day in 1967, as Kerry Chater pulled his well-traveled powder blue Dodge van into Columbia Records' parking lot just off Sunset Boulevard, he couldn't have been any happier. Having recently signed a much-coveted recording contract with the giant label as one of the members of an up-and-coming rock-and-roll band out of San Diego called the Union Gap, Chater and his four fellow musicians had finally hit the big time. After years of scuffling around, playing everything from tiny clubs and parties to a standing weekend residency at the local bowling alley, their hard work had paid off. They now had a major record deal, with a major producer.

With Chater ever the pragmatist, the sheer good fortune of it all made him chuckle for a moment, especially as he and the band got out of the van and took a peek at the vehicle parked next to them.

"Well, somebody's sure hit the jackpot," Chater commented.

Shining bright in the morning LA sun sat a stunning brand-new cherry red Ferrari 275 GTB, complete with a 300-horsepower engine and mobile telephone—a rare and expensive accessory in the pre–cell phone days of the 1960s.

"It belongs to Mark Lindsay of Paul Revere and the Raiders, in case you're wondering," a security guard said. "Beautiful, isn't it?"

Chater just smiled. He was never materially oriented; his goal—rather than to own an expensive Italian sports car—was to become the best songwriter and recording artist he could be, to carve out a long-standing successful career. It was the creative challenge of crafting the perfect song that fueled his dreams. And today was the day he planned to start taking it all to the next level.

But within seconds of walking through the control booth door of Columbia's cavernous Studio A, Chater knew something was wrong. Very wrong.

As a skilled musician, he had naturally brought along his favorite '64 Fender Precision Bass and Dual Showman amp, expecting to plug in and play. Just like he always did during the group's live gigs. But a quick glimpse through the double-thick glass that separated the booth from the main tracking room told him something different. In front of Chater's startled eyes sat what he momentarily thought to be someone else's session: a full fifteen-piece orchestra, along with several additional musicians he didn't recognize, including a drummer, a guitarist, a piano player, and some guy with a huge handlebar moustache cradling an electric bass.

Kerry Chater felt sick.

"Who are all those guys?" he asked the band's producer, Jerry Fuller, who was standing nearby.

"That's the orchestra," Fuller replied.

"But where do *we* set up?"

"Oh, you guys don't need to set up for this session. Just grab a seat and you can do the vocals later."

As Chater listened in dismay, not quite believing what he was hearing, his mind began to race. This session? You mean *our* band's session? The same band you recently came to see at the Quad Room in San Diego and sweet-talked into signing with you?

"Well, *I* need to set up," Chater responded.

"Kerry, I said that you guys don't have to set up your equipment today."

"No," said Chater, looking the producer square in the eye. "I told you that I *am*."

Kerry Chater wasn't about to let the first recording date of his major-label career slip away without actually playing on any of the songs. To hell with that. His name was going to be listed on the band's upcoming album cover as the bass player. It was now a matter of principle.

Grabbing his bass in one hand and his amp in the other, Chater instantly knew what he had to do. He was going to play anyway. Let them try to fire me, he thought. I have a contract. I'm already *in* the band, for crying out loud.

With necessity fast becoming the mother of sheer audacity, Chater strode out of the control booth and into Studio A's adjacent tracking room where all the musicians were sitting. Silently sliding onto an empty metal folding chair, the bassist hoped he might somehow just blend in. But it didn't really matter, anyway. He wasn't going anywhere. Most of Fuller's hand-picked Wrecking Crew guys looked Chater's way as he sat down but paid him little heed. They were hired to play, nothing more.

There was the other bass player, all right, the one with the distinctive facial hair. Next to him sat a tall, blond, cherubic-looking drummer. And on the other side of the drum kit, the lead guitar player wordlessly waited—a clean-cut guy of about thirty who seemed oblivious to Chater's presence. But then, by this point, with only four months left in yet another frustrating year without a hit record to call his own, Glen Campbell very much had other things on his mind.

At the end of the Union Gap's first recording session that day at Columbia Records, the confident, determined Chater felt a surge of satisfaction. He had managed to play on both songs cut during the three-hour date. True, he had disobeyed the band's producer in doing so, not the best idea for a guy just starting out. And he wasn't really sure if his bass work had actually even made it to tape. Too hard to tell in the huge sound mix swirling inside his headphones. But hey, he *had* played, and that's what mattered most. Chater could hold his head high. And one of the songs they laid down that morning, "Woman, Woman," took everyone by surprise a few months later by reaching number four on the national pop charts. The Union Gap had arrived.

But for Campbell, who had played guitar on the two Union Gap tracks along with fellow Wrecking Crew chums Jim Gordon on drums (a protégé of Hal Blaine's), Larry Knechtel on piano, and Ray Pohlman on bass, an "arrival" had yet to materialize. To Campbell, the session over at Columbia was just another day at the office. Something to keep the money coming in the door while he focused on what mattered to him more than anything in the world: becoming a major performing star in his own right. He had come too long and too far from his impoverished Arkansas roots to now settle for anything less.

It almost added insult to injury that Campbell had actually found "Woman, Woman" first. While he was listening one day to KGBS, the main country station in Los Angeles, something about the recording (performed by Nashville act Jimmy Payne) caught his ear. Maybe it was the mellifluous melody. Or maybe it was the fresh twist on the oft-told tale of a man's jealousy over a woman's wandering eye. Radio always did seem to have room for another good cheatin' song.

Thinking he might want to cut it for himself, Campbell gave the station a call and asked the disc jockey if he could get a copy of the record.

"Heck, you can have the forty-five right off our turntable. There's no interest in it anyway."

Campbell came away delighted with his find.

Though he figured "Woman, Woman" had a chance to make some real chart noise, it also presented a significant dilemma for the ambitious singer/guitarist. Campbell had been thinking about another tune he also wanted to put out, one that he almost liked better. And he knew that his good friend the producer Jerry Fuller—a guy who had helped him out plenty over the years—was looking for a strong first release for his new band, the Union Gap. So Campbell, after much deliberation, decided to go with "By the Time I Get to Phoenix" as his next single, giving "Woman, Woman" to Fuller.

Recorded just one day apart, in nearby studios, with several of the same Wrecking Crew musicians on board, the two songs provided strikingly different results. The Union Gap ended up with a career-defining smash; Glen Campbell did not.

To be fair, Campbell's version of "By the Time I Get to Phoenix" *did* become a mid-level pop hit—a big step in the right direction. And he was grateful. He knew firsthand how tough it could be getting any song into the Top 40. Plus, the single had done extremely well on the country charts. But it still wasn't good enough to establish him as a headlining act. You needed a Top 10 mainstream hit for that, maybe even a chart topper. Campbell desperately sought a new song, something so powerful, so transcendent, that it would catapult his career right out of session work for good. He wanted another "Phoenix," only better. And there was just one place to turn: Jimmy Webb.

✳

Sitting behind a funky green baby grand piano, high in the Hollywood Hills inside an old mansion that used to be the Philippine Embassy, Jimmy Webb heard his telephone ring. He had been sequestering himself lately in his recently purchased home in an effort to write some new material, all the while surrounded by a hard-partying group of live-in pals he jokingly referred to as "fifty of my closest friends."

"Jimmy, hey, it's Glen Campbell."

"Glen, good to hear from you, man! What's going on?"

"Well, DeLory and I are over here at Capitol cutting a new album and we're short on material. We need something really strong. Do you think you could write us another 'By the Time I Get to Phoenix'?"

Writing a hit song is hard enough, let alone one that is made-to-order. But Jimmy Webb liked a challenge. And he knew with Campbell's singing career on the rise, there might be some good publishing money in the deal.

"Okay," Webb finally said. "Let me see what I can come up with."

Despite his reservations about outright copying a previous hit, even his own, Webb thought perhaps that again using a geographical reference in the title might at least be a good place to start. And he had an idea.

Sometime earlier, Webb had been driving through an especially flat and remote area of northern Oklahoma, absorbing the almost surreal nature of its isolation and seemingly endless horizons. As he motored along, he had quite unexpectedly come across a utility worker perched high up on a telephone pole. The curious image of the anonymous, lone figure toiling away in a wilting heat in the middle of nowhere stuck in Webb's mind. What might be the circumstances of this solitary man's life?

Turning back to his piano after the phone call with Campbell, Webb spent the next two hours crafting a song around the mysterious individual he had encountered. Liking the sound and feel of what he had come up with, Webb asked Campbell and DeLory to swing by the house that evening to take a listen.

"It's not finished yet," Webb warned them as they sat down. "There's no middle part."

As Webb began playing and singing the basic verses of his new tune, Glen Campbell simply flipped. He immediately knew that this was the song he'd been hoping and praying for. A story of desolation and longing, it spoke to the human condition, the universal need for love. What could be better than that? And it was *real*. The imagery about singing in the wires and searching in the sun for overloads was out of this world. Campbell also felt it perfectly suited his voice and singing style. DeLory, too, agreed that the song was special. He particularly related to the lyrics, since his own uncle had coincidentally climbed poles for a California company.

"What's it called?" Campbell finally asked excitedly.

"'Wichita Lineman,'" came the reply.

∗

By the time the Union Gap's third single, "Lady Willpower," began powering its way up the pop charts in the summer of '68 (toward an eventual peak position of number two, just behind Hugh Masekela's jazzy Afropop instrumental version of "Grazing in the Grass"), internal dissension had begun to cripple the band. Producer Jerry Fuller, along with other Columbia execs, clearly now saw lead singer Gary Puckett as the star attraction. His soaring, world-class tenor vocals on a string of lush ballads had come to define the quintet's sound among the record-buying public. Puckett was also handsome, personable, and easy to work with—a marketing department's dream.

To compound matters, the group's name had finally, perhaps almost inevitably, morphed into the grandiloquent Gary Puckett and the Union Gap. Top billing for the top guy. Now even the *pretense* of a five-man democracy, something that had at least somewhat sustained them as a functioning unit over the past year, had dissolved. Kerry Chater, Paul Wheatbread, Dwight Bement, and Gary "Mutha" Withem had been effectively reduced to nothing more than Puckett's sidemen.

Naturally, none of this sat well with any of the four, especially Chater. His burning desire to be allowed to play bass on the songs the band recorded in the studio—and to have at least some of his compositions considered for release as singles—remained a major point of contention. He took pride in the quality of his musicianship and felt he could play alongside anyone, the Wrecking Crew included. After all, it was no fluke that he had long been the Union Gap's musical director on tour. That *had* to count for something.

But after more than a year of getting nowhere with Fuller (who had himself written or co-written several of the Union Gap's hits, a shrewd and lucrative move), Chater could take no more. He decided to schedule a one-on-one, sit-down meeting with Columbia's Vice-President of Artists & Repertoire, the man who happened to be Jerry Fuller's boss. Maybe this would finally help grease the wheels, Chater reasoned.

Sidestepping the label's carefully proscribed corporate chain of command, though, didn't come without potential fallout. Being branded a malcontent could quickly ruin a musician's career in the ultracompetitive Hollywood recording industry of the 1960s, where a hundred other guys were begging for a chance—*any* chance—to step in and take the instrument right out of your hands. For an increasingly angry and frustrated Kerry Chater, however, it was a shot he had to take.

A few days later, Chater found himself sitting in a chair in Jack Gold's office at Columbia, waiting on the other side of a large, cluttered desk as the busy head of the label's A & R department finished a call.

"Thanks for being patient," Gold said at last, swiveling toward Chater as he hung up the phone. "So, what can I do for you?"

"Well, I'm a writer and a musician here at Columbia. Very few of my songs are making the albums and I'm not playing bass on them, either. I don't think I'm even being considered."

Gold, squinting intently at Chater, paused for several seconds as if to scan his memory banks for the name of a long-forgotten girlfriend who had suddenly sidled up to him at a forty-year high school reunion.

"Ah ... it's the Union Gap, right?" he finally said.

"Right."

"Okay, good. Now, tell me, what was your first single and how many copies did it sell?"

"It was 'Woman, Woman' and a million-four," Chater replied.

"What about your second single?"

"'Young Girl' and it did around two million–six."

"And how many copies has your third single sold so far?"

"Roughly a million-two, I think."

When a band's first three singles sell well over a million copies each, the last thing any record label wants to do is screw up a winning formula. Especially when it involves some no-name bass player who just wants a bigger role.

After a brief, intense silence—with Chater looking at Gold and Gold looking at Chater—the label exec let out a sigh and wearily rose to his feet. He gestured toward the door.

"Get out of my office."

*

A number of months after Kerry Chater's dispiriting short-lived meeting with Jack Gold at Columbia, the musician decided to quit Gary Puckett and the Union Gap (just before they released their sixth and final Top 40 single, "This Girl Is a Woman Now"). Like Michael Clarke from the Byrds and Creed Bratton from the Grass Roots before him, Chater simply could take no more of being relegated to a bit role in his own band. Even with a new producer on board—Jerry Fuller having parted ways with Puckett over "artistic" differences—little room remained for Chater's contributions. His songs were still not being considered for the A-sides of singles and he found himself perpetually vacating his position as the band's bassist to whichever Wrecking Crew player the latest producer wanted to use in the studio.

With his unerring belief in his own abilities proving to be well founded, the multi-talented Chater, having cannily saved his money along the way, subsequently forged a highly successful career as a songwriter, penning a variety of hits for major country acts. For Kerry Chater, the agonizing days of watching from the sidelines were finally, mercifully, over.

✳

Wondrous things can sometimes happen in a recording studio when inspiration becomes contagious.

As Glen Campbell and Al DeLory worked on setting up the "Wichita Lineman" session inside Capitol A, something kept bothering bassist Carol Kaye. One of Campbell's longtime Wrecking Crew friends, the gifted player was on hand to help him cut this most important of records.

Having looked at the basic chord sheets, the experienced Kaye could see that the song lacked an identifiable lick to really kick things off, an attention getter. The biggest hits always had something to catch the listener's ear right up front. Just like she had created a couple of years before for Sonny Bono on "The Beat Goes On."

Drawing on her considerable jazz background, where less almost always meant more, Kaye worked out a simple six-note intro she thought just might do the trick.

"Glen, what would you think about opening the tune with something like this?"

As Kaye played the series of notes on her bass, Campbell thought it the perfect suggestion, immediately adding it to the song. Another great idea from a great player, one of the reasons he loved having her on his solo projects whenever possible.

But Campbell also loved the *tone* of her bass. It was a Danelectro, a solid-body electric bass guitar (made out of Masonite, of all things), often used in studios to add a "higher" sound than that of a standard Fender electric bass or an acoustic stand-up bass. In fact, some producers, like Brian Wilson, were well known for recording all three basses simultaneously, thereby "stacking" the distinctive qualities of each in order to provide the fattest possible bottom end.

In his own moment of inspiration, Campbell asked Kaye if he could borrow her Danelectro to play a "guitar" solo during that middle section Jimmy Webb had never finished. An unconventional but brilliant choice, the deep, resonant passage scored a direct hit, giving the song just the right quavering, tremolo-fueled melancholic interlude.

Almost like rural neighbors joyfully gathering at an old-fashioned barn raising, Jimmy Webb, too, chipped in with some delightfully appropriate inspiration of his own. Showing off his vintage Gulbranson church organ to Campbell one afternoon up at the house (during a few days off from the recording process while DeLory wrote the orchestral score), Webb mentioned how he thought the keyboard's unique bubbling sound evoked what he imagined to be the noise of signals passing through telephone wires. Campbell was so taken with the idea that he had a cartage company immediately come over and dismantle the monstrous keyboard and then reassemble it in the studio. Webb himself came into Capitol and played just three notes on it, over and over, during the song's fade. It proved to be the final piece to a masterfully executed production puzzle.

With Glen Campbell's plaintive vocals adding just the right touch of wistfulness and heartache, "Wichita Lineman" did indeed become the smash he had so desperately sought. There would be no more anonymous guitar playing on everybody else's hit records for this country boy. No more wondering whether he really had what it took to break out, to headline his own shows. The proof was all over America's radio dial.

As "Wichita Lineman" rocketed to number three on the national pop charts (and number one on the country charts), it became Glen Campbell's springboard to more success than even he dared to dream possible. The erstwhile Wrecking Crew guitarist with the off-the-chart skills and sunny, down-home disposition had finally crossed over into that rarefied realm where no session player had gone before: stardom.

16

MacArthur Park

I'll have that, Jimmy Webb.
—RICHARD HARRIS

As thirty-four-year-old Bones Howe zipped his way through morning Hollywood traffic one day during the fall of 1967 in his red Alpha Romeo convertible—an unexpected, middle-of-the-night Christmas gift from the four members of the Mamas & the Papas—the tall, rail-thin onetime Georgia Tech engineering grad had a lot on his mind. Having recently ventured out on his own as an independent producer, after years of being one of the best studio soundboard men in the business, Howe had just started work on the all-important second album by the 5th Dimension, *The Magic Garden*. Not wanting any kind of sophomore jinx to happen on his watch after their breakout success with the *Up, Up and Away* LP, Howe had been mentally mapping out each song, and he was eager to get to Western Recorders to continue cutting all the basic tracks with the Wrecking Crew.

Stopping off en route to pick up the songwriter Jimmy Webb, who had composed all of the music for the project, Howe saw Webb motioning for him to come inside.

"Bones, I've got the greatest idea for the Association," Webb said excitedly, sitting down at the piano in his living room. Howe's first solo production effort had been for that very band several months before, and the resulting album, *Insight Out,* had gone gold, with two Top 5 singles leading the charge ("Windy" and "Never My Love"). Juggling several projects at once, he was now in preproduction on their next LP, to be called *Birthday*.

"Listen to this," Webb enthused as he began to play. "It's written to be the entire side of an album. I'm calling it *The Cantata.*"

As Howe followed along, he found himself knocked out by the beauty and intricacy of the piece. Compositions like this just didn't come along every day. Not in a pop context, anyway.

"That is *fantastic,* Jimmy." Howe said as Webb finished. "I have a meeting later this week with the guys in the band at the studio. I'll take you over there and I want you to play it for them."

With the talented tandem of Webb and Howe firmly behind the song, it seemed as though the Association's next hit record was all but assured. Now the band members just needed to give it their approval.

*

As Jimmy Webb sat down at the Steinway Grand in Western 3 to demo *The Cantata* for the Association, expectations were running high. Earlier that day, Bones Howe had told the band about Webb's marvelous new composition, that it would perfectly match his vision for their voices. And they were looking forward to hearing it. But they were also leery.

By this, their fourth album, the six members of the Association were becoming ever more restive and resentful; they wanted to record as many of their own songs as possible. They also wanted to play their own instruments as a band in the studio, something they were never permitted to do. Howe considered them to be excellent singers, specifically in terms of their vocal blend. He did not, however, consider them to be excellent instrumentalists. They were capable enough for playing live gigs but not for the exacting demands of cutting a record. "I have to run the sessions my way, with my musicians," Howe had made clear to the Association's manager when they all started working together.

When the red light went on and the tape started rolling, Howe wanted his favorite Wrecking Crew rhythm section of Hal Blaine, Joe Osborn, and

Larry Knechtel laying down the groove, no substitutions allowed. He also wanted some combination of Dennis Budimir, Al Casey, Mike Deasy, and Tommy Tedesco on the guitars. Howe's job, as he saw it, was to create a hit record. And to that end, only the best would do.

While Webb played the roughly twenty-minute musical arrangement on the battered and scarred yet exquisite-sounding old piano that had been in the studio for years (the same one Webb had so nervously sat behind two years before on Johnny Rivers's version of "By the Time I Get to Phoenix"), he carefully explained along the way where the instrumental interludes and the vocals should be inserted. Howe, for one, was enthralled. This is going to be great, he thought. It's the ideal vehicle to showcase the Association's unique harmony-singing abilities.

But the boys in the band had other ideas. At the conclusion of Webb's mini-concert, one of the guys politely said, "Okay, Jimmy, thanks very much. Could you wait outside? We'd like to talk it over as a group."

With Webb safely out of earshot, Terry Kirkman, the group's leader and the talented songwriter behind "Cherish," their number-one hit from the year before, along with the rhythm guitarist, Russ Giguere, were the first to offer their opinions.

"Man, any two guys in this band could write something better than that," Giguere said, with Kirkman adding that it was "too long."

Howe was stunned. He was sure the suite of interconnected songs would be an automatic. Looking at the half-dozen faces in front of him, however, he could see that they were all in assent. The producer's standing agreement with the band was that if either he or they didn't like a piece of material, then it wouldn't be recorded. And for reasons that he couldn't fully comprehend, the Association had just voted him down, six thumbs to one.

Breaking the news to the anxious Webb waiting outside in the hall, Howe tried to soften the blow as much as possible.

"Well, you know," he offered, "the group just doesn't want to give up a whole side of an album."

A dejected Webb said he understood, though his eyes indicated otherwise. Sensitive by nature, most songwriters can't help but take rejection personally. Especially when the work is so heartfelt and autobiographical, as with *The Cantata*. Still pining for his ex-girlfriend Susan—the one who had inspired him to write "By the Time I Get to Phoenix"—Webb had created this Baroque-style song cycle about her, too. And it needed to somehow find a good home.

"Thanks anyway, Bones," he said. "At least you tried."

*

A couple of months after the deflating turn of events in the studio with the Association, Jimmy Webb found himself playing the piano one evening at a fund-raiser he had agreed to attend in West LA. While the well-heeled crowd mingled and drank, Webb informally entertained them on the ivories with both his own repertoire and some personal favorites from the Great American Songbook. As the evening rolled along, Webb, out of the corner of his eye, happened to notice a looming figure approach. Someone who seemed like he had something on his mind.

"Do ya know any good Irish pub songs, lad?" came the booming brogue of an obviously inebriated man. "I'm lookin' to sing me some 'Molly Malone' or 'Rocky Road to Dublin.'"

Recognizing the rugged, party-worn face to be that of the well-known actor Richard Harris, he of King Arthur in *Camelot*, Webb obligingly launched into comping his way through a few tunes that he vaguely recalled. As the vodka flowed and the ditties rolled, the unlikely duo began taking a shine to each other. So much so that, with a twinkle in his eye, Harris remarked just before leaving, "Let's make a record, Jimmy Webb."

Focused on his career, Webb subsequently shrugged off the evening's encounter, paying Harris's comment little heed. Following his recent release from contractual obligations with Johnny Rivers, Webb already had a busy existence as a freelancer, with songs to write and pitch. And Hollywood party talk was usually just that, anyway—talk. Then, several weeks later, a telegram arrived.

JIMMY WEBB, COME TO LONDON AND MAKE A RECORD. LOVE, RICHARD.

And so Webb did.

Or at least he flew to London with the actor footing the bill to see whether there was any suitable material *worth* recording. Harris, though he had sung a little here and there in the movies and onstage, was hardly known as a professional vocalist. But he had ambitions—and very selective tastes. Over pitchers of Pimm's Cup (a libation made in England from dry gin, liqueur, fruit juices, and spices), Webb played and sang every song he had to his name. But with nothing catching the fancy of the gregarious, high-octane Limerick, Ireland, native, Webb then looked one last time into the leather sheet music satchel he had brought with him. At the bottom sat *The Cantata.*

With some dread, he pulled it out and began to play. It had already been rejected once by a big-time act. He was wary of getting his feelings bruised all over again. But it was all he had left. As Webb sang a particularly poignant and poetic section of the lengthy piece about, among other things, someone leaving a cake out in the rain, his host's eyes grew moist.

"I'll have that, Jimmy Webb."

✳

In the middle of the night, at his palatial Castilian Drive home high up in the Hollywood Hills, Hal Blaine heard his telephone ring. And ring and ring.

Jolted from a deep sleep, the thirty-nine-year-old drummer groggily guessed that it must be some kind of an emergency. If it were any kind of a regular recording-session call, it would have gone through his answering service. He fumbled for the receiver.

"Hello?" he mumbled.

"Hal Blaine?"

"Yeah?"

"It's Richard Harris."

A couple of weeks before, Jimmy Webb had phoned Blaine from London, telling him that he had met an actor. They were going to do an album together and Webb wanted Blaine to fly over and play the drums on the project. By this time, having worked together on the 5th Dimension's first two albums, the two had become good friends. And Webb, like just about everybody else in town, wanted Blaine's skills on everything he did.

"Sure, I'd be glad to, Jimmy," Blaine had said. "I just need some lead time. I'm booked solid around three or four months ahead right now."

Webb agreed, Blaine went about his business, and suddenly, two weeks later, Richard Harris was on the line.

"We've got a seat reserved for you on a TWA flight out of LAX tomorrow," the actor said.

"Oh, my God," Blaine replied, sitting upright. "You know, I thought I was going to get some notice on this thing."

After some fast-talking and adept schedule shifting by Blaine's trusty secretary, the next thing the drummer knew, he was sitting across the breakfast table from Harris inside the thespian's opulent London apartment. As they ate and chatted, Harris had an important question on his mind.

"Hal, you came highly recommended to me by Jimmy Webb. Do you know any other good musicians like yourself that we could get to come over here and play on this project?"

For Blaine, the surprises just kept on coming. He assumed that Harris or Webb or at least *somebody* had already booked all the players.

"Well, jeez, Richard, I do know a lot of guys, " Blaine responded. "But they're like me, usually busy months in advance."

Then Harris asked his other question.

"Uh, one more thing. Do you happen to know of any good studios over here?"

There obviously wasn't going to be any recording done in England. Nothing had even been scheduled. Webb had cooked up an elaborate plan with Harris to get Blaine to fly over for what essentially would be a ten-day vacation. Blaine never seemed to take time off and his friend Webb wanted him to start enjoying life for a change. For the next week and a half, the trio caroused about merry old London like their very lives depended on it.

But the threesome would also soon reconvene for real back in Los Angeles, along with several other members of the Wrecking Crew, where they would see about proving the Association wrong.

*

By the middle of 1968, popular music was changing once again. In fact it was getting downright heavy. In the aftermath of the recent Bobby Kennedy and Martin Luther King, Jr., slayings, the bloody Tet Offensive in Vietnam, and the ever-growing level of campus unrest at universities around the country, Top 40 AM radio gradually began to lose step with the times.

In response, so-called underground FM stations like KSAN in San Francisco, WNEW in New York, and both KMET and KLOS in Los Angeles began easing into the mix, clearly distinguishing their formats from the frenetic presentations and three-minute song limits favored by their mono brethren. Instead, this new kind of progressive, free-form radio specialized in playing many seldom-heard album cuts, along with longer versions of some of the hit songs that did make the regular singles charts from bands like Iron Butterfly ("In-A-Gadda-Da-Vida"), the Chambers Brothers ("Time Has Come Today"), and Creedence Clearwater Revival ("Suzie Q"). Pioneering disc jockeys like Tom Donahue, Scott Muni, Jim Ladd, Raechel Donahue (Tom's wife), and Dusty Street played whatever they wanted, when they wanted.

Gathering at the noted engineer Armin Steiner's Sound Recorders on Selma Avenue in Hollywood in mid-May of 1968, Hal Blaine, Mike Deasy, Larry Knechtel, Joe Osborn, Jimmy Webb, and the redoubtable Richard Harris set about making some music. With the entire album, *A Tramp Shining*, written, arranged, and produced by Jimmy Webb, it was the twenty-one-year-old's baby all the way. And with it finally came a home for *The Cantata*.

As the recording progressed over several days, it all built toward a critical mass, to the one piece that had caught Harris's attention back in London. Called "MacArthur Park" (written as the final movement of *The Cantata*), it also put the Wrecking Crew's skills to the test like no song before it. A spectacular production with innumerable complex chords and polyrhythms, it was the furthest thing possible from a normal rock-and-roll date. And they simply loved it.

With Knechtel channeling the likes of Handel and Vivaldi on piano and with Webb sitting right next to him on harpsichord, they were joined by Blaine keeping rock-solid time in a variety of changing signatures and

Osborn just staring at the charts, moving his fingers up and down the neck of his bass as fast as he could. It was the musical challenge of a professional lifetime; for once, the Wrecking Crew were able to *stretch* and really strut their stuff. After they ran through the lengthy song over and over until they could play everything perfectly from beginning to end without stopping, the tenth take proved to be the keeper. Webb wanted to avoid any after-the-fact editing at all costs. One slip of the razor blade on the cutting block and the delicate sixteen-track tape easily could be ruined.

After Harris added his dramatic vocal reading, where through either stubbornness or too much alcohol—with a pint next to him at all times—he incorrectly kept singing the lyrics as "*MacArthur's* Park," the recording was almost complete. Webb then brought in a myriad of horns and strings to put the lush finishing touches on what had become his personal master-piece. Now it would be a matter of getting some airplay.

By this time, with a passel of Grammys to his credit, Jimmy Webb had a name that could open doors in the music world. Taking advantage of this, Dunhill Records, Harris's label, did their best to talk KHJ into putting "MacArthur Park" into immediate rotation. The station had enjoyed great success with the Webb-penned "Up, Up and Away," and Dunhill execs hoped KHJ would see the same promise in his latest composition. And they did, except for one thing: It was too long. *Way* too long. At well over seven min-utes, it was positively colossal, clocking in at twice the length of almost any other song on their playlist.

Webb then received a phone call from Ron Jacobs at KHJ.

"Jimmy, we'll go on 'MacArthur Park'," he said, "but you'll have to edit it down for us."

When Jacobs had initially listened to the song, he found it hard to be-lieve that it was really by Richard Harris. It was like nothing Jacobs had heard before, certainly not by some actor. And unlike his experience with "California Dreamin'," he immediately recognized that Webb's uniquely crafted production had all the earmarks of becoming an instant Top 40 smash. But first there was the little matter of trimming it all down to work-able AM radio size.

A resolute Jimmy Webb, however, very much had other ideas about how "MacArthur Park" was to be treated.

"No, I'm not going to do that," he replied.

Jacobs was taken aback. Turning down a guaranteed "add" on powerful KHJ was tantamount to heresy, at least by music business standards. *Nobody* did that.

"Do you realize what you're doing, then?" the gruff program director practically snorted through the receiver. "You're throwing away a hit record."

Despite the rosy promise of commercial success that so tantalizingly lay before him, Webb's artistic integrity was now on the line, too. And that he could not compromise, hit or no hit. Being true to his songs meant everything to him.

"Well, I'm not going to do that. I'm not going to edit it because it is what it is."

But the promotions men at Dunhill were savvy. They knew ahead of time that the length might be a problem. So they also pitched "MacArthur Park" to a bunch of underground FM stations, who jumped all over it. The song then built such a buzz in such a short period that within a week KHJ broke its own rules and added all seven minutes and twenty-one seconds of it anyway.

From there, it would take barely a month for the epic recording to go all the way to number two in the country, sandwiched between a couple of other Wrecking Crew efforts: "This Guy's in Love with You" by Herb Alpert and "Mrs. Robinson" by Simon and Garfunkel. Webb also won the 1968 Grammy for best arrangement accompanying vocalist(s), beating out, among others, the Association.

Webb's creation additionally generated another unexpected consequence, one that would begin to subtly affect the Wrecking Crew's livelihood. Because the song had broken through the AM radio barrier, it had suddenly made it okay for lengthier songs to make the playlist. And the longer each song, the fewer minutes left during each hour for the station to play *other* songs. That was the unfair, mathematical irony of the whole equation; the Wrecking Crew had just played their hearts out on an all-time award-winning hit, yet its very success directly contributed toward a drop in the total number of songs making it on the air. And with fewer songs finding airtime, there gradually evolved a diminishing number of rock-and-roll recording dates for them to play on. The days of the three-minute (or less) single were fading. But for several in the Wrecking Crew, despite these changes in the business, arguably their greatest recording glory lay just around the corner.

17

Bridge Over Troubled Water

Let's do the Phil Spector production idea.
—ART GARFUNKEL

By early 1969, Carol Kaye and Glen Campbell found themselves headed in opposite career directions. And both were moving on from the Wrecking Crew.

After playing on literally thousands of songs in the recording studios since her defection from the world of live jazz back in the Fifties, Kaye was just plain burned out. With so much of what she had been asked to play on standard rock-and-roll dates requiring little of her skills, particularly in regard to groups like the Monkees, the cumulative effect made her want to leave the business. So she did.

Always fond of teaching since her days with Horace Hatchett back in Long Beach during the late Forties, Kaye came up with the idea to start her own music book publishing company. With her first title, *How to Play the Electric Bass,* immediately becoming a strong seller, Kaye also went back into working directly with students, primarily focusing on those with more advanced skills. It also gave her a chance to rest her wrist, which had become arthritic from the intense, unrelenting use on the fret boards of her bass and guitar during her years of studio work. And, as an added bonus, with her no longer being away from home all day (and often much of the night) while playing on sessions, the newfound freedom allowed her to spend more time with her three growing children.

In contrast, by the end of the Sixties Glen Campbell's public profile had zoomed into the stratosphere. Following his chart success with "By the Time I Get to Phoenix" and by virtue of several well-received TV guest spots on *The Smothers Brothers Comedy Hour,* Campbell had been asked to host *The Summer Brothers Smothers Show* in 1968, the replacement for their much-publicized variety series during its three-month hiatus. When he scored surprisingly high among audiences during his summertime stint, CBS soon gave the telegenic and politically conservative Campbell—to the network, a welcome relief from the vexing Smothers Brothers—a musical variety show of his own.

Hitting the air in mid-season during January of 1969, *The Glen Campbell Goodtime Hour* was an immediate smash. Opening every show with a trademark high-pitched, "Hi, I'm Glen Campbell," he and his good buddy the banjo-playing Johnny Hartford would then launch into a quick version of the Hartford-penned "Gentle on My Mind." The weekly musical guests were top-notch, too, including many people Campbell used to play guitar for during his time with the Wrecking Crew, including Ricky Nelson, Nancy Sinatra, and the Righteous Brothers.

With the cash flowing along with the acclaim, Campbell also started construction on a mammoth 16,500-square-foot house on a hill at the top of Laurel Canyon. With a sweeping view of the San Fernando Valley and enough room to fit his boyhood home inside many times over, it was more than he ever imagined possible. Maybe too much. But it made his wife and their three kids happy, so he went along with it. Besides, he was rarely around, anyway. Always a whirlwind of activity, if the in-demand Campbell wasn't recording a new album or taping his weekly show, he was on the road performing scores of weekend concert dates around the country. Though by no means a trained actor, he also somehow found time to co-star in the motion picture *True Grit* with John Wayne, playing a hard-nosed Texas Ranger by the name of LaBoeuf. Despite all his newfound wealth, having grown up poor, Campbell just hated to say no to an offer, even to acting. He had seen careers start to slide in the entertainment world just as fast as they had begun. Campbell hoped it wouldn't happen to him.

✳

Growing up during the Forties as the only child of a young single mother, Gary Coleman never did know who his father was. Despite his repeatedly asking her questions over the years, his mom always told him the same thing: "Your dad went out for a pack of cigarettes one day and just never came back." Whatever the actual truth might have been, the Pennsylvania-born Coleman always knew that he was unlike most of the kids in his neighborhood. Not in a bad way, just different. Others had the luxury of fathers to talk with, to brag about, to emulate. Coleman, never knowing what having an old man was actually like, instead made up an imaginary mental picture of what he *wanted* his dad to be. He then modeled himself accordingly.

Like many children of his era, Coleman also took piano lessons for a time, dutifully practicing each day after school on an old upright. An indifferent student, however, he much preferred to go outside and horse around with his friends than to sit on a wooden bench endlessly learning scales. By the age of eight, he had retired from the piano for good.

In 1949, at the age of thirteen, after having moved to Alhambra, California, (about eight miles northeast of downtown LA) with his mother to live rent-free with her parents, Coleman made a life-changing discovery. One afternoon, while poking around in the cellar of the old home, he found a series of large black hard-shell travel cases all lined up against a wall. Peering closer, he could just make out the name of his mother's brother, Carson Meade Davis, stenciled on the sides. Flipping one of them open, Coleman saw a strange series of metal bars. And then it occurred to him: this must be his uncle's vibraphone set. Struck with a yarn-covered, rubber-tipped pair of mallets and somewhat similar to the smaller wooden bar-style percussion instruments like the xylophone and the glockenspiel, the vibes were the undisputed granddaddy of them all.

Coleman had heard the stories, too. Davis, now working a regular day job up in San Francisco, had once been a Big Band musician, playing the hotel circuit throughout the country during the Thirties and Forties. Starting as a pianist, he had switched to the vibes somewhere along the way. And word was, he had been pretty good.

Fascinated with what he had unearthed, Coleman lugged each piece up two flights of stairs to his bedroom and assembled the whole thing, playing along as best he could with the radio and some old records. For the introverted teen, it was a transformative experience. The instrument took him to a place that provided a sense of accomplishment and pleasure he had never experienced. A welcoming destination that was a million emotional miles away from his often-lonely, fatherless existence. Instinctively, Gary Coleman knew that he would be playing the vibes for the rest of his life.

*

By the mid-Sixties, after having graduated from college and entered the working world, Gary Coleman found himself surrounded by a wife, three kids, a mortgage, and a job as a public school music teacher that was going nowhere. To supplement his meager salary, to maybe someday save enough money to actually get his family out of the cockroach-infested dump of a duplex they lived in right next to the freeway—where the noxious pollution actually ate the curtains right off the rods—Coleman also moonlighted when he could on his uncle's vibes at various jazz clubs. But with the combined pay still low, Coleman was open to *anything* that might help change his circumstances.

Walking down the street one day in Alhambra in 1965, deep in thought as always, the angular, rangy Coleman looked up just in time to see the familiar face of a blond-haired woman coming toward him. It was Carol Kaye.

"Hi, Carol," he said, surprised to see his old friend again. They had played together years earlier at least a handful of times around town.

"Hey, Gary, good to see you," she replied, giving him a warm hug.

"How've you been?" Coleman asked. "Are you still playing casuals?"

"No, I'm not doing that anymore. I'm now just working in the recording studios. In fact, I worked a date this morning."

When she happened to mention in passing the amount she had earned, Coleman did a double take.

"That's really something, Carol," he marveled. "You made as much before noon today as I make all week teaching school *and* playing in the clubs!"

Always generous in helping other musicians, Kaye then made an offer to the struggling Coleman that he couldn't refuse.

"I'm having a get-together next week at my house. Some friends from the business. Why don't you come by? I'll introduce you to some people."

✳

Sometimes in the music business, one well-timed party or one fleeting connection can make a career on the spot. And so it was for Gary Coleman. At the big soiree over at Carol Kaye's North Hollywood home, the bassist made a point of introducing Coleman to her gathered guests as "the greatest vibist west of the Mississippi." Though an accolade that at first embarrassed him—if I'm so great, aren't they going to wonder why they've never heard of me?—he couldn't help but enjoy the praise. It meant a lot coming from someone as important as Kaye.

More important, however, by virtue of a few choice introductions made by his friend, Coleman's downwardly mobile life suddenly did an almost 180-degree turn. The twenty-nine-year-old unexpectedly found himself by the next week on his first professional session, playing for the prominent producer David Axelrod at Capitol Records. Taking the miraculous opportunity as the sign that he long had been looking for, Coleman immediately retired from teaching, taking his four-thousand-dollar early-retirement payout to buy a bunch of pro-quality instruments. He knew that those who did the hiring in the studios expected a percussionist to come equipped with all the tools of the trade, not just a paltry set of vibes. These necessary items included chimes, bells, tympanis, xylophones, marimbas, congas, bongos, castanets, maracas, vibraslaps, rain sticks, and shakers of all kinds.

Buoyed by Kaye's continued encouragement and words of wisdom—she had told him after the Axelrod date, "You're going to make it, Gary, but you've also got to make yourself available"—Coleman soon started playing on anywhere from twelve to twenty sessions a week, taking anything that came his way. He also decided early on that, to make his work really stand out, he needed to become a *part* of what he was doing. It was no good to just show up and shake some things around. Anybody could do that. Coleman wanted to make sure that what he played was right for rock and roll, a genre that was new to him. So he made up his mind that if a producer or arranger wanted him to do something as pedestrian as merely striking a tambourine on the two and the four beats throughout an entire three-hour session, then he was going give it everything he had. And his efforts paid off. By the late Sixties, Coleman had become an accepted part of the Wrecking Crew, a first-call percussionist playing on songs for dozens of major artists like the Monkees and the 5th Dimension—even on the Beach Boys' *Pet Sounds.*

Unlike Glen Campbell, Carol Kaye, Hal Blaine, and most of the other established Wrecking Crew regulars, however, Gary Coleman also liked to get high, sometimes in the studio. It was not uncommon for him to smoke some pot or even snort a little cocaine during a session. Given that he was usually far in the back, at least partially obscured by his large equipment cases, it was not difficult for him to partake in his favorite substances while the producer busied himself in the booth. And in this regard, Coleman fit in nicely with a number of the performers themselves.

One evening, during early 1968, while inside the secret home recording studio that John and Michelle Phillips of the Mamas & the Papas had illegally built in the attic of their Bel Air home—a beautiful Tudor-style mansion that once belonged to the singer and actress Jeanette MacDonald—Gary Coleman joined in as a couple of joints were passed around. After everyone enjoyed getting sufficiently pie-eyed before finally settling down to business to cut "Dream a Little Dream of Me" (a love song first recorded by Ricky Nelson's father, Ozzie, in 1931), the lead singer on the tune, Mama Cass Elliot, suddenly couldn't remember the words. And neither could any of her now-fried group mates.

"I'm gonna have to call Wallichs!" she laughingly exclaimed, referring to the musical instrument, sheet music, and record store located in Hollywood on the corner of Sunset and Vine.

Coleman, for one, had never seen anything like it. It was certainly a first to watch a major singing star unable to perform in the studio. But then this *was* the Mamas & the Papas.

Elliot eventually got on the phone after someone dialed the number for her.

"Yes, this is Mama Cass," she said, pen in hand. "Could you please read me the lyrics to 'Dream a Little Dream of Me'?"

With the store clerk suitably stunned by the out-of-the-blue request from such a famous celebrity, Elliot, pro that she was, scribbled down the words, said, "Thank you very much," and then proceeded to step up to the mic in the cozy, haze-filled room and belt out a number-twelve hit on the spot.

＊

One day during the late summer of 1969, as Gary Coleman went through the usual time-consuming process of packing up his tymps, vibes, marimbas, and other gear after a session at Columbia Records in Hollywood, he heard someone calling his name. The busy musician had just finished working on an Andy Williams Christmas album, along with several other Wrecking Crewers and a large orchestra. As he turned around, he saw that it was Hal Blaine.

"Hey, Gary, could I get you to come overdub something next door in Studio A?" Blaine asked hopefully. "It won't take long, plus you'll get paid the full three-hour scale, of course."

"Sure," said Coleman, who never strayed far from Carol Kaye's original advice about making himself available. He also knew who was recording in the other studio. Everyone did. It was Simon & Garfunkel.

Having become one of the biggest acts in the world on the heels of songs like "I Am a Rock," "Homeward Bound," and "Scarborough Fair," the two were now painstakingly piecing together their most important work to date, an album they planned to call *Bridge Over Troubled Water.* They also had become ardent admirers and employers of Blaine, Joe Osborn, and Larry Knechtel from the Wrecking Crew. The undeniable creative symbiosis between the drummer, bassist, and keyboardist had been in place since Lou Adler first hired them to play together on Johnny Rivers's "Mountain of Love" in 1964. More recently, the three had played drums, bass, and piano as a unit on the *Age of Aquarius* album for Bones Howe and the 5th Dimension, yet another gold record for all involved.

Simon & Garfunkel also had used the trio extensively on their previous LP *Bookends,* which contained the Grammy-winning number-one hit "Mrs. Robinson." Originally starting with the working title of "Mrs. Roosevelt," the song featured a bare-bones trio of just Simon, Blaine, and Knechtel (who came up with the signature opening riff) on all the instruments. But with Knechtel soon wearying of doing double duty for the demanding duo on both bass and keyboards, Blaine suggested that they bring in Osborn to help finish the album. And the fit was perfect. By 1969, with a comfortable and highly successful working relationship firmly in place, it only made sense for Simon & Garfunkel to bring the three sidemen back, this time along with the guitarist Fred Carter, Jr., of Nashville's fabled A-Team.

In composing the title song for *Bridge,* which Clive Davis, the head of Columbia Records, adamantly wanted as the first cut on side one of the album—the lead track—Paul Simon knew precisely what kind of feel he was looking for. And on the first day of recording, with Knechtel sitting behind the studio's nine-foot Steinway concert grand, Simon carefully laid out his vision.

"I want this to be on piano," he said. "It's going to be just you and Artie most of the way through."

Knechtel nodded.

"I also have this phrase," Simon continued, nimbly running down the song's basic chord changes on his Guild acoustic guitar. "But it needs an introduction."

With his creative juices now beginning to flow, the twenty-nine-year-old Knechtel mentally flashed on several possibilities. Piano (and organ) riffs were his specialty. Producers all over town knew that. After growing up in nearby Bell, California, and playing several years right out of high school for Duane Eddy, Knechtel had gotten his studio start with the Wrecking Crew (courtesy of Steve Douglas) back in 1963 on Phil Spector's *A Christmas Gift for You from Philles Records* album. Since then, Knechtel had amassed years of studio experience in coming through time and again with exquisite, uncanny appropriateness.

John Phillips of the Mamas & the Papas, who held Knechtel's abilities in awe, even had a pet nickname for the keyboardist, calling him Third Hand.

And Bones Howe routinely encouraged Knechtel to cut loose with whatever came to mind, just like on his memorable, off-the-cuff, one-take Hohner pianet solo during the bridge section on "Never My Love" by the Association. Howe had also employed Knechtel's superior electric bass–playing skills on Elvis Presley's so-called comeback special broadcast on NBC in December 1968 (along with Blaine, Tedesco, Deasy, and several others), a prestigious gig. Through it all, no matter the request, if there was one thing the reserved blond-haired, multi-instrumental Knechtel could do maybe better than anybody inside (or out) of the Wrecking Crew, it was improvise. And that's one big reason why both Simon and Garfunkel loved working with him.

Back in the studio at Columbia, Paul Simon still wasn't quite through with Knechtel, however. Simon had one last dangling, absolutely crucial caveat about "Bridge Over Troubled Water" to impart to the gifted piano player sitting before him. "I want it to be gospel," Simon said, pausing. "Not white gospel, *black* gospel."

Well, now, that was something else again. Larry Knechtel, the king of the keys, rarely was asked to play gospel of any kind, let alone the real deal. He had been ready to go with a variation or two of what was usually asked of him on a rock-and-roll date, generally a bunch of seventh chords. But the more he thought about it, the more he realized that Simon was dead-on. With Garfunkel's angelic high tenor voice slotted as the song's signature element, there needed to be some kind of almost religious-like instrumental lead-in that would set just the right emotional tone for the delicate, heartfelt lyrics to follow.

Knechtel subsequently spent the next hour playing various chording and melody ideas for Simon until the singer/songwriter heard exactly the kind of piano prelude he wanted. They then decided to do the whole thing in E-flat, the only key in which the complex piece Knechtel had crafted would lie the right way. "Okay, Larry, I think that's it," Simon finally said, rising. Time to roll some tape.

Garfunkel, in the meantime, had taken position behind an ultrasensitive (and -expensive) German-made Neumann M49 mic inside an isolation (ISO) booth at the opposite end of the hundred-plus-foot-long, high-ceilinged room. With headphones firmly in place, Knechtel and Garfunkel then proceeded to run down everything together, intently listening to each other as they went. Hour after hour the two worked on melding their parts, with Garfunkel altering his phrasing as he saw fit on a not-quite-finished set of lyrics by Simon, searching for just the right gossamery nuance and inflection. The vocal and piano arrangements needed to subtly build in tandem toward a powerful climax, to cap off the song's overriding message of selflessness with a soaring, orchestral-like crescendo of practically biblical proportions. That was the plan the duo formulated early on, with Garfunkel telling Simon, "Let's do the Phil Spector production idea that we loved when we heard the Righteous Brothers' recording of 'Old Man River.'"

After a grueling marathon of seventy-two takes spread over several days, with the perfectionist Garfunkel at one point breaking into tears in front of Knechtel, the superstar recording duo, along with Roy Halee, their indispensable voice of reason, finally had the ideal marriage of gospel-style piano and inspirational vocals. Secular though it may have been lyrically, the overwhelming spiritual quality of the arrangement rivaled anything put to vinyl by such celebrated church-reared practitioners as the Swan Silvertones or the Dixie Hummingbirds. Not bad for a couple of white twentysomethings from Queens and their equally Caucasian pianist. Now the song needed just the right addition of some Wall of Sound–like production elements to really put it over the top. And Hal Blaine had yet another of his ideas.

While listening to the playback in the booth after Garfunkel and Knechtel had finished their magnificent collaboration, Blaine, for some reason, kept picturing a troubled man shuffling along a dirt road as part of a chain gang. Just as he had done so many times before in the studio with Jimmy Bowen, Brian Wilson, and even Phil Spector himself, Blaine approached Simon and said, "If you'll allow me, I'd like to try something here. It may seem odd, but I think it just might work."

Of course, contributing something unusual to a Simon & Garfunkel session was hardly a first for Blaine. Some months before, during the recording of "The Boxer" (the first track cut for the *Bridge Over Troubled Water* album), the duo had decided that they wanted to add an exploding sound as an emphatic point of emphasis between the song's repeated vocal choruses of "lie-la-lie." Needing an enclosure that could provide the maximum possible echo, Simon had asked Blaine to fly to New York, where Halee then recorded the drummer whacking a snare while sitting at the bottom of an elevator shaft at Columbia's 52nd Street studios.

This time around, with Simon's blessing, Blaine stepped out to his car and brought in a set of snow chains from his trunk. Spending the next few hours on his knees in an old microphone storage room, Blaine alternately slammed the heavy-duty galvanized steel links onto the cement floor while being remotely recorded. Drag on one, smack on two, drag on three, smack on four. The brilliant maneuver ended up being incorporated as a dramatic percussion element from the song's third verse all the way through its epic conclusion.

But as the recording of the album's namesake title tune wound down, there were still a few finishing touches left to add. And that's when Gary Coleman got to make his mark.

After Coleman and Blaine rolled the big rack of vibes down the hall into Studio A, Paul Simon stepped out into the studio and introduced himself to the young percussionist, adding a quick, "Thanks very much for coming." Simon then showed Coleman where he wanted the vibraphone's notes to be inserted within the arrangement, and the recording swiftly began. With Blaine overdubbing a set of tom-toms right next to him, Coleman was in and out within thirty minutes, on his way to his next gig. It always seemed like there was a next gig, too, leaving the hardworking musician little time to reflect on anything as momentous as playing for Simon & Garfunkel. But at least he *had* gotten to be a part of what would become one of the biggest songs of all time.

As for Larry Knechtel, his indelible piano arrangement on "Bridge Over Troubled Water" ended up winning him a Grammy, making the keyboardist the only Wrecking Crew player to ever take home one of the statuettes for his instrumental prowess as a hired gun. Perhaps more important, at least in terms of income, with "Bridge" enjoying a six-week run at number one on the Hot 100 during the early part of 1970, Knechtel, along with Blaine and Osborn, suddenly became *the* hottest rhythm section in rock and roll. The three essentially entered the new decade as a super-hit-making Wrecking Crew inside of the Wrecking Crew. Producers, arrangers, and others started referring to the talented troika as the Hollywood Golden Trio. And even if the public had never heard of them, with most record labels still avoiding the placement of any credits on album jackets that would refer to the Wrecking Crew's contributions, everybody on the recording side of the ledger knew *exactly* who Hal, Joe, and Larry were. In particular, that included a young brother and sister combo from Downey, California, who quietly sat on the verge of becoming, like Simon & Garfunkel before them, one of the biggest-selling music acts in the world.

18

(They Long to Be) Close to You

Please, just get back inside and close the door.
—GARY COLEMAN

By early 1970, Herb Alpert, another in the long line of ambitious, music-obsessed onetime Fairfax High School grads like Steve Barri, P. F. Sloan, and Phil Spector, was sitting on an empire. A veritable Renaissance man, the trumpeter, singer, songwriter, producer, arranger, hit maker, and frequent Wrecking Crew employer also owned a thriving record label called A&M (for Alpert and Jerry Moss, his partner). Located within a series of unique Tudor-style bungalows on the old Charlie Chaplin Studios lot along North La Brea Avenue on the border of West Hollywood, the eight-year-old company had enjoyed success throughout the Sixties with acts like Alpert's own Tijuana Brass ("The Lonely Bull"), Sérgio Mendes & Brazil '66 ("The Look of Love"), and Chris Montez ("The More I See You").

Having released a debut album several months back by a wholesome-looking twenty-three-year-old piano player and his nineteen-year-old kid sister who played the drums, Alpert had been looking for some quality follow-up material to cut for their next LP. Remembering a love song that his friends Burt Bacharach and Hal David had written a number of years before called "They Long to Be Close to You," which had been recorded by

Dusty Springfield, Dionne Warwick, and even Bacharach himself—all to little success—Alpert thought he would see about using the tune for his current duo. He felt it could be a hit if done the right way.

"I'm going to give you this lead sheet," Alpert had said one day to Richard Carpenter, the older brother of Karen, the duo's lead singer. "I want you to do your own arrangement of the song." And so Carpenter did.

On March 24, 1970, at a little before eleven at night, Joe Osborn and Hal Blaine arrived at A&M's funky-looking studio complex, ready to work once more for the Carpenters. Osborn had known the pair since April of 1966 when a trumpet player brought them along one night to play for him in Osborn's well-equipped garage studio at his North Hollywood home. Though the horn guy never came back, the two kids began regularly recording song demos of their own with Osborn. Working together over about a two-year period, they cut a number of what they thought were promising records, but nothing seemed to catch the right ear at the right label at the right time. Finally, through a friend of a friend of a friend of Richard's, one of their demos made it into the hands of Herb Alpert, who liked it enough to sign the duo to a contract.

As the Carpenters began their recording career at A&M in 1969, they made sure to employ the Louisiana-born-and-raised Osborn as their bass player; it was the least they could do to repay his kindness. Plus, there was simply no better choice. As Roy Halee, Simon & Garfunkel's engineer and co-producer, liked to say, "You never have to stop the tape because of a mistake by Joe Osborn. There just aren't any." Alpert, in turn, recommended Osborn's Wrecking Crew chum Hal Blaine to become the Carpenters' in-studio drummer (Karen mainly sat behind the kit on tour only). Blaine, of course, had played many times for Alpert over the years on the huge-selling Tijuana Brass records. The record mogul felt that the combination of Blaine and Osborn was especially strong at making a song really *groove.*

As they all began running down the Bacharach/David tune, along with Louie Shelton on guitar, Blaine, with his acute ingrained sense of meter, noticed that Richard Carpenter's piano playing had been going faster and faster as the song had progressed. A stickler for proper, steady tempo, having worked for so long on so many hit records, Blaine felt compelled to speak up. He was the band's quarterback, after all. It was his job to make sure that everything stayed tight.

Ironically, a handful of years earlier Blaine had observed a similar scenario with a very green Shelton during that guitarist's first time in the studio with the Wrecking Crew. Blaine had told him, "I really like your guitar work, Louie, and I think you're going to do great in this town. But you're playing slightly ahead of the beat. Remember, when we're recording, the drummer is god. Don't get to the backbeat before I do. Just lock in with me."

Shelton, who would go on to play the famous opening guitar riff on "Last Train (to Clarksville)" by the Monkees, among many other notable musical accomplishments (including eventually producing all of Seals & Crofts's hit records), took Blaine's words to heart. He felt it was a great lesson, something that had never dawned on him. Not trained in the disciplined ways of the studios, Shelton hadn't been conscious of what he should be listening to during a take. He just went for it, like so many other guitarists who were accustomed to playing mostly live shows. Once Blaine, the dean of rock-and-roll session men, set Shelton straight, it helped the quiet, self-effacing Arkansas-born guitarist (and good friend of Glen Campbell's) to become what was known in the business as a "pocket player." And Shelton was forever grateful for the advice, particularly since it also helped him become a highly sought-after Wrecking Crew regular.

Now Hal Blaine just had to find a way to impart the same kind of wisdom to Richard Carpenter, who was not only a fellow musician but also the drummer's employer. Diplomacy would be the better part of valor.

"Hold it, Richard," Blaine said, calling a brief halt to the action. "Do you want the song to go this fast?"

"What do you mean?"

Carpenter, though a brilliant keyboardist and arranger, hadn't noticed the subtle shift in pace. In Blaine's experience, nondrummers, especially pianists, sometimes had a tendency to rush while playing. He had seen it before.

"Well, the piano part seems to be speeding up a little bit. Why don't we use a click track?"

A click track, common in recording studios, was just that: an automated sound that went *click-click-click* while keeping absolute, unvarying time. Like someone tapping their foot or snapping their fingers, it was similar in concept to the metronome often used by piano teachers.

Being relatively new to the recording game, at least on a more sophisticated, technical level, Richard Carpenter and his sister wanted no part of a click track. They thought it would be heard on the record, like the hokey percussion sound coming from some cheesy home organ straight out of Grandma's living room.

However, once Blaine patiently explained that it was merely a guide, that it could only be heard in their headphones—that it would *never* make it to tape—the pair relented. And from that song forward, much of the Carpenters' output was recorded using that exact tool.

As the recording of "(They Long to Be) Close to You" continued, now in perfect cadence (the parentheses had been added by Richard Carpenter), another thought occurred to Blaine. He decided to approach Karen during a break.

"Listen, this is none of my business," Blaine began carefully, "but I think maybe you're singing in the wrong key."

Having played for major artists over the years like Petula Clark, Patti Page, and Barbra Streisand, the drummer had developed a sixth sense about what brought out the best in female vocalists. And, in this case, he felt that the beyond-talented Carpenter was performing too high in pitch, that her ideal recording range was in a lower register.

"That's how we rehearsed it," Karen replied, glancing quickly at her parents for reassurance, who were sitting nearby. And Harold and Agnes Carpenter didn't care for Blaine butting in one bit.

"No, that's how she sings," Agnes said icily. "Besides, Richard is the star here. Karen is just the drummer."

Blaine immediately backed off, letting the subject drop. No need to overstep his bounds. Maybe he already had. Getting in the middle of family dynamics was risky business. But as the musicians finalized the recording of the song later that night, he noticed that Karen did end up singing it in a different key, helping "(They Long to Be) Close to You" to become a number-one hit for four weeks in the summer of 1970. Though Blaine wasn't sure that he could take credit for the change, his suggestion sure couldn't have hurt. And from that point forward, it became apparent that one thing the public especially loved about listening to Karen Carpenter sing was her soulful, melancholy way with the lower notes. Or, on a more practical level, as she came to tell people, "The money's in the basement."

✳

As the Sixties moved into the Seventies, Glen Campbell could no longer lay sole claim to his status as the only breakout star among the Wrecking Crew. One other sideman had recently joined his ranks. Leon Russell, the shy, prematurely graying piano-playing phenom who, like so many, had gotten his studio start with Spector and Wilson back in the early days, had now become a name-brand act of his own.

Having developed his prodigious skills in high school back in Tulsa during the Fifties while playing in club bands alongside future music notables such as J. J. Cale and David Gates, the outwardly low-key Russell had a deceptively intense inner drive that few among the Wrecking Crew recognized. By 1967, after having worked closely with the producer Snuff Garrett (and several others, including Hal Blaine and Tommy Tedesco) in cutting the instrumental tracks on most of the Gary Lewis and the Playboys hits, Russell finally built a recording studio in his Hollywood Hills home on Skyhill Drive and promptly disappeared within its confines for the better part of a year.

Upon his emergence, the keyboardist had a new vision and a new mission: songwriter and producer. He and musician Marc Benno released an album of their own material called *Look Inside the Asylum Choir* in 1968, followed in 1969 with Joe Cocker's successful cover of Russell's "Delta Lady" (inspired by Russell's then-girlfriend, future solo star Rita Coolidge). It was through this new musical relationship with Cocker (yet another A&M artist) that, in the spring of 1970, Leon Russell had his official coming-out party. He became the musical director and ringleader of the infamous Mad Dogs & Englishmen concert tour.

Traveling throughout America on a forty-eight-city jaunt over a sixty-day period, the caravan of over twenty musicians and more than twenty others was a merry band of music-making misfits that became the wildest traveling road show in rock and roll. Cocker and Russell, the two principals, joined forces with a crazed cast of characters like the Lunar Teacake Snake Man, the Ruby-Lipped Essence of Lubbock, Texas, and the Mad Professor to form a rolling revue of unprecedented creativity, revelry, and utter debauchery.

From the Fillmore East to the Fillmore West and everywhere in between, the music soared, the junkies scored, and the orgies roared. Children took acid at a picnic. Nightly sex partner swaps were de rigueur. Tempers flared. And yet, through it all, during sixty-five shows, the band and crew—night after night—somehow managed to deliver riveting versions of soon-to-be classics like "The Letter," "Superstar" (co-written by Russell and a future hit for the Carpenters), and "Feelin' Alright" to sold-out audiences across America. Not only did the tour jump-start Cocker's career; the massive publicity and exposure also provided the distinctive-looking (and -sounding) Russell the springboard *he* was looking for. Russell began working with a series of high-profile British acts like George Harrison, Badfinger, and Dave Mason, and he put out several more albums of his own during the early Seventies, one of which included his first Top 20 hit single, "Tight Rope." He also became a headlining concert draw, assuming the role of star attraction, just like the many well-known acts he had anonymously played piano for in the studios back in his Wrecking Crew days.

Another musician on the Mad Dogs & Englishmen excursion was a guy by the name of Jim Gordon. A young drummer and Hal Blaine acolyte, he had gradually become a valued part of the Wrecking Crew by the latter half of the Sixties, playing on big hits like "Classical Gas," "Wichita Lineman," and "Woman, Woman," among many others. An extremely likable character with spot-on timing and a groove to be reckoned with whenever the sticks were in his hands, Gordon had zipped his way into becoming a first-call sideman. He had also begun accepting live work, something the other Wrecking Crew players seldom did, with studio pay being far too consistent and lucrative to jeopardize by being out of town. It was just too easy to lose your place in line. But unlike his friend Leon Russell's headline-making

ascent during and after the big Mad Dogs tour, Jim Gordon's own career—
and life—would soon come crashing to the ground.

*

Growing up in Southern California during the Fifties was, for many children, just about as idyllic as life can get. Nuclear families with a dad and
a mom were still standard issue, and the happy, innocent structure of it all
often seemed like something straight out of a Norman Rockwell painting.
Backyard barbecues and Little League baseball games became weekend
rituals. Neighborhood churches stood on just about every third corner,
filled with worshipers on Sunday mornings. PTA meetings were standing-
room-only affairs. Post-war job opportunities were plentiful, too, at places
like Lockheed, Raytheon, and Douglas Aircraft.

And how could you beat the weather? Abundant year-round sunshine
gave rise to acres of lush orange groves and added an irresistible sparkle to
the blue of the nearby Pacific Ocean. If this wasn't paradise, then it sure
wasn't far from it.

Or so it seemed on the surface.

From all outward appearances, the Gordon family of Sherman Oaks per-
sonified the stereotypical San Fernando Valley suburban existence. Dad was
an accountant; Mom was a nurse. Two well-mannered boys always answered
the phone, "Gordon residence." They all lived in a tidy home with a big yard
in a neighborhood teeming with other children. Life was a wholesome sit-
com in the making.

But for little James Beck Gordon, trying to make sense of his place in
this sun-drenched template of the American dream proved to be a struggle
from the beginning. Always anxious, Gordon often felt left out, even though
his parents doted on him as the baby of the family. Shy, too, he never made
friends easily. Eating made him feel better, but it caused him to gain weight,
which further compounded his insecurities. The last thing he wanted was
for the other kids at Dixie Canyon Elementary School to laugh at him and
call him fat. No, that wouldn't do at all.

With all the inner turmoil Gordon experienced, there was one place he
knew he could turn for consolation, no questions asked. Whispered words

that offered him relief from all his imagined worries. A comforting presence he knew simply as "the voices." They had been around as long as he could remember and were his true friends. Yes, the voices were always there for him, giving him guidance, soothing his torment.

By all accounts an energetic, creative child, Jim Gordon decided at the age of eight to rig up a makeshift set of drums from some trash cans. He then enthusiastically played along with the radio as often as possible and showed enough early talent that his parents decided to help him take the next logical step by buying him a real drum kit and springing for a series of lessons from a local pro.

As he sailed through his weekly instructions in remarkable fashion, Gordon remained focused and disciplined, practicing day and night on the brand-new drum kit his parents had recently purchased for him. As he got better by the week, the word "prodigy" started to come to mind. "Genius," too. By the time he was fifteen, many considered Gordon to be world-class.

A tall, handsome, curly-haired boy—if always a little on the heavy side—Jim Gordon also to his surprise began to turn into a school leader, somehow overcoming the terrible shyness that had held him back socially in his younger years. His fellow junior high students elected him class president and he later became head yell leader at U. S. Grant High School in Van Nuys. Gordon even found himself a girlfriend, a beautiful young blonde named Jill.

Life was good. Even the voices approved.

But no matter his other activities, drumming always came first. Gordon's skills were by now stupefying. His almost freakish knack for laying down a perfect beat for any style of song made him a popular choice to play with local bands like Frankie Knight and the Jesters. His new success also gave Gordon a feeling of accomplishment that appealed to his fragile psyche. When he played the drums—especially live on stage—he was *somebody*, and no one could take that away.

As he neared high school graduation, his parents urged him to consider attending a four-year university. UCLA had offered a music scholarship and it seemed like a great opportunity. But Gordon left them crestfallen, especially his mother, Osa, when he announced that he was forgoing his

free ride in order to start making music his career, beginning with a touring job with the Everly Brothers. It was a fantastic, once-in-a-lifetime
chance to play with a famous band and to see the world, he explained.

Though Gordon's parents strongly disapproved of his decision to skip
college, the voices were all for it. And that's what really mattered. They
always did know what was best for him.

*

In mid-1963, with the aid of a piece of fake ID, the almost-eighteen-year-old
clean-cut, all-American-looking Jim Gordon flew across the globe with the
Everly Brothers to England (along with a twenty-two-year-old Don Peake).
Returning to the LA area after the well-received tour's conclusion, a stoked
Gordon enthusiastically began playing in local bands, taking music classes
at a local junior college, and trying to get his foot in the door in the studios.
Anything, *anything,* to be involved in music. Michel Rubini, who had met
Gordon through a mutual friend, gave the young drummer a valuable boost
along the way by scoring him some basic percussion work on several Sonny
& Cher recording dates. Gordon's reputation was starting to build.

Through glowing recommendations from just about everyone with
whom he worked—"have you heard this new kid play?"—Gordon soon
found himself employed by no less than the exalted Brian Wilson in early
1966, where the up-and-comer joined in on a few tracks during the epic *Pet
Sounds* sessions. From there, Gordon's career simply took off, especially
when Hal Blaine generously began tossing him a bunch of his overflow dates
with one A-list act after another. By the late Sixties, behind only Blaine and
Earl Palmer, Jim Gordon had become the most-requested rock-and-roll
session drummer in town.

But during this period, Gordon's squeaky-clean image gradually started
taking on a slightly less than shiny patina, at least behind closed doors. By
the end of the Sixties, he had been secretly smoking pot for several years.
He had also begun trying harder drugs, too, with far more halucinogenic
effects. Something that didn't always mix well with his innate paranoia
or with the voices, which had turned increasingly malevolent. But Gordon
had to do something. He always felt like he was being watched, and the

self-medication, however illegal, helped keep the demons at bay. Some of the time, anyway.

One afternoon, during the colorful two-month-long Mad Dogs extravaganza in 1970, for no apparent reason, Gordon suddenly hauled off and punched his girlfriend, the beautiful Rita Coolidge, flat in the face. Having split from Leon Russell some time before, she was now singing backup for Cocker and dating Gordon. The blow sent Coolidge sprawling to the floor in the hallway of the hotel where they were all staying, leaving her with a black eye for the rest of the tour. Stunned and scared, she immediately ended the relationship with Gordon, having nothing more to do with him.

To some, though, it seemed like Gordon's violent outburst was probably just one of those weird, inexplicable, random things that sometimes happen on the road, where the chaos and pressure can do crazy things to the best of people. It all seemed so out of character for the unfailingly pleasant drummer. A sunnier, more kindhearted person would have been hard to find. Certainly, few in the music business had any awareness of his mental instability. The kid seemed like a throwback to *Leave It to Beaver* or something. Frank Zappa even took to calling him Skippy. Gordon's playing, too—for the time being, anyhow—remained immaculate. And for quite a while, the skillfully deceptive drummer kept mostly to himself when on gigs, leaving his co-workers and others fooled.

Perhaps most notably during this period, Gordon fell into a musical relationship with the guitarist Eric Clapton through their brief association on tour as part of Delaney & Bonnie & Friends (a rootsy, R & B–flavored husband-and-wife outfit that opened for Clapton's then-band, Blind Faith, on a brief run through England). Following this and after finishing up his Mad Dogs duties by the early summer of 1970, Gordon then joined Clapton, Leon Russell, Dave Mason, and many other mostly British musicians in playing at Abbey Road Studios in London for producer Phil Spector on George Harrison's breakout solo album, *All Things Must Pass*.

Soon thereafter, with his LA-based Wrecking Crew session work on permanent hold, Gordon accepted an invitation to hook on with Clapton and fellow Delaney & Bonnie alums Bobby Whitlock (keyboards) and Carl Radle (bass) to form a new band called Derek and the Dominos.

Moving to Clapton's beautiful hillside estate deep within the lush woodlands of the English countryside, the reunited friends immediately immersed themselves in trying to find their sound, playing day and night while simultaneously fortifying themselves on staggering amounts of heroin, cocaine, and hard liquor.

After several weeks of woodshedding, the newly minted group broke camp, gathered their instruments, and caught a plane for the States, setting up shop at Criteria Studios in Miami during the late summer of 1970. With the foursome soon being joined by guest slide guitarist extraordinaire Duane Allman (of the Allman Brothers), a double album's worth of strong material quickly took shape. In particular, their output included a song that Clapton had written about his secret, unrequited love for his best friend George Harrison's wife, Pattie. Called "Layla," it featured a half dozen intricately layered guitar parts, with Allman supplying the trademark opening riff and playing bottleneck slide throughout. Though Clapton felt all along that the power ballad had the possibility of becoming a standout, after they cut it he also realized that it had no suitable ending. The whole thing just kind of stopped.

Then one day in the studio, while Jim Gordon sat at a grand piano, playing around with some chord changes and melody ideas, a nearby Clapton stopped in his tracks. There it was: the perfect ending for "Layla." Clapton and the rest of the band hadn't even *thought* about adding a keyboard piece as the outro.

"What about *that*?" Clapton asked Gordon excitedly. "That's good."

Following a bit of arm-twisting, Gordon obligingly agreed to donate his composition to the common cause. Though he had been working on it for inclusion on a possible solo album, at least this way there would be a guaranteed co-writing credit alongside one of the biggest music stars around *and* probably some pretty good publishing royalties, too. Plus, as an added bonus, Clapton wanted Gordon to play the beautiful piano coda himself on the record, an unexpected honor for the multi-talented drummer.

For a little while, life in Laylaland was golden. The camaraderie of the whole adventure seemed like it had been practically torn right from the pages of Dumas's classic French novel, *The Three Musketeers*—*tous pour un, un pour tous!*—with Clapton, especially, enjoying the exhilaration of being one of four kindred spirits made from the same musical mold. He also grew to consider Jim Gordon to be the greatest rock-and-roll drummer in the world, no small praise coming from a man who had just been in *two* bands (Cream and Blind Faith) with another drummer's drummer, Ginger Baker.

But even with the superior, simpatico quality of their shared creativity, the quartet's incessant drug use began to overshadow everything. It led to a growing number of arguments and a general paralysis; after a hot start, followed by a couple of tours, work had come to a standstill just as they had begun recording their second LP. The substances were now more important. Suddenly, being rock and roll's answer to d'Artagnan and his three pals, Athos, Porthos, and Aramis, wasn't so fun anymore. The inevitable end for everyone came one day after a heated disagreement between Clapton and Gordon resulted in the superstar guitarist storming out of the studio in a rage. Their once-promising dream team collaboration had lasted but months.

Though Derek and the Dominos' one-and-only album, *Layla and Other Assorted Love Songs,* did manage to climb to number sixteen on the U.S. charts, most of the public never even knew that "Derek" was really Eric, a major selling point. As for the single version of "Layla," after a couple of edits and unsuccessful releases over nearly a two-year period it finally made its way to number ten on the U.S. Top 40 during the summer of 1972.

Despite the dispiriting demise of Derek and the Dominos, Jim Gordon's career behind the kit never even skipped a beat. The virtuoso stick man smoothly slid on to playing the drums on many other high-profile album projects for acts like John Lennon (*Imagine*), Harry Nilsson (*Nilsson Schmilsson*), and Traffic (*The Low Spark of High Heeled Boys*). With his résumé now certifiably chockablock with an astounding array of world-class credits, Gordon sat among rock and roll's elite. It seemed like everybody wanted him. If it wasn't Steely Dan calling one day, it was Gordon Lightfoot or Hall & Oates calling the next. The hits just kept on coming, too. But, unfortunately, so did the voices and the drugs.

By the mid-Seventies, having returned to the LA area for good after intermittent periods of living in England, Gordon's mental decline began to accelerate, making his previously hidden problems now painfully obvious to almost everyone. While he was riding one day in the backseat of a VW Camper Van being driven by Gary Coleman on the Hollywood Freeway, Gordon's dark side emerged once more, this time in a far more public setting.

Coleman and Gordon had become fast friends through working together in the LA studios as part of the Wrecking Crew, sharing a common fondness for all things percussion *and* of a mind-altering nature. The supposedly square Gordon had even gotten Coleman to take LSD for the first time. But the drummer's ability to adequately handle his own substance intake—and the mounting cacophony of voices—was fading fast.

"If you knew who I am, you'd want my autograph," Gordon maniacally yelled at startled motorists while hanging as far as he could by one arm from the vehicle's open sliding door. "I'm a star!"

Petrified for Gordon's safety, Coleman struggled to avoid swerving into the other lanes of traffic as he simultaneously tried to coax his out-of-control colleague away from an accidental tumble onto the rushing pavement below.

"Jimmy, come on, man," Coleman pleaded, slowing down as much as he dared on the crowded five-lane northbound thoroughfare. "Please, just get back inside and close the door."

But Gordon refused to listen. He needed to let the world know who he was. Didn't these drivers realize that *he* was the one playing the drums on their car radios on hits like "Summer Breeze" and "You're So Vain"? That he also co-wrote the song "Layla" with Eric Clapton? Or that he had worked with both George Harrison and John Lennon, two-fourths of the Beatles?

Finally, fed up with Gordon's childish, bizarre behavior, Coleman's wife, Mary Lou, who was riding in the passenger seat up front, turned around, narrowed her eyes, and said in an ominous, do-not-even-*think*-about-messing-with-me tone, "Sit the fuck down and shut up."

And, surprisingly, Jim Gordon did.

Perhaps it was the sound of a woman that made him snap to. His mother's voice had always been the loudest of the bunch in his head. The dominant one. Always telling him what to do. Where to be. How to act. And even though he hated her for it, he had to comply. He *had* to.

When Gary and Mary Lou Coleman finally made it home that night after safely dropping Gordon off at his house, they both breathed a sigh of relief. Drugs were one thing. This *was* the music business, after all. But the harrowing events on the freeway were way over-the-top. Something was seriously wrong with Gordon. It was now patently obvious. The guy was addled, touched even. And, friend or no friend, Coleman's wife had experienced enough.

"I don't want you to ever go near him again," she said, her worry evident.

"Why?"

"Because he's going to kill someone someday."

*

Creativity at the genius level has never been known as a hotbed of mental health. High art, in its purest form, requires the unflinching exposure of the human heart—a vulnerable, and, for some, exceedingly dangerous place to go. Especially for Jim Gordon.

By the late Seventies, heroin had already been in Gordon's life for a number of years, causing further damage, especially with his predilection for mixing it with cocaine, the result known as a "speedball." And his unexpected violent outbursts, fueled by the voices and the drugs, became more frequent, sometimes even occurring behind studio walls, once an unthinkable act. "You're messing with my time," he screamed at an innocent, bewildered session guitarist one day while menacingly eyeing him. "You're moving my hands." Another time Gordon showed up a half hour late for an important recording date with a well-known producer, started to play, missed his crash cymbal entirely, and fell to the floor, too crocked to continue. The session had to be canceled.

Not only had Gordon become notoriously unreliable, but his presence, when he could muster it, was by now corrosive also. Nobody in the studios wanted to be near him. Two marriages had failed. His drug use and drinking were at an all-time high. More than a dozen trips to local psychiatric hospitals had done little. The drummer's life was in tatters.

On the evening of June 3, 1983, mentally and emotionally exhausted from years of existing under the strict control of the incessant voices raging inside his head, Jim Gordon just wanted to make it all stop. They were monitoring his every move, telling him what to eat, how much, and when. They also didn't want him to play the drums anymore, either. In Gordon's view, the voices had become one with that of his real-life mother. Something had to give.

Carefully placing a hammer and an eight-and-a-quarter-inch kitchen knife into a leather attaché case, Gordon got into his white Datsun 200SX and eased his way into busy mid-Valley traffic. He then drove east from his Van Nuys condo toward his mother's small North Hollywood apartment, careful to obey all traffic laws along the way. The voices were sticklers about that.

Sliding into an available parking spot on the street out front, Gordon grabbed the two implements he had brought along and hopped out of the car. After making his way up the walkway toward the building, he then rang the bell. As his seventy-two-year-old mother shuffled over and opened the door, she found, to her surprise, the towering, glowering figure of her youngest son staring down at her. Now face-to-face with the imagined source of all his suffering, Gordon knew what had to be done. In his crazed mind, it had all come down to a matter of self-defense. She was the enemy. It was either kill or be killed. And the look on his face said it all.

Before Osa Gordon could move or even yell for help, Gordon barged his way inside and viciously attacked. In a blur of motion, he smashed in her skull with his hammer, then repeated the act three more times for good measure. As she screamed and crumpled to the floor, he swiftly switched to the knife, plunging its gleaming, serrated edge over and over into his still-conscious mother's chest in order to make sure he finished the job. The voices—her voice—had finally fallen silent.

When the police found Gordon the next day, facedown and moaning in psychic agony on his living room rug, they had merely come to inform him about her death. But he quickly confessed, telling them as he sobbed uncontrollably in the back of the patrol car that he was sorry, so very sorry, but she had tortured him for years.

At his subsequent bench trial in Los Angeles in 1984, the judge found Gordon guilty of second-degree murder and sentenced him to sixteen years to life in state prison. And there the drummer remains. One of the greatest Wrecking Crew talents of them all, a Grammy winner (for co-writing "Layla") who so masterfully laid down the beat for the biggest names in music, has permanently settled into a quiet life behind bars, taking his daily medications and occasionally playing in the prison band.

19

Love Will Keep Us Together

Thanks very much, everybody. You've been great.
—Phil Spector

Six years after they first hit the American charts with "I Want to Hold Your Hand," the Beatles were done. Having grown increasingly acrimonious, the quartet shocked the world by releasing their final album, *Let It Be,* in the spring of 1970, no ordinary recording. The Beatles left the tapes in the vault for the better part of a year before John Lennon finally hired Phil Spector to fly across the pond to see if he could make something out of them.

Slowly returning to limited recording action after his meltdown following the "River Deep, Mountain High" debacle back in 1966, Spector duly slapped a heaping helping of echo and strings on the Beatles' record, helping to push it (and its namesake single) to the top of the charts. Delighted with the outcome, Lennon and fellow Beatle George Harrison brought Spector back for an encore, having him produce "Instant Karma" and "Imagine" for Lennon and the triple LP *All Things Must Pass* for Harrison. The master of the Wall of Sound was back, if only as an overseas producer.

In the fall of 1973, Lennon asked Spector to come aboard one more time. Obligated to quickly cut an album as part of a legal settlement (to be called *Rock 'n' Roll*), the former Beatle wanted to record a bunch of his favorite oldies from the late Fifties and early Sixties. And, he reasoned, who better to head the project than the man who put now-vintage acts like the Ronettes, the Crystals, and the Righteous Brothers on the musical map? With Spector's favorite engineer, Larry Levine, having moved over to A&M Studios in the late Sixties at the request of Herb Alpert, the producer decided to use that facility instead of the tried-and-true Gold Star or EMI's Abbey Road in London, the Beatles' usual recording home.

Aside from booking the studio, Spector also had one more task at hand. He needed to hire the Wrecking Crew. Calls went out to people like Hal Blaine, Dennis Budimir, Gary Coleman, Leon Russell (who, though now a star, couldn't resist playing with Lennon), Nino Tempo, and others from the old gang who were still around town and available for playing some rock and roll. The word was out: Phil was back. It was going to be just like old times.

Only it wasn't.

One of the Wrecking Crew keyboard players hired to be part of the massive group of musicians was Mike Melvoin. An Ivy Leaguer from Dartmouth with a degree in English literature, Melvoin was a longtime, classically trained, first-call pianist (and organist) in the LA studios who had played on everything from the Beach Boys' *Pet Sounds* to all the music for the Partridge Family (which he also arranged) to many earlier Spector dates. Melvoin had learned to play rock and roll by teaching his left hand to do whatever the drummer Earl Palmer's bass drum did while his right mimicked Palmer's work on the snare. Highly intelligent, with an innate sense of fairness, Melvoin was also an unyieldingly principled man, something that soon would prove to be oil to Spector's water.

As the session got under way on the evening that they were to cut what was expected to be the album's first single, "Stand by Me," it became clear that things were altogether different; yet in some ways, they seemed very much the same. With a huge entourage and a couple of beefy bodyguards on hand, Spector had a vastly different attitude this time around. And he was drinking in the studio, something that rarely, if ever, occurred a decade prior. Maybe it was the presence of Lennon. Or maybe it was the added pressure of trying to re-create history on Spector's home turf. Whatever the reason, the musicians sensed a different vibe. They also found themselves playing the one song over and over for three hours, just like back at Gold Star. That part hadn't changed.

As they cruised into overtime, closing in on the four-hour mark, Spector finally came out of the booth and said, "I'd like to make this a double session. Is that okay with everybody?"

A double session meant having back-to-back three-hour blocks of time, payable at the regular union rate. Overtime, which producers tried to avoid, paid time and a half starting with the first minute beyond three hours.

As the gathered musicians all said, "Sure, Phil," a lone voice of dissent rang out in the room. It was that of Mike Melvoin.

"You mean starting now, right?"

Spector stared.

"No, it started at the end of hour three."

"Phil, if you'd like to start a double session right now, that's fine," Melvoin replied. "But you can't ask my permission to do something you already did almost an hour ago. Union rules prohibit that."

Like the mythological Prometheus stealing fire from the all-powerful Zeus and then giving it back to mere mortals, Spector was accustomed to divining a record from the studio heavens and then grandly presenting it to the adoring masses. He was not, however, used to being challenged in front of others, especially on such an important night.

"You motherfucking prick, you're fired," he screamed as the studio fell silent.

Spector then marched back to the control booth, with a dumbfounded Melvoin trailing behind.

"Listen to me, Phil. Just listen for a minute."

But Spector wouldn't engage with him. Melvoin had broken the rule of all rules and now he had to pay the ultimate price.

As Melvoin glanced at Spector's two hulking protectors, they began very conspicuously patting their chests, implying that the tiny, irate producer was packing some heat. With Melvoin fully aware of the story about Spector allegedly firing a round into the studio's ceiling only the night before, he decided to back off.

Stepping out into the hall, the keyboard player soon had company. It was John Lennon.

"Oh, Spike, he don't mean it," the ex-Beatle said in his best faux Cockney accent. The two had been joshing around earlier in the evening about an old TV program called *The Goon Show* that ran on the BBC in the early Fifties starring the comedians Spike Milligan and Peter Sellers.

But Melvoin, understandably, was no longer in the mood for humor.

"John! He's fucking crazy. He *definitely* means it. And he's armed."

Lennon thought it over for a moment.

"C'mon, man. Let's just finish the music," he finally said, putting his hand on Melvoin's shoulder. "It'll be okay."

With John Lennon's insistence and clout, Melvoin reluctantly returned to the session. And though the pianist would never work for Spector again, the famed producer still had one last little bit of unfinished business to come with several other members of the Wrecking Crew.

∗

By the time Lennon's *Rock 'n' Roll* album recording sessions finally wrapped in December of 1973 (the former Beatle would do more work on the project later in New York), the Wrecking Crew were feeling the effects of an obvious employment downturn. In fact, most of them had been noticing a reduction in the number of bookings for rock-and-roll dates for some time. Partly due to the decreasing influence of Top 40 AM radio (and the growing length of songs), it also had as much or more to do with the overall musical climate itself. The way things were done in the business had started to change. Producers and arrangers were moving away from the once-dominant desire to hire freelance sidemen to play all the parts for various bands. Even established, insular LA-based hit makers like America and the Doors, who had used the occasional help of a few Wrecking Crewers to supplement some of their earliest work (e.g., Hal Blaine and Joe Osborn on "Ventura Highway"; Larry Knechtel on "Light My Fire"), had ultimately chosen to go it alone.

Attempting to reflect the attitudes of American youth in the music they released, if often a step or two behind, the major record labels began signing artists by the late Sixties and early Seventies who insisted upon playing their own instruments. Slick packaging was no longer hip. Authenticity—being *real*—was the new philosophy. So as self-contained bands like the Eagles, Three Dog Night, Chicago, the Doobie Brothers, Fleetwood Mac, and others grew in popularity, the job prospects for the Wrecking Crew suffered accordingly.

In addition, technological advances were making an impact. With the advent of synthesizers and drum machines, not to mention forty-eight-track studios, in many cases (especially where it was only a singer) it became easier and more cost-effective to just bring in one or two players, as needed, to then lay down multiple bass and guitar parts, which would be recorded one at a time onto discrete tracks. The producers and arrangers found, too, that they could often supply the electronically generated keyboard and drum programming themselves, thereby further eliminating the need to bring in outside help. With so many more individual tracks now available, the once-pressing need to record a huge number of highly paid pros all at once in a big room (like Spector did) no longer existed. Times had changed. Now most projects could be done piecemeal and on the cheap.

To compound matters, a new crop of young, hungry session cats were lining up to snatch whatever gigs *were* still available—much like the Wrecking Crew had done with the blue-blazer-and-necktie men who had come before them. These new players also had a more contemporary, "California" sound and sensibility, which fit well with the mellow, acoustic, singer/songwriter trend of the mid-Seventies. Acts that regularly recorded in Los Angeles like Jackson Browne, Carole King, Loggins and Messina, Joni Mitchell, Linda Ronstadt, Boz Scaggs, and James Taylor—even longtime Wrecking Crew employers like Neil Diamond and Johnny Rivers—now preferred to go with various combinations of guys like Richard Bennett, Larry Carlton, Andrew Gold, Danny Kortchmar, Dean Parks, Fred Tackett, and Waddy Wachtel on guitar; Kenny Edwards, Bob Glaub, David Hungate, and Lee Sklar on bass; Mike Botts, Jim Guerin, Jim Keltner, Russ Kunkel, and Jeff Porcaro on drums; and Craig Doerge, Michael Omartian, and David Paich on keyboards. Like it or not, the torch was being passed.

By the middle of the decade, Carol Kaye (who had returned to bass-playing action after her brief retirement), along with Gary Coleman, Earl Palmer, Don Peake, Bill Pitman, Michel Rubini, Tommy Tedesco, and several others, had, for the most part, already shifted gears into doing film and TV soundtrack work, with occasional forays into jazz. Rock and roll just couldn't pay the bills anymore. A few, like Barney Kessel, put out solo albums, too. Joe Osborn took off for Nashville, as did Billy Strange (Frank Sinatra had asked Strange to run his music publishing company there). Larry Knechtel joined the band Bread. Mike Deasy became a born-again rock-and-roll-style preacher. Lyle Ritz settled in as arguably the world's greatest ukulele player. Al Casey moved home to Phoenix to play on sessions and teach. The Wrecking Crew, for the most part, had scattered.

And then there was Glen Campbell. At the same time his star turn as the host of *The Glen Campbell Goodtime Hour* had come to a close in June of 1972, the hits had been drying up, too. For over four years, from early 1971 through the summer of 1975, Campbell never so much as dented the Top 40 pop charts. His worry about things all going away seemed to be well founded. But then along came something called "Rhinestone Cowboy."

Written by a little-known singer/songwriter named Larry Weiss, it was another one of those songs that Campbell knew he just had to record. The resulting single became the biggest of his career, going all the way to number one (his first). "Rhinestone Cowboy" also provided him with enough momentum to coast through the rest of the Seventies with several more big hits and to establish a permanent post–Wrecking Crew career headlining live shows at theaters, casinos, and state fairs around the country. The boy from Arkansas had finally achieved his dream.

Hal Blaine, however, was one of the few from the old days still standing, taking whatever rock-and-roll session dates came his way. Since his first job in that genre back in the late Fifties playing for Tommy Sands, a whole lot of life-altering history had washed across the American landscape. After almost fifteen grisly, divisive years, the last of the U.S. troops were finally home from combat in Southeast Asia. JFK, MLK, and RFK all had been assassinated. NASA somehow, astoundingly, found a way to land a man on the moon not once but many times over. And through talent, savvy, and an unrivaled Rolodex, Blaine managed to professionally thrive right along-side every bit of it. But the big-name session calls were now slowing to a trickle, even for him. He had begun supplementing his income by doing an increasing amount of advertising jingle work for big corporations like Bud-weiser, Coca-Cola, and Goodyear. Good pay, though not always the most satisfying way to make a buck. Yet the artful drummer, despite the rapidly changing face of his chosen industry, still had one last huge Top 40 record-ing about to fall right into his lap.

✳

One day in the early winter of 1975, Hal Blaine picked up a message from his answering service. It was from a little-known keyboardist by the name of Daryl Dragon who wanted to hire Blaine to play on a session over at Paramount Recording on Santa Monica Boulevard, across the street from Gold Star. The two knew each other in passing from working with the Beach Boys on some of that band's post–Brian Wilson output in the early Seventies. Blaine liked the introverted Dragon and also knew him to be exceptionally skilled at playing anything with a set of keys attached to it—pianos, organs, harpsichords, synthesizers, and more. He was also the son of the well-known Oscar-winning conductor, composer, and arranger Carmen Dragon, so mu-sical talent obviously ran in the Dragon family.

Agreeing to do the date, Blaine reported for duty on Saturday, January 25, at a little before 3:00 P.M. Dragon was already there, along with his wife, Toni, and also his younger brother, Dennis. As had become common on recording projects for Blaine by this point, there were no other Wrecking Crew players in attendance. In fact, there were no other outside musicians in the studio at all. Dragon (the co-producer and arranger) and his brother (the recording engineer) planned to overdub all the keyboard, bass, and stray percussion parts themselves.

After they worked together for three and a half uneventful hours, the basic instrumental tracks for the two songs scheduled for that day were complete. Everything went smoothly, an ordinary recording date in Blaine's opinion. More important, it was another four hundred dollars in his pocket, for which he was appreciative. Weekend union scale rates were known as "golden time" and the pay was good. At a little after 6:30 P.M., the drummer packed up his gear, thanked the Dragons, and walked out to his car, giving the session little further thought.

Around five months later, after Blaine had returned from touring with John Denver, for whom the drummer had become part of both the singer's road and recording bands—a fantastic gig that had materialized just in time—Blaine's new wife, a stunning six-foot-tall blonde from Texas, happened to mention a song she had heard on the radio. "I think it might be you playing," she said. "It's called 'Love Will Keep Us Together.'" Blaine looked at her for a moment while running the title through his mind. "Nope," he concluded, "never heard of it."

A few days later, while down at Local 47's office to pick up a paycheck, Blaine happened to run into Dennis Dragon. Life was like that in Hollywood, especially for a guy like Blaine, who had been around a long, long time. Coming across a friend or aquaintance was practically a daily occurrence.

After they had exchanged pleasantries, Dragon excitedly shared the thought that seemed to be uppermost in his mind. "We've got a hit, man!" he exclaimed, smiling from ear to ear. "We've got a *hit*."

Thinking that Dragon was speaking about some new project he had recently played on for somebody, Blaine said, "Oh, that's great, Dennis. I'm really happy for you." The way the business was going in the mid-Seventies for a lot of freelance studio musicians, good news was always nice to hear.

"Yeah, you know," Dragon continued, "the Captain and Tennille. Looks like the record is going to be huge."

Blaine was perplexed. Though certainly aware of plenty of music acts around town, he had never heard of that particular group or duo or whatever they were. And it seemed like Dragon assumed that he had.

"Please excuse my ignorance, Dennis, but who the heck are the Captain and Tennille?"

Dragon smiled.

"You *know*," he replied, hoping to jog Blaine's memory, "the session we did with my brother and his wife over at Paramount Recording early this year? Remember?"

Oh, that session. Maybe *this* was the song his wife had been talking about.

Blaine never had any reason to think that anything from that date back in January would see the light of day, let alone become a big deal. Who knew? For one thing, he had never heard any of the vocals. Toni had planned to add those later.

Once she did, however, "Love Will Keep Us Together" didn't just become a hit. It didn't just go to number one, either. It simply exploded everywhere, turning the Captain & Tennille into overnight sensations. The Captain's tight, effervescent production values and Tennille's powerful, uplifting singing performance combined to make the up-tempo love song (co-written by Neil Sedaka) a simply irresistible piece of pop confection. It became both the biggest-selling single of 1975 and the Grammy winner for record of the year (Blaine's record-setting eighth).

But for Hal Blaine, "Love Will Keep Us Together" proved to be the high-water mark of an unparalleled career. As the Seventies became the early Eighties, with the John Denver gig long gone and calls to play on any kind of session becoming as scarce as the four-track tape machines they were once recorded on, Blaine finally just stopped. It was time to move on, like the rest of the Wrecking Crew. Nobody lasts forever in the music biz, and he had lasted longer than most.

✳

On December 3, 1992, Michel Rubini sat down to enjoy a delightfully un-expected fiftieth birthday present, something he never thought would come to pass. There he was, after well over two decades, enthusiastically manning a set of keyboards in a recording studio for none other than Phil Spector.

To be precise, it had been twenty-six and a half years since Rubini had last seen Spector, not since that strange, unnerving evening at Gold Star back in the summer of 1966 when the producer appeared to be in the mid-dle of some kind of breakdown. In the meantime, Rubini's career had been on a sharp trajectory. He had gone from playing (mostly) rock-and-roll ses-sions to producing, arranging, and even scoring films. And, at the personal request of Sonny Bono, Rubini spent several years in the early Seventies as the musical director, conductor, and arranger on *The Sonny & Cher Comedy Hour* on CBS and on the singing duo's live, sold-out appearances at the

Sahara Hotel in Las Vegas. The keyboardist hadn't done what might be considered a true Wrecking Crew date in what seemed like forever. But the out-of-the-blue message from Spector had been intriguing. It said to be at a place called Studio 56 at 7000 Santa Monica Boulevard in Hollywood for an 8:00 P.M. start. And the way Rubini understood it, a bunch of his onetime session buddies were going to be there, too. That in itself would make it worth doing.

Spector recently had come out of one of his many mini-retirements and the reenergized producer now wanted to cut a record. Though he would have preferred to do it at Gold Star, home of his greatest triumphs, that landmark studio had unfortunately closed in 1984, a victim of hard times. After a subsequent fire burned the place to the ground, the parcel of land it sat on then became home to a slick, prefab-looking strip mall, which served to add an it-figures, Nineties-style insult to the whole injury.

With the Gold Star option now forever off the table, Spector instead decided to book some time for his new project at Studio 56, an ultramodern complex located about eight blocks farther to the west on Santa Monica Boulevard in a building that used to house the old Radio Recorders (ironically one of Gold Star's early competitors). Spector assumed that the facilities would be similar to what he was accustomed to using. But he was wrong.

From the start, it was clear that Studio 56's young owners had no clue how the legendary Phil Spector liked to record. With a giant multi-track console yet just a handful of available microphones, the whole setup obviously had been designed for doing endless overdubs, not to record a group of almost thirty people all at once, each of whom needed a separate input signal. Spector wanted to do it all *live*, just like in the old days. That's how he created his masterpieces, by tinkering with the EQ and volume on a full complement of sounds at the precise moment they came together in the studio and went to tape. Not by editing some hodgepodge of separate tracks after the fact.

As Spector and his friends David and Dan Kessel (Barney's boys) worked to scrounge up enough workable mics and waited for Jack Nitzsche to show up with the arrangement, a good number of onetime Wrecking Crew regulars waited and watched along with Rubini. Those on hand included Hal Blaine, Dennis Budimir, Al DeLory, Steve Douglas, Don Peake, Don Randi, Tommy Tedesco, Nino Tempo, and Julius Wechter. Well-known musicans Paul Shaffer and Todd Rundgren were also in attendance to play on the date, having both been huge Spector fans for years. Some of the other horn guys who commonly played as part of the Wrecking Crew were there, too, including Jim Horn, Dick "Slide" Hyde, Lou McCreary, Jay Migliori, and Ollie Mitchell. It was a full house of eager, talented musicians, all just itching to create some magic for the master. The thought crossed more than a few minds that maybe, just maybe, if things went right, this could be the start of something big, a return to the happiest times they had ever known.

Finally, after three hours of sitting around, the musicians all ran through the song together for the first time. And it didn't sound half-bad from where Spector was sitting in the booth. They would, of course, need to play it many more times to get it where it needed to be. But hey, so far, so good.

And then came the playback.

As the young in-house engineer who had been assigned to the production rolled tape, there was music all right. Good music. But one crucial element was missing, Spector's signature element, the thing that glued everything he ever recorded together: echo. The producer had heard it when listening to the monitors as the Wrecking Crew played live. And now it was gone.

"Where's the echo?" he asked the engineer, baffled.

"Oh, well, we don't record here with echo," the kid casually replied. "We just monitor with it. That's something that can be added later during mixdown."

During *mixdown?* Spector was virtually speechless. These people had no idea what he had been trying to achieve for the past several hours. And there was no point in going any further. If this studio was set up this way, then they probably all were. Good old Gold Star had been the last of its kind.

"That's it; session's over," the producer bluntly said over the talk-back mic to the roomful of musicians expectantly waiting on the other side of the glass. Then, with what seemed like a touch of melancholy, he softly added, "Thanks very much, everybody. You've been great." And that was that.

It didn't take an advanced degree in psychoanalysis to sense that Spector's wistful words reflected a whole lot more than just an evening's worth of frustration. It was as if the producer knew that this had been the last hurrah, their last time together. There would be no further shot at redemption or resurrection or glory for any of them. No more hits. The Wrecking Crew's unrivaled rock-and-roll recording legacy, along with that of the man who had first put them together in a studio some thirty years before, would have to stand as is.

Acknowledgments

Thank You (for the Interviews):
Lou Adler, Keith Allison, Herb Alpert, Don Altfeld, Ray Anthony, Renee Armand, John Bahler, Tom Bahler, Steve Barri, Richard Bennett, Chuck Berghofer, Ted Bluechel, Jr., the late Mike Botts, Jimmy Bowen, Dennis Budimir, Artie Butler, Glen Campbell, Frankie Capp, the late Fred Carter, Jr., Kerry Chater, David Cohen, Kane Cole, Joe Correro, Jr., Dave Costell, Kent Crowley, Nancy Deedrick, Al DeLory, the late Denny Doherty, Micky Dolenz, Leo Eiffert, Rick Faucher, Chuck Findley, Jerry Fuller, Snuff Garrett, David Gates, Arnie "Woo Woo" Ginsburg, David Gold, Roy Halee, Albert Hammond, Jimmie Haskell, Ron Hicklin, Danny Hutton, Ron Jacobs, Carol Kaye, Craig Kincaid, Terry Kirkman, the late Larry Knechtel, Lonnie Knechtel, Artie Kornfeld, Florence LaRue, David Leaf, Darlene Love, Roger McGuinn, Scott McKenzie, Mike Melvoin, Tommy Morgan, Art Munson, Michael Omartian, Joe Osborn, Gary S. Paxton, Michelle Phillips, Peter Pilafian, Bill Pitman, Guy Pohlman, Mike Post, Gary Puckett, Chuck Rainey, Don Randi, Emil Richards, Lyle Ritz, Johnny Rivers, Stan Ross, Louie Shelton, P. F. Sloan, Tommy Smothers, Armin Steiner, Sally Stevens, Billy and Jeanne Strange, Carmeline Tedesco, Dean Torrence, Mark Volman, Jackie Ward, Jimmy Webb, Mason Williams, and Linda Wolf.

Special Thanks To:
Helen Zimmermann at the Helen Zimmermann Literary Agency, for being the best.

Rob Kirkpatrick and Margaret Smith at Thomas Dunne, for being so welcoming (and patient).

Carl Lennertz, for being absolutely golden.

Larry Colton, for showing me the ABCs of it all.

Richard Snow, for graciously giving me my start.

Susan Gunderson, for Burt Bacharach, Woody Guthrie, and Rodgers and Hammerstein.

Naomi Rooney, for teaching me about Mother Treble Clef and Father Bass Clef.

Laura Hillenbrand, for all things *Seabiscuit*.

Shirley Manson, for being the kindest and the coolest.

Linda Ronstadt, for her gratefully received comments.

Dusty Street, for allowing me to fly low and avoid the radar with her.

Denny Tedesco, for his generosity and for carrying the torch all these years.

Bones Howe, for always being so helpful, forthcoming, and insightful.

Hal Blaine, for endlessly answering my questions and being a real friend to the book.

Don Peake, for all the well-told tales.

Michel Rubini, for so openly sharing his life's story.

Gary Coleman, for coming out in the rain to tell me even more.

Creed Bratton, for honesty, humor, inspiration, and a great new album.

Cactus, for keeping it lean and swampy.

Steve DiTullio, for Conner Henry, Craning-it-up, and laughter nonpareil.

Charlie Faust, for introducing me to Larry C. and Betty D.

Macy Lawrence, for the Bartell tutorials.

Steve Roth, for the best pass in history.

Mark and Deb Lindsay, for all the shared adventures.

Terry and Anna Finley, for being as solid as they come.

Kosh and Susan, for the astounding creativity and continued friendship.

Jane Allen and Jeff Worrell, for all the great music conversations.

Sabrina, for just being her.

Valerie, for more love, enthusiasm, and encouragement than I could imagine possible.

My dad, George Hartman, for simply being the finest father in the world.

The Usual Suspects

A List of Those Among the Wrecking Crew Who Commonly Played in Various Combinations on the Biggest Rock-and-Roll Recordings Coming Out of LA During the Sixties and Early Seventies

Keyboards: Al DeLory, Larry Knechtel, Mike Melvoin, Don Randi, Michel Rubini, and **Leon Russell***

Guitar: Dennis Budimir, James Burton, Glen Campbell, Al Casey, David Cohen, Jerry Cole, Mike Deasy, Barney Kessel, Lou Morrell, Don Peake, Bill Pitman, Mac Rebennack (aka Dr. John), Howard Roberts, Louie Shelton, Billy Strange, and Tommy Tedesco

Upright (string) bass: Chuck Berghofer, Jimmy Bond, and Lyle Ritz

Electric bass: Max Bennett, Carol Kaye, Joe Osborn, Ray Pohlman, and Bob West

Drums: **Hal Blaine,*** Frank Capp, Jim Gordon, and **Earl Palmer***

Percussion: Larry Bunker, Gary Coleman, Gene Estes, Emil Richards, and Julius Wechter

Harmonica: Tommy Morgan

Horns: Allan Beutler (sax), Roy Caton (trumpet), Gene Cipriano (sax), **Steve Douglas*** (sax), Chuck Findley (trumpet), Bill Green (sax), Jim Horn (sax, flute), Dick "Slide" Hyde (trombone), Plas Johnson (sax), Jackie Kelso (sax), Lou McCreary (trombone), Jay Migliori (sax), Ollie Mitchell (trumpet), and Nino Tempo (sax)

*Rock and Roll Hall of Fame inductee

Time Line

A Small Sample from Among the Wrecking Crew's Hundreds of Hit Recordings

The Lonely Bull	Herb Alpert & the Tijuana Brass	1962
Zip-a-Dee-Doo-Dah	Bob B. Soxx and the Blue Jeans	1962
He's a Rebel	The Crystals	1962
Surfer Girl	The Beach Boys	1963
Surfin' USA	The Beach Boys	1963
Da Doo Ron Ron (When He Walked Me Home)	The Crystals	1963
Surf City	Jan and Dean	1963
Be My Baby	The Ronettes	1963
I Get Around	The Beach Boys	1964
Dead Man's Curve	Jan and Dean	1964
Little Old Lady (from Pasadena)	Jan and Dean	1964
You've Lost That Lovin' Feelin'	The Righteous Brothers	1964
Mountain of Love	Johnny Rivers	1964
Help Me, Rhonda	The Beach Boys	1965
Mr. Tambourine Man	The Byrds	1965
This Diamond Ring	Gary Lewis and the Playboys	1965
California Dreamin'	The Mamas & the Papas	1965

Eve of Destruction	Barry McGuire	1965
I Got You Babe	Sonny & Cher	1965
Good Vibrations	The Beach Boys	1966
Poor Side of Town	Johnny Rivers	1966
Monday, Monday	The Mamas & the Papas	1966
(You're My) Soul and Inspiration	The Righteous Brothers	1966
I Am a Rock	Simon & Garfunkel	1966
Strangers in the Night	Frank Sinatra	1966
These Boots Are Made for Walkin'	Nancy Sinatra	1966
Never My Love	The Association	1967
Up, Up and Away	The 5th Dimension	1967
San Francisco (Be Sure to Wear Flowers in Your Hair)	Scott McKenzie	1967
Woman, Woman	Gary Puckett and the Union Gap	1967
Him or Me (What's It Gonna Be)	Paul Revere & the Raiders	1967
The Beat Goes On	Sonny & Cher	1967
Wichita Lineman	Glen Campbell	1968
Midnight Confessions	The Grass Roots	1968
MacArthur Park	Richard Harris	1968
Mrs. Robinson	Simon & Garfunkel	1968
Valleri	The Monkees	1968
Young Girl	Gary Puckett and the Union Gap	1968
Classical Gas	Mason Williams	1968
Galveston	Glen Campbell	1969
Holly Holy	Neil Diamond	1969
Aquarius/Let the Sunshine In	The 5th Dimension	1969
Dizzy	Tommy Roe	1969
The Boxer	Simon & Garfunkel	1969
(They Long to Be) Close to You	The Carpenters	1970
Cracklin' Rosie	Neil Diamond	1970
Arizona	Mark Lindsay	1970
I Think I Love You	The Partridge Family	1970
Bridge Over Troubled Water	Simon & Garfunkel	1970

Rainy Days and Mondays	The Carpenters	1971
Gypsys, Tramps & Thieves	Cher	1971
Sooner or Later	The Grass Roots	1971
Don't Pull Your Love	Hamilton, Joe Frank & Reynolds	1971
Indian Reservation	Raiders	1971
Hurting Each Other	The Carpenters	1972
Last Night (I Didn't Get to Sleep)	The 5th Dimension	1972
It Never Rains in Southern California	Albert Hammond	1972
Rockin' Pneumonia and the Boogie Woogie Flu	Johnny Rivers	1972
Mother and Child Reunion	Paul Simon	1972
Yesterday Once More	The Carpenters	1973
Half-Breed	Cher	1973
All I Know	Art Garfunkel	1973
The Night the Lights Went Out in Georgia	Vicki Lawrence	1973
Chevy Van	Sammy Johns	1974
The Way We Were	Barbra Streisand	1974
Rhinestone Cowboy	Glen Campbell	1975
Love Will Keep Us Together	Captain & Tennille	1975

Source Notes

1. California Dreamin'

AUTHOR INTERVIEWS with Hal Blaine (11/21/05; 9/28/07; 2/21/09), Glen Campbell (12/9/05; 3/12/10), and Carol Kaye (11/16/05).

BOOKS: Blaine with Mr. Bonzai, *Hal Blaine and the Wrecking Crew: The Story of the World's Most Recorded Musician;* Campbell with Carter, *Rhinestone Cowboy;* O'Nan, *The Circus Fire: A True Story of an American Tragedy.*

ARTICLES: Chircop, "The Last Days of the Elks Lodge," *Everett Daily Herald,* 2007. Duersten, "The Lady at the Bottom of the Groove," *LA Weekly,* 2004. Head, "The Ol' 'Gee-tar' Comes Back," *Press-Telegram,* 1958. Hopper, "Ace of Bass: Carol Kaye," *LA Weekly,* 2010. Moseley, "Carol Kaye: Think Extensive," *Vintage Guitar,* 2001.

WEB SITES: www.thirteen.org/unsungheroines/2009/03/25/carol-kaye-youve -heard-her-bass-but-not-her-name/; www.carolkaye.com; www.glencampbellshow.com.

2. Limbo Rock

AUTHOR INTERVIEWS with Ray Anthony (9/16/91), Hal Blaine (11/21/05; 9/28/07), Glen Campbell (12/9/05; 3/12/10), Jerry Fuller (7/24/09), Arnie "Woo Woo" Ginsburg (1/23/06), Mark Lindsay (11/20/04), Gary S. Paxton (8/11/09), and Billy Strange (11/21/05).

BOOKS: Blaine with Mr. Bonzai, *Hal Blaine and the Wrecking Crew: The Story of the World's Most Recorded Musician;* Bronson, *The Billboard Book of Number 1 Hits;* Brooks and Marsh, *The Complete Directory to Prime Time Network and Cable Shows: 1946–Present;* Brown, *Tearing Down the Wall of Sound: The Rise and Fall of Phil Spector;* Campbell with Carter, *Rhinestone Cowboy;* Dannen, *Hit Men;* Fisher, *Something in the Air: Radio, Rock, and the Revolution That Shaped a Generation;* Fong-Torres, *The Hits Just Keep On Coming: The History of Top 40 Radio;* Jackson, *American Bandstand: Dick Clark and the Making of a Rock 'n'*

Roll Empire; Ribowsky, *He's a Rebel: Phil Spector: Rock 'n' Roll's Legendary Producer;* Whitburn, *Billboard Hot 100 Charts: The Sixties;* Whitburn, *Billboard Pop Charts 1955–1959.*

ARTICLES: Perrone, "Obituary: Lou Chudd," *The Independent,* 1998. Severo, "Mitch Miller, Maestro of the Singalong, Dies at 99," *New York Times,* 2010. "Xavier Cugat, 'Rumba King' in 1930s, '40s; Band Leader Also Was Violin Prodigy," *Washington Post,* 1990.

WEB SITES: www.billystrangemusic.com; www.garyspaxton.org/Biography /index.htm; www.jerryfuller.com.

OTHER: "Limbo Rock" AFM session date contract (November 16, 1961).

3. He's a Rebel

AUTHOR INTERVIEWS with Hal Blaine (11/21/05; 9/28/07; 2/21/09), Glen Campbell (12/9/05; 3/12/10), Al DeLory (1/7/07), Jerry Fuller (7/24/09), Snuff Garrett (8/3/09), Dave Gold (10/26/08), Carol Kaye (11/16/05), Darlene Love (2/9/10), Joe Osborn (12/6/05), Bill Pitman (2/22/09), Guy Pohlman (1/8/11), Stan Ross (10/26/08), and Billy Strange (11/21/05).

BOOKS: Blaine with Mr. Bonzai, *Hal Blaine and the Wrecking Crew: The Story of the World's Most Recorded Musician;* Bronson, *The Billboard Book of Number 1 Hits;* Brown, *Tearing Down the Wall of Sound: The Rise and Fall of Phil Spector;* Campbell with Carter, *Rhinestone Cowboy;* Leiber and Stoller with Ritz, *Hound Dog: The Leiber and Stoller Autobiography;* Love with Hoerburger, *My Name Is Love: The Darlene Love Story;* Ribowsky, *He's a Rebel: Phil Spector: Rock 'n' Roll's Legendary Producer;* Whitburn, *Billboard Hot 100 Charts: The Sixties.*

ARTICLES: "Henry Busse, Band Leader Dies; Wrote Song Hit, 'Hot Lips,'" *Chicago Daily Tribune,* 1955. "Henry Busse Estate Left to Widow," *Los Angeles Times,* 1955. "The Making of a Hit Record," CNN.com, 2003. "Studio Savant," *Fretboard Journal,* 2007.

WEB SITES: www.songsofsamcooke.com/sar_records.htm; www.jerryfuller.com; www.billystrangemusic.com; www.redhotjazz.com/henrybusse.html.

OTHER: Commentary by Larry Levine from DVD documentary *Da Doo Ron Ron: The Story of Phil Spector.*

4. The Little Old Lady (from Pasadena)

AUTHOR INTERVIEWS with Lou Adler (11/9/05), Don Altfeld (3/6/10), Hal Blaine (11/21/05; 9/28/07; 2/21/09), Glen Campbell (12/9/05; 3/12/10), Al DeLory (1/7/07), Artie Kornfeld (4/2/10), Bones Howe (7/28/10), Carmie Tedesco (6/27/09), Denny Tedesco (3/25/09), and Dean Torrence (2/18/10).

BOOKS: Blaine with Mr. Bonzai, *Hal Blaine and the Wrecking Crew: The Story of the World's Most Recorded Musician;* Brown, *Tearing Down the Wall of Sound: The Rise and Fall of*

Phil Spector; Campbell with Carter, *Rhinestone Cowboy;* Feldman, *The Billboard Book of No. 2 Singles;* Fong-Torres, *The Hits Just Keep On Coming: The History of Top 40 Radio;* Love with Hoerburger, *My Name Is Love: The Darlene Love Story;* Passmore, *Dead Man's Curve and Back: The Jan & Dean Story;* Ribowsky, *He's a Rebel: Phil Spector: Rock 'n' Roll's Legendary Producer;* Spector with Waldron, *Be My Baby: How I Survived Mascara, Miniskirts, and Madness or My Life as a Fabulous Ronette;* Tedesco, *Confessions of a Guitar Player;* Whitburn, *Billboard Hot 100 Charts: The Sixties;* Wilson with Gold, *Wouldn't It Be Nice: My Own Story.*

ARTICLE: Purdy, "Remembering Tommy: Family and Friends Remember Niagara Falls' Best 'Known-but-Unknown' Guitarist," *Niagara Gazette,* 2007.

WEB SITES: www.promusic47.org; www.tournamentofroses.com/the-rose-parade; www.rockradioscrapbook.ca/radkfwb.html; www.niagarafallsinfo.com/history-item.php?entry_id=1411&current_category_id=108; www.lavasurfer.com/cereal-shreddedwheat-history.html; www.madehow.com/Volume-3/Cereal.html; www.carborundumabrasives.com/aboutCarborundum.aspx; www.youtube.com/watch?v=SR8MgBulXD8.

OTHER: Commentary by Nino Tempo from DVD documentary *Da Doo Ron Ron: The Story of Phil Spector;* "Be My Baby" AFM session date contract (July 5, 1963); "Little Old Lady (from Pasadena)" AFM session date contract (March 21, 1964).

5. What'd I Say

AUTHOR INTERVIEW with Don Peake (11/21/09).

BOOKS: Charles with Ritz, *Brother Ray: Ray Charles' Own Story;* Evans, *Ray Charles: The Birth of Soul;* Guralnick, *Last Train to Memphis:The Rise of Elvis Presley;* Lydon, *Ray Charles: Man and Music;* Whitburn, *Billboard Hot 100 Charts: The Sixties;* Whitburn, *Billboard Pop Charts 1955–1959.*

ARTICLE: "Music: Crow Jim," *Time,* 1962.

WEB SITES: www.museum.tv/eotvsection.php?entrycode=godfreyarth; www.archives.state.al.us/govs_list/inauguralspeech.html; www.nationalaviationmuseum.com/Martin-404-Museum.aspx.

6. I Got You, Babe

AUTHOR INTERVIEWS with Arnie "Woo Woo" Ginsburg (1/23/06), Ron Jacobs (1/9/10), Don Peake (11/21/09), and Michel Rubini (3/4/10).

BOOKS: Bono, *And the Beat Goes On;* Dannen, *Hit Men;* Brown, *Tearing Down the Wall of Sound: The Rise and Fall of Phil Spector;* Fisher, *Something in the Air: Radio, Rock, and the Revolution That Shaped a Generation;* Fong-Torres, *The Hits Just Keep On Coming: The History of Top 40 Radio;* Jackson, *American Bandstand: Dick Clark and the Making of a Rock 'n' Roll Empire;* Ribowsky, *He's a Rebel: Phil Spector: Rock 'n' Roll's Legendary Producer;* Whitburn, *Billboard Hot 100 Charts: The Sixties.*

WEB SITE: www.youtube.com/watch?v=SR8MgBulXD8.

OTHER: Commentary by Sonny Bono from DVD documentary *Da Doo Ron Ron: The Story of Phil Spector;* "I Got You Babe" AFM session date contract (June 7, 1965); liner notes from CD *A Christmas Gift for You from Phil Spector.*

7. Mr. Tambourine Man

AUTHOR INTERVIEWS with Hal Blaine (2/21/09), Mark Lindsay (11/20/04), Roger McGuinn (10/19/09), Larry Knechtel (7/13/97; 11/17/02), and Lonnie Knechtel (10/7/09).

BOOKS: Blaine with Mr. Bonzai, *Hal Blaine and the Wrecking Crew: The Story of the World's Most Recorded Musician;* Bronson, *The Billboard Book of Number 1 Hits;* Brown, *Tearing Down the Wall of Sound: The Rise and Fall of Phil Spector;* Hjort, *So You Want to Be a Rock 'n' Roll Star: The Byrds Day-by-Day, 1965–1973;* Miller, *The Complete Idiot's Guide to Playing Drums;* Marmorstein, *The Label: The Story of Columbia Records;* Ribowsky, *He's a Rebel: Phil Spector: Rock 'n' Roll's Legendary Producer;* Whitburn, *Billboard Hot 100 Charts: The Sixties.*

ARTICLE: "Rock 'n' Roll: Message Time," *Time,* 1965.

WEB SITES: www.lbjlib.utexas.edu/johnson/inauguration/index.shtm; www.youtube.com/watch?v=76QCvFhpUtM; www.spectropop.com/TerryMelcher/index.htm.

OTHER: Liner notes from CD *Terry Melcher;* "Hey, Little Cobra" AFM session date contract (October 16, 1963); "Mr. Tambourine Man" AFM session date contract (January 20, 1965).

8. River Deep, Mountain High

AUTHOR INTERVIEWS with Hal Blaine (11/21/05; 9/28/07), Larry Knechtel (11/17/02), Lonnie Knechtel (10/7/09), and Michel Rubini (3/4/10; 7/15/10).

BOOKS: Brown, *Tearing Down the Wall of Sound: The Rise and Fall of Phil Spector;* Ribowsky, *He's a Rebel: Phil Spector: Rock 'n' Roll's Legendary Producer;* Turner with Loder, *I, Tina;* Whitburn, *Billboard Hot 100 Charts: The Sixties.*

ARTICLE: Francis and Rowesome, "Chrysler Lifts Hood on Most Powerful Car Engine," *Popular Science,* 1951.

WEB SITES: www.beverlyhills.org/about/radio/default.asp; www.dss.cahwnet.gov/cdssweb/PG190.htm.

OTHER: Chrysler print advertisement, 1956 (from unknown magazine); "Let's Go" AFM session date contract (April 13, 1962); "Out of Limits" AFM session date contract (September 18, 1963); "River Deep, Mountain High" AFM session date contract (March 7, 1966).

9. Eve of Destruction

AUTHOR INTERVIEWS with Lou Adler (11/9/05), Steve Barri (11/13/09), Hal Blaine (9/28/07), Denny Doherty (11/7/05), Bones Howe (6/24/09), Ron Jacobs (1/9/10), Larry Knechtel (11/17/02), Michelle Phillips (11/20/09), Peter Pilafian (1/19/10), Don Randi (10/13/07), and P. F. Sloan (10/28/09).

BOOKS: Blaine with Mr. Bonzai, *Hal Blaine and the Wrecking Crew: The Story of the World's Most Recorded Musician;* Cogan and Clark, *Temples of Sound: Inside the Great Recording Studios;* Jacobs, *KHJ: Inside Boss Radio;* Kubernik, *Canyon of Dreams: The Magic and the Music of Laurel Canyon;* Phillips with Jerome, *Papa John: An Autobiography;* Phillips, *California Dreamin': The True Story of the Mamas and the Papas;* Whitburn, *Billboard Hot 100 Charts: The Sixties.*

ARTICLES: Cogan, "Bill Putnam," *Mix,* 2003. Sutheim, "An Afternoon With: Bill Putnam," *Journal of the Audio Engineering Society,* 1989. Hevesi, "Gene Chenault, Who Changed Rock Radio, Dies at 90," *New York Times,* 2010. "Programming: The Executioner," *Time,* August 23, 1968. "What Goes On!: Smells like Teen Spirit,"*Mojo,* 2002.

WEB SITES: www.barrymcguire.com; www.uaudio.com/about/our-story; www.emmytvlegends.org/blog/?p=1273.

OTHER: "California Dreamin'" AFM session date contract (November 4, 1965). *T.A.M.I Show* DVD.

10. Strangers in the Night

AUTHOR INTERVIEWS with Herb Alpert (1/8/10), Hal Blaine (10/25/08), Chuck Berghofer (12/2/05), Jimmy Bowen (12/13/05), Glen Campbell (12/9/05; 3/12/10), and Michel Rubini (3/4/10).

BOOKS: Bowen and Jerome, *Rough Mix;* Bronson, *The Billboard Book of Number 1 Hits;* Campbell with Carter, *Rhinestone Cowboy;* Granata, *Sessions with Sinatra: Frank Sinatra and the Art of Recording;* Kaplan, *Frank: The Voice;* Tosches, *Dino: Living High in the Dirty Business of Dreams;* Whitburn, *Billboard Hot 100 Charts: The Sixties;* Whitburn, *The Billboard Book of Top 40 Hits.*

ARTICLE: "Recordings: Hitting Big with Hummables," *Time,* 1969.

WEB SITE: www.grammy.com.

OTHER: "A Taste of Honey" AFM session date contract (March 10, 1965). "Strangers in the Night" AFM session date contract (April 11, 1966).

11. Good Vibrations

AUTHOR INTERVIEWS with Hal Blaine (11/21/05; 9/28/07), Glen Campbell (12/9/05; 3/12/10), Frank Capp (12/7/09), Kane Cole (8/27/09), Al DeLory (1/7/07), Carol Kaye (11/16/05), Larry Knechtel (7/13/97; 11/17/02), David Leaf (10/26/09),

Mike Melvoin (7/23/09), Bill Pitman (2/22/09), Guy Pohlman (1/18/11), Don Randi (10/13/07), Emil Richards (8/7/09), Lyle Ritz (11/23/05), Billy Strange (11/21/05), and Dean Torrence (2/18/10).

BOOKS: Benarde, *Stars of David: Rock 'n' Roll's Jewish Stories;* Blaine with Mr. Bonzai, *Hal Blaine and the Wrecking Crew: The Story of the World's Most Recorded Musician;* Brooks and Marsh, *The Complete Directory to Prime Time Network and Cable Shows: 1946–Present;* Crosby and Gottlieb, *Long Time Gone, the Autobiography of David Crosby;* Emerick and Massey, *Here, There and Everywhere: My Life Recording the Music of the Beatles;* Gaines, *Heroes & Villains: The True Story of the Beach Boys;* Lewisohn, *The Beatles Recording Sessions: The Official Abbey Road Studio Session Notes 1962–1970;* Miles, *Paul McCartney: Many Years from Now;* Passmore, *Dead Man's Curve and Back: The Jan & Dean Story;* Whitburn, *Billboard Hot 100 Charts: The Sixties;* Whitburn, *Billboard's Top Pop Albums 1955–2001;* Wilson with Gold, *Wouldn't It Be Nice: My Own Story.*

ARTICLES: Crisafulli, "Endless Strummers: The Studio Heavyweights Behind the Beach Boys Sound," *Guitar Player,* 1993. Fricke, "Leon Russell: The Master of Space and Time Returns," *Rolling Stone,* 2010. Rasmussen, "Closing of Club Ignited the 'Sunset Strip Riots,'" *Los Angeles Times,* 2007. "Troubled Beach Boys Genius Finds Renewed Joy," CNN.com, 2008.

WEB SITES: www.billystrangemusic.com; www.radiocityhollywood.com/?p=18; www.norimuster.com/history/capitoldaysintro.html; www.lib.umich.edu/node/11736.

OTHER: Audio outtakes (mp3), "Help Me, Rhonda" session, Western Recorders, January 8, 1965. "God Only Knows" AFM session date contract (March 10, 1966). "Good Vibrations" AFM session date contracts (1966: February 17, April 9, May 4, May 25, May 27, and June 16). Interviews from the CD box set *The Pet Sounds Sessions,* by the Beach Boys (Capitol Records, 1997). "Sloop John B" AFM session date contract (July 12, 1965). "These Boots Are Made for Walkin'" AFM session date contract (November 19, 1965).

12. Let's Live for Today

AUTHOR INTERVIEWS with Steve Barri (11/13/09), Creed Bratton (1/24/10), Micky Dolenz (6/30/09), Bones Howe (7/28/10), Carol Kaye (11/16/05), Don Peake (11/21/09), Mike Post (1/7/10), Michel Rubini (3/4/10), and P. F. Sloan (10/28/09).

BOOKS: Bono, *And the Beat Goes On;* Bronson, *Hey, Hey, We're the Monkees;* Dolenz and Bego, *I'm a Believer: My Life of Monkees, Music, and Madness;* Friedan, *The Feminine Mystique;* Graham and Greenfield, *Bill Graham Presents: My Life Inside Rock and Out;* Massingill, *Total Control: The Monkees Michael Nesmith Story;* Sandoval, *The Monkees: The Day-by-Day Story of the 60s TV Pop Sensation;* Whitburn, *Billboard Hot 100 Charts: The Sixties;* Whitburn, *Billboard's Top Pop Albums 1955–2001.*

ARTICLES: Fox, "Betty Friedan, Who Ignited Cause in 'Feminine Mystique,' Dies at 85," *New York Times,* 2006. Segal, "Return of the Hit Man," *Washington Post,* 2004. Sisario, "Don Kirshner, Shaper of Hit Records, Dies at 76," *New York Times,* 2011.

OTHER: "Midnight Confessions" AFM session date contract (May 14, 1968). "The Beat Goes On" AFM session date contract (December 13, 1966).

13. Up, Up and Away

AUTHOR INTERVIEWS with Hal Blaine (11/21/05; 9/28/07; 10/25/08), Glen Campbell (12/9/05; 3/12/10), Al DeLory (1/7/07), Bones Howe (11/2/05; 6/24/09; 1/26/10; 7/28/10), Larry Knechtel (11/17/02), Chuck Rainey (2/23/06), Johnny Rivers (12/13/05), Armin Steiner (7/7/09), and Jimmy Webb (7/27/09).

BOOKS: Blaine with Mr. Bonzai, *Hal Blaine and the Wrecking Crew: The Story of the World's Most Recorded Musician;* Bowman, *Soulsville, U.S.A.: The Story of Stax Records;* Brokaw, *Boom!: Voices of the Sixties: Personal Reflections on the '60s and Today;* Bronson, *The Billboard Book of Number 1 Hits;* Campbell with Carter, *Rhinestone Cowboy;* Kranow, *Vietnam: A History;* McCoo with Davis and Yorkey, *Up, Up and Away;* Katz, *The Film Encyclopedia;* Posner, *Motown: Music, Money, Sex, and Power;* Webb, *Tunesmith: Inside the Art of Songwriting;* Whitburn, *Billboard Hot 100 Charts: The Sixties;* Whitburn, *Billboard's Top Pop Albums 1955-2001;* Whitburn, *The Billboard Book of Top Country Hits.*

ARTICLES: Johnson, "Grammy Awards Bestowed," *Los Angeles Times,* 1968. Reitman and Landsberg, "Watts Riots, 40 Years Later," LATimes.com, 2005. Piorkowski, "Jimmy Webb Talks About His Acclaimed Songs and Troubled Life," *Euclid Sun Journal,* 2009. Sisario, "Pierre Cossette, Who Brought Grammys to TV, Dies at 85," *Los Angeles Times,* 2009. Weiner, "This Is Where I Came In: The Song Cycles of Jimmy Webb," *Stylus,* 2005.

WEB SITES: www.grammy.com; www.laconservancy.org/centuryplaza/century _moments.php4; www.examiner.com/movie-in-baltimore/biggest-box-office-bombs -6-cleopatra-1963; www.nashvillesound.net/current/ateam.htm; www.wattstax.com /backstory/staxhistory.html; www.india-server.com/awards/features/grammy-awards -1968-218.html.

OTHER: "Up, Up and Away" AFM session date contract (February 22, 1967).

14. Classical Gas

AUTHOR INTERVIEWS with Gary Coleman (12/16/09; 1/17/10), Larry Knechtel (1/17/02), Mike Post (1/7/10; 1/26/10), Tommy Smothers (10/21/06), and Mason Williams (8/17/09).

BOOKS: Bianculli, *Dangerously Funny: The Uncensored Story of the Smothers Brothers Comedy Hour;* Brooks and Marsh, *The Complete Directory to Prime Time Network and Cable*

Shows: 1946–Present; Feldman, *The Billboard Book of No. 2 Singles*; Sandoval, *The Monkees: The Day-by-Day Story of the 60s TV Pop Sensation*; Whitburn, *Billboard Hot 100 Charts: The Sixties*.

ARTICLE: Taubman, "Hair and the 20's: Pert Musical on Lafayette Street Recalls Another Era's Off-Broadway Revues," *New York Times*, 1967.

WEB SITE: www.july4th.org; www.grammy.com.

OTHER: "Classical Gas" AFM session date contract (November 14, 1967).

15. Wichita Lineman

AUTHOR INTERVIEWS with Kerry Chater (12/31/09), Glen Campbell (12/9/05; 3/12/10), Al DeLory (1/7/07), Jerry Fuller (7/24/09), Carol Kaye (11/16/05), Gary Puckett (11/23/09), and Jimmy Webb (7/27/09).

BOOKS: Campbell with Carter, *Rhinestone Cowboy*; Webb, *Tunesmith: Inside the Art of Songwriting*; Whitburn, *Billboard Hot 100 Charts: The Sixties*; Whitburn, *Billboard's Top Pop Albums 1955–2001*; Whitburn, *The Billboard Book of Top Country Hits*.

ARTICLES: Black, "The Greatest Songs Ever! Wichita Lineman," *Blender*, 2001 (online edition). Hunter, "Arkansas to Hollywood to Phoenix," *The Beat*, 2005.

OTHER: "By the Time I Get to Phoenix" AFM session date contract (August 17, 1967). "Wichita Lineman" AFM session date contract (May 27, 1968). "Woman, Woman" AFM session date contract (August 16, 1967).

16. MacArthur Park

AUTHOR INTERVIEWS with Hal Blaine (10/25/08; 2/21/09), Ted Bluechel, Jr. (12/30/09), Bones Howe (11/2/05; 6/24/09; 1/26/10; 7/28/10), Terry Kirkman (12/17/09), Larry Knechtel (11/17/02), Ron Jacobs (1/9/10), and Jimmy Webb (7/27/09).

BOOKS: Blaine with Mr. Bonzai, *Hal Blaine and the Wrecking Crew: The Story of the World's Most Recorded Musician*; Feldman, *The Billboard Book of No. 2 Singles*; Fong-Torres, *The Hits Just Keep On Coming: The History of Top 40 Radio*; Webb, *Tunesmith: Inside the Art of Songwriting*; Whitburn, *Billboard Hot 100 Charts: The Sixties*; Whitburn, *Billboard's Top Pop Albums 1955–2001*.

ARTICLES: Amendola, "Hal Blaine," *Modern Drummer*, 2006 (online edition). Boucher, "'MacArthur Park' Jimmy Webb," *Los Angeles Times*, 2007. Piorkowski, "Jimmy Webb Talks About His Acclaimed Songs and Troubled Life," *Euclid Sun Journal*, 2009. Wapshott, "That Soggy Cake and Other Stories: Jimmy Webb Looks Back on 'MacArthur Park', and the Songs He Wrote for Barbra Streisand and Himself," *The Independent*, 1994. Weiner, "This Is Where I Came In: The Song Cycles of Jimmy Webb," *Stylus*, 2005.

WEB SITE: www.grammy.com.

OTHER: "MacArthur Park" AFM session date contract (December 21, 1968).

17. Bridge Over Troubled Water

AUTHOR INTERVIEWS with Hal Blaine (11/21/05; 2/21/09), Glen Campbell (12/9/05; 3/25/10), Fred Carter, Jr. (2/25/10), Gary Coleman (12/6/10; 1/17/10), Roy Halee (8/10/09), Bones Howe (1/26/10), Carol Kaye (11/16/05), Larry Knechtel (11/17/02), Joe Osborn (12/6/05), and Michelle Phillips (11/20/09).

BOOKS: Blaine with Mr. Bonzai, *Hal Blaine and the Wrecking Crew: The Story of the World's Most Recorded Musician;* Bronson, *The Billboard Book of Number 1 Hits;* Brooks and Marsh, *The Complete Directory to Prime Time Network and Cable Shows: 1946–Present;* Campbell with Carter, *Rhinestone Cowboy;* Humphries, *Paul Simon: Still Crazy After All These Years;* Katz, *The Film Encyclopedia;* Luftig, *The Paul Simon Companion: Four Decades of Commentary;* Morella and Barey, *Simon and Garfunkel: Old Friends;* Whitburn, *Billboard Hot 100 Charts: The Sixties;* Whitburn, *Billboard Hot 100 Charts: The Seventies;* Whitburn, *Billboard's Top Pop Albums 1955–2001.*

ARTICLES: Evans, "The Making of 'Bridge Over Troubled Water,'" *Goldmine,* 2010. Hunter, "Arkansas to Hollywood to Phoenix," *The Beat,* 2005. Kienzle, "Hired Gun," *Fretboard Journal,* 2008. Manno, "Joe Osborn: A Few Hundred Hits," *Vintage Guitar,* 2006. Schneider, "Nashville Guitar Legend Fred Carter Jr. Dies at 76," *Exclaim!* 2010.

WEB SITE: www.grammy.com.

OTHER: "Bridge Over Troubled Water" AFM session date contracts (August 1, 1969, August 6, 1969, August 7, 1969, August 13, 1969, August 14, 1969, and August 21, 1969). "Mrs. Robinson" AFM session date contracts (February 1, 1968, and February 2, 1968).

18. (They Long to Be) Close to You

AUTHOR INTERVIEWS with Herb Alpert (1/8/10), Tom Bahler (10/02/09), Hal Blaine (10/25/08), Gary Coleman (12/6/10; 1/17/10), Snuff Garrett (8/3/09), Roy Halee (8/10/09), Joe Osborn (12/6/05), Michel Rubini (3/4/10), Louie Shelton (7/5/09), and Linda Wolf (12/17/09).

BOOKS: Bronson, *The Billboard Book of Number 1 Hits;* Clapton, *Clapton: The Autobiography;* Coleman, *The Carpenters: The Untold Story;* Dumas, *The Three Musketeers;* Evslin, *Heroes, Gods and Monsters of the Greek Myths;* Schmidt, *Little Girl Blue: The Life of Karen Carpenter;* Whitburn, *Billboard Hot 100 Charts: The Seventies;* Whitburn, *Billboard's Top Pop Albums 1955–2001.*

ARTICLES: Booe, "Bang the Drum Slowly: The Tragedy of Jim Gordon, Percussionist, Songwriter, Paranoid Schizophrenic, Murderer," *Washington Post,* 1994. Elder, "So, Let's Get Started . . . Gonna Make You Feel Good," *Distinctly Oklahoma,* 2009. Fricke, "Leon Russell: The Master of Space and Time Returns," *Rolling Stone,* 2010. Manno, "Joe Osborn: A Few Hundred Hits," *Vintage Guitar,* 2006. "100 Greatest Guitar Solos," *Guitar World,* 2008. Rehfeld, "When the Voices Took Over," *Rolling Stone,* 1985.

Speed, "At One with Leon Russell," souvenir program from the Bare Bones International Film Festival, 2006.

WEB SITES: www.songfacts.com/blog/interviews/bobby_whitlock; www.richardandkarencarpenter.com; www.grammy.com; www.louieshelton.com.

OTHER: "(They Long to Be) Close to You" AFM session date contract (March 24, 1970).

19. Love Will Keep Us Together

AUTHOR INTERVIEWS with Richard Bennett (10/23/09), Hal Blaine (2/21/09), Mike Botts (11/17/02), Glen Campbell (12/9/05; 3/25/10), Gary Coleman (12/6/10; 1/17/10), Carol Kaye (11/16/05), Larry Knechtel (7/13/97; 11/17/02), Mike Melvoin (7/23/09), Michael Omartian (3/12/10), Don Peake (11/21/09), Bill Pitman (2/20/09), Johnny Rivers (12/13/05), Lyle Ritz (11/23/05), Michel Rubini (3/4/10), and Billy Strange (11/21/05).

BOOKS: Blaine with Mr. Bonzai, *Hal Blaine and the Wrecking Crew: The Story of the World's Most Recorded Musician;* Brokaw, *Boom!: Voices of the Sixties: Personal Reflections on the '60s and Today;* Bronson, *The Billboard Book of Number 1 Hits;* Brooks and Marsh, *The Complete Directory to Prime Time Network and Cable Shows: 1946–Present;* Brown, *Tearing Down the Wall of Sound: The Rise and Fall of Phil Spector;* Campbell with Carter, *Rhinestone Cowboy;* Eliot, *To the Limit: The Untold Story of the Eagles;* Fleetwood with Davis, *Fleetwood: My Life and Adventures in Fleetwood Mac;* Kranow, *Vietnam: A History;* Lewisohn, *The Beatles Recording Sessions: The Official Abbey Road Studio Session Notes 1962–1970;* Miles, *Paul McCartney: Many Years from Now;* Negron, *Three Dog Night: The Continuing Chuck Negron Story;* Pang and Edwards, *Loving John: The Untold Story;* Ribowsky, *He's a Rebel: Phil Spector: Rock 'n' Roll's Legendary Producer;* Scherman, *Backbeat: Earl Palmer's Story;* Whitburn, *Billboard Hot 100 Charts: The Seventies;* Whitburn, *Billboard's Top Pop Albums 1955–2001;* Wood, *How Apollo Flew to the Moon.*

ARTICLE: Eden, "The Mike Deasy Story," *Mojo,* 2001 (unpublished).

WEB SITES: www.billystrangemusic.com; www.grammy.com; www.rockchurchse.com.

OTHER: "Love Will Keep Us Together" AFM session date contract (January 25, 1975). Phil Spector AFM session date contract (December 7, 1992).

Bibliography

BOOKS

Badman, Keith. *The Beach Boys: The Definitive Story of America's Greatest Band on Stage and in the Studio*. San Francisco: Backbeat Books, 2003.

Benarde, Scott. *Stars of David: Rock 'n' Roll's Jewish Stories*. Waltham, MA: Brandeis University Press, 2003.

Bianculli, David. *Dangerously Funny: The Uncensored Story of the Smothers Brothers Comedy Hour*. New York: Touchstone, 2009.

Blaine, Hal, with Mr. Bonzai. *Hal Blaine and the Wrecking Crew: The Story of the World's Most Recorded Musician*. Alma, MI: Rebeats Publications, 2010.

Bono, Sonny. *And the Beat Goes On*. New York: Pocket Books, 1991.

Bowen, Jimmy, and Jim Jerome. *Rough Mix*. New York: Simon & Schuster, 1997.

Bowman, Rob. *Soulsville, U.S.A.: The Story of Stax Records*. New York: Schirmer Trade Books, 2006.

Brokaw, Tom. *Boom!: Voices of the Sixties: Personal Reflections on the '60s and Today*. New York: Random House, 2007.

Bronson, Fred. *The Billboard Book of Number 1 Hits*. New York: Billboard Books, 2003.

Bronson, Harold. *Hey, Hey, We're the Monkees*. Santa Monica: Rhino Records, 1996.

Brooks, Tim, and Earle Marsh. *The Complete Directory to Prime Time Network and Cable Shows: 1946–Present*. New York: Ballantine Books, 1995.

Brown, Mick. *Tearing Down the Wall of Sound: The Rise and Fall of Phil Spector*. London: Bloomsbury, 2007.

Campbell, Glen, with Tom Carter. *Rhinestone Cowboy*. New York: St. Martin's Press, 1995.

Carlin, Peter Ames. *Catch a Wave: The Rise, Fall & Redemption of the Beach Boys' Brian Wilson*. Emmaus, PA: Rodale, 2006.

Cassidy, David, with Chip Deffaa. *C'mon, Get Happy...* New York: Warner Books, 1994.

Charles, Ray, with David Ritz. *Brother Ray: Ray Charles' Own Story.* Cambridge, MA: Da Capo Press, 2004.

Clapton, Eric. *Clapton: The Autobiography.* New York: Broadway Books, 2007.

Cogan, Jim, and William Clark. *Temples of Sound: Inside the Great Recording Studios.* San Francisco: Chronicle Books, 2003.

Coleman, Ray. *The Carpenters: The Untold Story.* New York: HarperCollins, 1994.

Crosby, David, and Carl Gottlieb. *Long Time Gone, the Autobiography of David Crosby.* New York: Dell, 1990.

Dannen, Fredric. *Hit Men.* New York: Vintage Books, 1991.

Dolenz, Micky, and Mark Bego. *I'm a Believer: My Life of Monkees, Music, and Madness.* New York: Cooper Square Press, 2004.

Dumas, Alexandre. *The Three Musketeers.* Calgary: Qualitas Publishing, 2010.

Eliot, Marc. *To the Limit: The Untold Story of the Eagles.* New York: Little Brown and Company, 1998.

Emerick, Geoff, and Howard Massey. *Here, There and Everywhere: My Life Recording the Music of the Beatles.* New York: Gotham Books, 2007.

Evans, Mike. *Ray Charles: The Birth of Soul.* London: Omnibus Press, 2005.

Evslin, Bernard. *Heroes, Gods and Monsters of the Greek Myths.* New York: Laurel Leaf, 1984.

Feldman, Christopher. *The Billboard Book of No. 2 Singles.* New York: Billboard Books, 2000.

Fisher, Marc. *Something in the Air: Radio, Rock, and the Revolution That Shaped a Generation.* New York: Random House, 2007.

Fleetwood, Mick, with Stephen Davis. *Fleetwood: My Life and Adventures in Fleetwood Mac.* New York: William Morrow and Company, 1990.

Fong-Torres, Ben. *The Hits Just Keep On Coming: The History of Top 40 Radio.* San Francisco: Backbeat Books, 1998.

Fornatale, Pete. *Simon & Garfunkel's Bookends.* Emmaus, PA: Rodale, 2007.

Friedan, Betty. *The Feminine Mystique.* New York: W. W. Norton & Co., 1963.

Gaines, Steven. *Heroes & Villains: The True Story of the Beach Boys.* Cambridge, MA: Da Capo Press, 1995.

Graham, Bill, and Robert Greenfield. *Bill Graham Presents: My Life Inside Rock and Out.* New York: Dell Publishing, 1992.

Granata, Charles. *Sessions with Sinatra: Frank Sinatra and the Art of Recording.* Chicago: A Cappella Books, 2004.

Guralnick, Peter. *Last Train to Memphis: The Rise of Elvis Presley.* New York: Little Brown and Company, 1994.

Hjort, Christopher. *So You Want to Be a Rock 'n' Roll Star: The Byrds Day-by-Day, 1965–1973.* London: Jawbone Press, 2008.

Humphries, Paul. *Paul Simon: Still Crazy After All These Years.* New York: Doubleday, 1988.

Jackson, John A. *American Bandstand: Dick Clark and the Making of a Rock 'n' Roll Empire.* New York: Oxford University Press, 1999.

Jacobs, Ron. *KHJ: Inside Boss Radio.* Kailua, HI: Zapoleon Publishing, 2010.

Jorgensen, Ernst. *Elvis Presley: A Life in Music—the Complete Recording Sessions.* New York: St. Martin's Griffin, 2000.

Kaplan, James. *Frank: The Voice.* New York: Doubleday, 2010.

Katz, Ephraim. *The Film Encyclopedia.* New York: HarperPerennial, 1994.

Kranow, Stanley. *Vietnam: A History.* New York: Viking Adult, 1983.

Kubernik, Harvey. *Canyon of Dreams: The Magic and the Music of Laurel Canyon.* New York: Sterling Publishing, 2009.

Leiber, Jerry, and Mike Stoller with David Ritz. *Hound Dog: The Leiber and Stoller Autobiography.* New York: Simon & Schuster, 2009.

Lewisohn, Mark. *The Beatles Recording Sessions: The Official Abbey Road Studio Session Notes 1962–1970.* New York: Harmony Books, 1988.

Love, Darlene, with Rob Hoerburger. *My Name Is Love: The Darlene Love Story.* New York: William Morrow and Company, 1998.

Luftig, Stacey. *The Paul Simon Companion: Four Decades of Commentary.* New York: Schirmer Books, 1997.

Lydon, Michael. *Ray Charles: Man and Music.* New York: Routledge, 2004.

Marmorstein, Gary. *The Label: The Story of Columbia Records.* New York: Thunder's Mouth Press, 2007.

Massingill, Randi. *Total Control: The Monkees Michael Nesmith Story.* Carlsbad, CA: FLEX-quarters Publishing, 2005.

McCoo, Marilyn, with Billy Davis, Jr., and Mike Yorkey. *Up, Up and Away.* Chicago: Northfield Publishing, 2004.

Miller, Michael. *The Complete Idiot's Guide to Playing Drums.* Royersford, PA: Alpha Publishing House, 2004.

Miles, Barry. *Paul McCartney: Many Years from Now.* New York: Henry Holt and Company, 1997.

Morella, Joseph, and Patricia Barey. *Simon and Garfunkel: Old Friends.* New York: Birch Lane Press, 1991.

Nash, Alanna. *The Colonel: The Extraordinary Story of Colonel Tom Parker and Elvis Presley.* New York: Simon & Schuster, 2003.

Negron, Chuck. *Three Dog Night: The Continuing Chuck Negron Story.* Indianapolis: Literary Architects, 2008.

O'Nan, Stewart. *The Circus Fire: A True Story of an American Tragedy.* New York: Anchor Books, 2000.

Pang, May, and Henry Edwards. *Loving John: The Untold Story.* New York: Warner Books, 1983.

Passmore, Mark Thomas. *Dead Man's Curve and Back: The Jan & Dean Story.* Bloomington, IN: 1st Books Library, 2003.

Phillips, John, with Jim Jerome. *Papa John: An Autobiography.* New York: Dolphin Books, 1986.

Phillips, Michelle. *California Dreamin': The True Story of the Mamas and the Papas.* New York: Warner Books, 1986.

Posner, Gerald. *Motown: Music, Money, Sex, and Power.* New York: Random House, 2002.

Ribowsky, Mark. *He's a Rebel: Phil Spector: Rock 'n' Roll's Legendary Producer.* Cambridge, MA: Da Capo Press, 2006.

Sandoval, Andrew. *The Monkees: The Day-by-Day Story of the 60s TV Pop Sensation.* San Francisco: Backbeat Books, 2005.

Scherman, Tony. *Backbeat: Earl Palmer's Story.* Cambridge, MA: Da Capo Press, 1999.

Schmidt, Randy L. *Little Girl Blue: The Life of Karen Carpenter.* Chicago: Chicago Review Press, 2010.

Spector, Ronnie, with Vince Waldron. *Be My Baby: How I Survived Mascara, Miniskirts, and Madness or My Life as a Fabulous Ronette.* New York: Harmony Books, 1990.

Tedesco, Tommy. *Confessions of a Guitar Player.* Fullerton, CA: Centerstream Publishing, 1993.

Tosches, Nick. *Dino: Living High in the Dirty Business of Dreams.* New York: Dell, 1992.

Turner, Tina, with Kurt Loder. *I, Tina.* New York: William Morrow, 1986.

Webb, Jimmy. *Tunesmith: Inside the Art of Songwriting.* New York: Hyperion, 1998.

Whitburn, Joel. *The Billboard Book of Top Country Hits.* New York: Billboard Books, 2006.

———. *The Billboard Book of Top 40 Hits.* New York: Billboard Books, 1992.

———. *Billboard Hot 100 Charts: The Seventies.* Menomonee Falls, WI: Record Research, 1990.

———. *Billboard Hot 100 Charts: The Sixties.* Menomonee Falls, WI: Record Research, 1990.

———. *Billboard Pop Charts 1955–1959.* Milwaukee, WI: Hal Leonard, 1995.

———. *Billboard's Top Pop Albums 1955–2001.* Menomonee Falls, WI: Record Research, 2002.

White, Timothy. *The Nearest Faraway Place: Brian Wilson, the Beach Boys, and the Southern California Experience.* New York: Henry Holt and Company, 1994.

Wilson, Brian, with Todd Gold. *Wouldn't It Be Nice: My Own Story.* New York: HarperCollins, 1991.

Wood, W. David. *How Apollo Flew to the Moon.* New York: Springer Praxis, 2008.

ARTICLES

Amendola, Billy. "Hal Blaine." *Modern Drummer,* April 18, 2006 (online edition).

Black, Johnny. "The Greatest Songs Ever! Wichita Lineman." *Blender,* September 15, 2001 (online edition).

Booe, Martin. "Bang the Drum Slowly: The Tragedy of Jim Gordon, Percussionist, Song-writer, Paranoid Schizophrenic, Murderer." *Washington Post,* July 3, 1994.

Boucher, Geoff. "'MacArthur Park' Jimmy Webb." *Los Angeles Times,* June 10, 2007.

Carlton, Jim. "Studio Savant." *Fretboard Journal,* Summer 2007.

Chircop, David. "The Last Days of the Elks Lodge." *Everett Daily Herald,* November 25, 2007.

Cogan, Jim. "Bill Putnam." *Mix,* October 1, 2003.

Crisafulli, Chuck. "Endless Strummers: The Studio Heavyweights Behind the Beach Boys Sound." *Guitar Player,* December 1993.

Duersten, Matthew. "The Lady at the Bottom of the Groove." *LA Weekly,* April 8, 2004.

Eden, Dawn. "The Mike Deasy Story." *Mojo,* August 2001 (unpublished).

Elder, Bud. "So, Let's Get Started...Gonna Make You Feel Good." *Distinctly Oklahoma,* September 2009.

Evans, Rush. "The Making of 'Bridge Over Troubled Water.'" *Goldmine,* February 20, 2010.

Fox, Margalit. "Betty Friedan, Who Ignited Cause in 'Feminine Mystique,' Dies at 85." *New York Times,* February 5, 2006.

Francis, Devon, and Frank Rowesome, Jr. "Chrysler Lifts Hood on Most Powerful Car Engine." *Popular Science,* March 1951.

Fricke, David. "Leon Russell: The Master of Space and Time Returns." *Rolling Stone,* November 11, 2010.

Head, Tim. "The Ol' 'Gee-tar' Comes Back." *Long Beach Press Telegram,* 1958.

"Henry Busse, Band Leader Dies; Wrote Song Hit, 'Hot Lips.'" *Chicago Daily Tribune,* April 24, 1955.

"Henry Busse Estate Left to Widow," *Los Angeles Times,* May 13, 1955.

Hevesi, Dennis. "Gene Chenault, Who Changed Rock Radio, Dies at 90." *New York Times,* March 4, 2010.

Hopper, Jessica. "Ace of Bass: Carol Kaye." *LA Weekly,* February 18, 2010.

Hunter, Graham. "Arkansas to Hollywood to Phoenix." *The Beat,* June 2005.

Johnson, Pete. "Grammy Awards Bestowed." *Los Angeles Times,* March 2, 1968.

Kienzle, Rich. "Hired Gun." *Fretboard Journal,* Winter 2008.

"Making of a Hit Record, The." CNN.com, February 20, 2003.

Manno, Joe. "Joe Osborn: A Few Hundred Hits." *Vintage Guitar,* July 19, 2006.

Moseley, Willie G. "Carol Kaye: Think Extensive." *Vintage Guitar,* May 16, 2001.

"Music: Crow Jim." *Time,* October 19, 1962.

"100 Greatest Guitar Solos." *Guitar World,* October 21, 2008.

Perrone, Pierre. "Obituary: Lou Chudd." *The Independent,* August 3, 1998.

Piorkowski, Jeff. "Jimmy Webb Talks About His Acclaimed Songs and Troubled Life." *Euclid Sun Journal,* July 10, 2009.

"Programming: The Executioner." *Time*, August 23, 1968.

Purdy, Kevin. "Remembering Tommy: Family and Friends Remember Niagara Falls' Best 'Known-But-Unknown' Guitarist." *Niagara Gazette*, November 2, 2007.

Rasmussen, Cecilia. "Closing of Club Ignited the 'Sunset Strip Riots.'" *Los Angeles Times*, August 5, 2007.

"Recordings: Hitting Big with Hummables." *Time*, January 17, 1969.

Rehfeld, Barry. "When the Voices Took Over." *Rolling Stone*, June 6, 1985.

Reitman, Valerie, and Mitchell Landsberg. "Watts Riots, 40 Years Later." LATimes .com, August 11, 2005.

"Rock 'n' Roll: Message Time." *Time*, September 17, 1965.

Schneider, Jason. "Nashville Guitar Legend Fred Carter Jr. Dies at 76." *Exclaim!* July 22, 2010.

Segal, David. "Return of the Hit Man." *Washington Post*, December 20, 2004.

Severo, Richard. "Mitch Miller, Maestro of the Singalong, Dies at 99." *New York Times*, August 2, 2010.

Sisario, Ben. "Don Kirshner, Shaper of Hit Records, Dies at 76." *New York Times*, January 18, 2011.

———. "Pierre Cossette, Who Brought Grammys to TV, Dies at 85." *Los Angeles Times*, September 13, 2009.

Speed, Carol. "At One with Leon Russell." Souvenir program from the Bare Bones International Film Festival, April 17–23, 2006.

Sutheim, Peter. "An Afternoon With: Bill Putnam." *Journal of the Audio Engineering Society* 37, no. 9 (September 1989).

Taubman, Howard. "Hair and the 20's: Pert Musical on Lafayette Street Recalls Another Era's Off-Broadway Revues." *New York Times*, November 14, 1967.

Thorn, Steve. "A Conversation with Jimmy Webb." *San Diego Troubadour*, February 2008 (online edition).

"Troubled Beach Boys Genius Finds Renewed Joy." CNN.com, August 26, 2008.

Wapshott, Tim. "That Soggy Cake and Other Stories: Jimmy Webb Looks Back on 'MacArthur Park', and the Songs He Wrote for Barbra Streisand and Himself." *The Independent*, August 20, 1994.

Weiner, Matthew. "This Is Where I Came In: The Song Cycles of Jimmy Webb." *Stylus*, February 28, 2005.

"What Goes On!: Smells like Teen Spirit." *Mojo*, December 2002.

"Xavier Cugat, 'Rumba King' In 1930s, '40s; Band Leader Also Was Violin Prodigy." *Washington Post*, October 28, 1990.

WEB SITES

www.archives.state.al.us/govs_list/inauguralspeech.html

www.artgarfunkel.com/articles/bookends.html

www.barrymcguire.com

www.beverlyhills.org/about/radio/default.asp

www.billystrangemusic.com

www.carborundumabrasives.com/aboutCarborundum.aspx

www.carolkaye.com

www.donrandi.com/home3_v4_content.html

www.dss.cahwnet.gov/cdssweb/PG190.htm

www.emmytvlegends.org/blog/?p=1273

www.emmytvlegends.org/interviews/people/steve-binder

www.examiner.com/movie-in-baltimore/biggest-box-office-bombs-6-cleopatra-1963

www.garyspaxton.org/Biography/index.htm

www.glencampbellshow.com

www.grammy.com

www.india-server.com/awards/features/grammy-awards-1968-218.html

www.jerryfuller.com

www.july4th.org

www.krlabeat.sakionline.net/cgi-bin/index.cgi

www.laconservancy.org/centuryplaza/century_moments.php4

www.lavasurfer.com/cereal-shreddedwheat-history.html

www.lbjlib.utexas.edu/johnson/inauguration/index.shtm

www.leonrussellrecords.com/memory_lane.shtml

www.lib.umich.edu/node/11736

www.louieshelton.com

www.madehow.com/Volume-3/Cereal.html

www.metrolyrics.com/1968-grammy-awards.html

www.museum.tv/eotvsection.php?entrycode=godfreyarth

www.museum.tv/eotvsection.php?entrycode=smothersbrot

www.nashvillesound.net/current/ateam.htm

www.nationalaviationmuseum.com/Martin-404-Museum.aspx

www.niagarafallsinfo.com/history-item.php?entry_id=1411&current_category_id=108

www.93khj.com

www.norimuster.com/history/capitoldaysintro.html

www.promusic47.org

www.radiocityhollywood.com/?p=18

www.redhotjazz.com/henrybusse.html

www.richardandkarencarpenter.com

www.rockabillyhall.com/JerryCole.html

www.rockabilly.nl/references/messages/champs.htm

www.rockchurchse.com

www.rockhall.com/inductees/alphabetical

www.rockradioscrapbook.ca/radkfwb.html

www.scottmckenzie.info/music.html

www.songfacts.com/blog/interviews/bobby_whitlock

www.songsofsamcooke.com/sar_records.htm

www.spectropop.com/TerryMelcher/index.htm

www.steveescobar.com

www.studioelectronics.biz/URCNewsletterindex-13.html

www.theenvelope.latimes.com/news/archives/env-1968grammystext,0,4857947.story?
    page=1

www.thirteen.org/unsungheroines/2009/03/25/carol-kaye-youve-heard-her-bass-but
    -not-her-name

www.tournamentofroses.com/the-rose-parade

www.uaudio.com/about/our-story

www.wattstax.com/backstory/staxhistory.html

www.youtube.com/watch?v=76QCvFhpUtM

www.youtube.com/watch?v=SR8MgBulXD8

OTHER

Audio outtakes (mp3), "Help Me, Rhonda" session, Western Recorders, January 8, 1965.

"Be My Baby" AFM session date contract (July 5, 1963).

"Beat Goes On, The" AFM session date contract (December 13, 1966).

"Bridge Over Troubled Water" AFM session date contracts (August 1, 1969, August 6, 1969, August 7, 1969, August 13, 1969, August 14, 1969, and August 21, 1969).

"By the Time I Get to Phoenix" session date contract (August 17, 1967).

"California Dreamin'" AFM session date contract (November 4, 1965).

Chrysler print advertisement, 1956 (from unknown magazine).

"Classical Gas" AFM session date contract (November 14, 1967).

Commentary by Sonny Bono, Larry Levine, and Nino Tempo from DVD documentary *Da Doo Ron Ron: The Story of Phil Spector* (Charly Films, 2009).

"God Only Knows" AFM session date contract (March 10, 1966).

"Good Vibrations" AFM session date contracts (1966: February 17, April 9, May 4, May 25, May 27, and June 16).

"Hey, Little Cobra" AFM session date contract (October 16, 1963).

"I Got You Babe" AFM session date contract (June 7, 1965).

Interviews from the CD box set *The Pet Sounds Sessions*, by the Beach Boys (Capitol Records, 1997).

"Let's Go" AFM session date contract (April 13, 1962).

"Limbo Rock" AFM session date contract (November 16, 1961).

Liner notes from CD *A Christmas Gift for You from Phil Spector*, by Phil Spector (Legacy Recordings, 2009).

Liner notes from CD *Terry Melcher*, by Terry Melcher (Collector's Choice, 2005).

"Little Old Lady (from Pasadena)" AFM session date contract (March 21, 1964).

"Love Will Keep Us Together" AFM session date contract (January 25, 1975).

"MacArthur Park" AFM session date contract (December 21, 1968).

"Midnight Confessions" AFM session date contract (May 14, 1968).

"Mr. Tambourine Man" AFM session date contract (January 20, 1965).

"Mrs. Robinson" AFM session date contracts (February 1, 1968, and February 2, 1968).

"Out of Limits" AFM session date contract (September 18, 1963).

Phil Spector AFM session date contract (December 7, 1992).

"River Deep, Mountain High" AFM session date contract (March 7, 1966).

"Sloop John B" AFM session date contract (July 12, 1965).

"Strangers in the Night" AFM session date contract (April 11, 1966).

T.A.M.I. Show, The, Collector's Edition DVD (Shout! Factory, 2010).

"Taste of Honey, A" AFM session date contract (March 10, 1965).

"These Boots Are Made for Walkin'" AFM session date contract (November 19, 1965).

"(They Long to Be) Close to You" AFM session date contract (March 24, 1970).

"Up, Up and Away" AFM session date contract (February 22, 1967).

"Wichita Lineman" AFM session date contract (May 27, 1968).

"Woman, Woman" AFM session date contract (August 16, 1967).

Index